Philosophical Exigencies of Christian Religion

THRESHOLDS IN PHILOSOPHY AND THEOLOGY

Jeffrey Bloechl and Kevin Hart, series editors

Philosophy is provoked and enriched by the claims of faith in a revealed God. Theology is stimulated by its contact with the philosophy that proposes to investigate the full range of human experience. At the threshold where they meet, there inevitably arises a discipline of reciprocal interrogation and the promise of mutual enhancement. The works in this series contribute to that discipline and that promise.

PHILOSOPHICAL EXIGENCIES OF CHRISTIAN RELIGION

MAURICE BLONDEL

Translated by
Oliva Blanchette

University of Notre Dame Press
Notre Dame, Indiana

Copyright © 2021 by the University of Notre Dame
Notre Dame, Indiana 46556
undpress.nd.edu
All Rights Reserved

Published in the United States of America

Library of Congress Control Number: 2021931602

ISBN: 978-0-268-20045-9 (Hardback)
ISBN: 978-0-268-20046-6 (Paperback)
ISBN: 978-0-268-20044-2 (WebPDF)
ISBN: 978-0-268-20047-3 (Epub)

NOTE TO THE FRENCH EDITION

Here will be found two studies complementary
to one another : *The Christian Sense* and
On Assimilation, brought together under the global title:
Philosophical Exigencies of Christian Religion

TABLE OF CONTENTS

Translator's Preface xi

1
THE CHRISTIAN SENSE

Foreword 3

Introduction 5

Chapter 1. The Historical Aspect: What Is Specific about It in Christian Religion 23

Chapter 2. The Intellectual Aspect and the Permanent Unity of the Christian Spirit 30

Chapter 3. The Internal Proofs and the Spiritually Vivifying Aspect of Catholicism 44

Chapter 4. Is It Possible to Define the Christian Spirit by Reducing It to a Principle of Essential Unity? 62

Chapter 5. On the Enabling Method for Acceding to the Domain Where Lives the Indissoluble Unity of the Christian Spirit 73

Chapter 6. The Catholic Unity 79

Chapter 7. The Inventions of Charity and the Supernatural 92

Chapter 8. The Destiny Offered and Imposed on Man 100

Chapter 9. Synthetic Exploration and Progressive Elaboration Starting from the Generative Idea of Christian Religion 110

Chapter 10. Unity of the Work of Creation for the External Glory of God through Supernatural Elevation 119

Chapter 11. The Conditions for Realizing the Divine Plan for Surmounting the Difficulty of Uniting Two Incommensurables, the Creator and the Creature: On the One Hand, the Invention of Divine Charity to Cross the Abyss through the "Verbum Caro Factum" [the Word Made Flesh] and the Hypostatic Union, on the Other Hand, the Testing Imposed on Man by the Transformative Union 126

Chapter 12. The Doctrine of the Supernatural Considered under Its Triple Metaphysical, Ascetic, and Mystical Aspect 131

Chapter 13. How the Order of Grace Completes the Natural Order and Forms with It in Us a Life and a Personality That Is Truly One 135

Chapter 14. The Union of Nature and Supernature in the Practical Order Itself 144

Chapter 15. The Philosophical Problem of Sanctity 155

Chapter 16. The Proof of Christian Religion through the Idea and the Very Word—Catholicism 160

Chapter 17. The Character of Apostolicity in Catholicism 164

Conclusion 170

2
ON ASSIMILATION AS FULFILLMENT AND TRANSPOSITION OF THE THEORY OF ANALOGY

Foreword 181

Chapter 1. Twofold Traditional Sense of the Word "Assimilation" 183

Chapter 2. Getting beyond the Metaphors That Risk Masking the True Problem 187

Chapter 3. Is the Issue One of a Simple Ideal Participation or Do We Have to Conceive of a Truly Vital Participation? 189

Chapter 4. Irreplaceable Role of a Laborious Trial of Parturition for the "New Birth"   191

Chapter 5. Paradox of the Tribulations of the Just and Scandal of the Sufferings Judged According to Our Human Views   193

Chapter 6. Supreme Objection: The Problem of Evil in Its Most Universal Form   198

Chapter 7. The Only Appeasing Solution of an Assimilative Theogony by Way of Renunciation and Even Death   201

Chapter 8. Exigencies of Divine Charity   205

3
RECONSIDERATION AND GLOBAL VIEW: CIRCUMINCESSION OF THE PROBLEMS AND UNITY OF PERSPECTIVES

1. Twofold Inspiration of Our Inquiries   213
2. Objections and Contradictions through Which the Enlightened and Enlightening Way Is Opened   219
3. How Philosophical Thought Can Resolve the Enigma of Our Indeclinable Destiny   225

4
APPENDIX: CLARIFICATIONS AND ADMONITIONS

1. Remarks on Our Method of Implication against the Abuses of Abstractive and Constructive Methods   231
2. Some Precisions on Terminology   244
3. On the Relation between the Philosophical Trilogy and the Study of Philosophy and the Christian Spirit   250
4. Appeasing Clarities for Reason Projected by Revelation   254

TRANSLATOR'S PREFACE

The relation between philosophy and theology has long been a bone of contention between the two as intellectual disciplines. In the West it began coming to a head as the Scholastics, who were mostly theologians, began to look more seriously into ancient Greek philosophy as a prelude of one kind or another, Platonic or Aristotelian, to their study of theology as based on revelation, even regarding rational human beings living in this world in anticipation of a final judgment regarding eternal life or death.

There were many ways of regarding this relationship between philosophy and theology in the transition from medieval thought to modern thought, depending mainly on the different modes of philosophical thinkers, such as the early nominalists or the later rationalists, Descartes, Hobbes, Wolff, and finally Kant and Hegel, all of whom took exception to the idea of theology as an intellectual discipline on a par with philosophy, even while admitting some value of religion in human consciousness and behavior.

This is the conception of philosophy that gave rise to what came to be called the "crisis of Modernism" for Catholic intellectuals in France at the turn of the twentieth century, the crisis Maurice Blondel was walking into as he was beginning his study of philosophy in the 1880s in Dijon, the capital of Burgundy wine country.

Blondel came from a long line of staunch Catholic lawyers and jurists dating from the Middle Ages. At the time there were two systems of education in France, one run by the government, which was indifferent, if not hostile to, religion, and another run by and for Catholics who wanted a Catholic education. In Dijon there was only a secular government system for Blondel to attend until he was in graduate school, studying philosophy, when a Jesuit school opened locally. Though one of his cousins transferred to the Jesuit college, Blondel did not. He remained in the state school to continue his study of philosophy.

In continuing to study philosophy at his strictly secular school, Blondel was not abandoning or setting aside his Catholic upbringing. He was activating it in a new way, in a more spiritual way, as he saw it relating to the modern way of thinking critically and dialectically. He remained a very devout Catholic all his life, while also being a forceful philosopher in the modern mode, even regarding the question of religion, not to mention the question of the supernatural in the practice of Christian religion.

From Dijon, Blondel was accepted into the École Normale Supérieure in Paris to work toward a doctorate that would qualify him to teach philosophy in France's own philosophy program on both graduate and undergraduate levels, and to supervise the teaching of others, as he did later when he came to be known as the "philosopher of Aix-en-Provence." At the École Normale, Blondel was identified as a practicing Catholic along with a few others, but his Catholicism did not end with his going to Sunday Mass. It also dictated what he would do for his doctoral dissertation, as no one else dared to allow.

He chose to write on "Action," which was unheard of as a theme for philosophy at the time, and from that to build up to the hypothetical necessity of a gift that is not only religious but also supernatural for the fulfilment of human action and its destiny. The proposal was at first rejected by the administration, but later on accepted at the insistence of Émile Boutroux, a well-known authority in philosophy at the time, who had agreed to direct work on that subject.

The result of that work has turned out to be the best known of Blondel's works: *L'Action: Essai d'une Critique de la Vie et d'une Science de la Pratique* (1893).[1] Blondel's defense of it was monumental: it lasted more than five hours, before it was finally approved for the doctorate in philosophy, but its conclusion about a necessary hypothesis of a super-

---

1. The 1893 edition soon sold out, much to the surprise of everyone. But Blondel did not allow it to be published again during his lifetime. It came to be known widely by reproductions of the 1893 edition. But it was published a second time by Presses Universitaires de France (PUF) (1950) soon after his death. The English translation is by Oliva Blanchette, *Action (1893): Essay on a Critique of Life and a Science of Practice* (Notre Dame, IN: University of Notre Dame Press, 1984).

natural religious gift was not accepted. The reaction on the Catholic side was also one of approval, but only for the conclusion, and not for the method by which the conclusion was arrived at. The Catholic approval came in the form of an article published in a prominent Catholic journal at the time, *Annales de Philosophie chrétienne*,[2] which praised Blondel for having gained a foothold for Catholics in the secular system of philosophy. What the article said about Blondel's method and his philosophy of action left Blondel aghast as the opposite of what he had intended, and he pleaded his right of reply, as if to an objection against what he had done. His reply took the form of several installments in the same *Annales*, almost the equal of a short book. It consisted of three parts: one critical of the various kinds of apologetics for Christianity common at the time, all of which proved ineffective for modern philosophy, according to Blondel; a second on how philosophy and religion can mutually reinforce one another; and a third to suggest ways in which the two can come together, rather than stay separate and opposed to one another. The reply is often referred to as the *Letter on Apologetics*, but that is misleading. *The Letter* was intended to show how the immanence of philosophy and the transcendence of religion come together in human consciousness and how they can grow together there, in this life and in the next.

That "letter" stirred up the crisis of Modernism even more among both Modernist philosophers, who became more entrenched in their rational immanentism, and Catholic thinkers who insisted even more than ever on distancing themselves further from anything having to do with the concrete historical order. Blondel remained a devout practicing Catholic, but without giving up his thinking as a modern philosopher dealing with the problem of religion, especially of the Catholic religion with its dogma of a supernatural life with God. He defended himself against his colleagues in philosophy, but he decided to stop writing on

---

2. See *Annales de Philosophie chrétienne*, edited at the time by a certain Abbé Denis. Blondel's rejoinder is available in English as one of two essays in Maurice Blondel, *"The Letter on Apologetics" and "History and Dogma,"* texts presented and trans. Alexander Dru and Illtyd Trethowan (Grand Rapids, MI: Eerdmans, 1974).

the problem of religion for fear of being unduly condemned by Catholic witch-hunters accusing him of heresy for trying to bring together modern philosophy and Catholic religion, even with its supernatural dimension in the spiritual practice of Catholicism.

The controversy over the Modernist crisis among Catholics continued through the turn of the century and troubled many young Catholic intellectuals, while Blondel continued his work as a philosopher in the modern secular system of France, keeping his resolution of the crisis pretty much to himself and to his friends in the Church. But two of these friends, both priests having to do with the formation of future intellectuals and priests, persuaded Blondel to break his silence again to help the young Catholic intellectuals who were still struggling with the Modernist crisis. So that in 1904 Blondel published one more article, entitled "Histoire et Dogme," dealing with the crisis, in which he showed how the crisis was aggravated by *extrinsicist* dogmatists in theology who only provoked the so-called *historicists* to cut themselves off from the extrinsicists, as if the two had nothing to do with each other in their way of dealing with the problem of religion in the historical order. Blondel criticized both camps for their one-sidedness, and showed how the two did come together in a *living tradition* going all the way back to the community that had gathered around Jesus at the beginning of an apostolic tradition that has adapted itself to the needs of different cultures in the historical order and in answer to the different problems for a religion that was supernatural from start to finish.

"Histoire et Dogme" is the article on the Modernist crisis that is usually associated with the earlier one of 1896, not so much on apologetics as on the "problem of religion" in modern thought. It was the final contribution of Blondel to the earlier Modernist crisis. It was mainly an expansion of the idea of tradition Blondel had alluded to in *Action* of 1893, and had been left undeveloped for decades to come, while Blondel was fulfilling his role as philosopher and supervisor in the secular system of philosophy that prevailed in the French university. Blondel had made his peace with the philosophers, but not with the Catholic theologians he had taken to task in the early Modernist crisis at the turn of the twentieth century. That crisis was still simmering twenty-five years later, and Blondel was once again the one to bring it to the forefront.

At the time Blondel was in the process of retiring from teaching in the university system, precipitated not just by his age, but also by problems of deafness and blindness, not in order to give up work altogether, but rather to devote himself entirely to the work he had been doing on the side while teaching in the secular philosophy system, work in the philosophy of religion, which remained his primary interest as a philosopher, to bring philosophy and religion back together, even in a context of supernatural religion, which by definition could not be fitted into the framework of a natural or a rational philosophy.

During this period of self-imposed public silence on how to relate modern philosophy to Christian religion, and reciprocally relate Christian religion to modern philosophy and its satisfaction with an exclusive framework of immanence, without any acknowledgment of a transcendent, let alone a supernatural order, Blondel continued to work in private on this question of bringing philosophy and Christian religion together, which he had launched in his doctoral dissertation on Action. He went back to look at the tradition of authors such as Aquinas, Augustine, and even Saint Bernard, whom he had quoted in his dissertation. And he explored ways of bringing that tradition forward in relation to modern philosophy.

It was not until 1930 that he went public again on this question, by publishing articles on Augustine, as a philosopher, on the occasion of a centenary of the saint's death.[3] That debate of the early 1930s in French philosophy and theology has been well documented. But it was not the end of Blondel's interest in the question. In fact, it was only the beginning of what was to be his intellectual task for the rest of his life. And the book we are presenting here was the pivotal piece for what was yet to come in Blondel's main systematic work as a philosopher of the Christian spirit: his trilogy on *Thought* (two volumes), *Being* (one volume), and *Action* (two volumes, with the second as an adaptation of the original dissertation), followed by another trilogy on *Philosophy and the*

---

3. See Maurice Blondel, "The Latent Resources of St. Augustine's Thought," in *A Monument to Saint Augustine: Essays on His Age, Life and Thought* (London: Sheed & Ward, 1930), 319–53, the only piece of writing published in English by Blondel in his lifetime. See also Blondel, "L'unité originale et la vie permanente de sa doctrine philosophique" and "La fécondité toujours renouvelée de la pensée augustinienne," both reproduced in *Dialogues avec les philosophes* (Paris: Bloud et Gay, 1966), and Blondel again, "Y a-t-il une philosophie chrétienne?," *Revue de Métaphysique et de Morale* 38, no. 4 (1931) : 599–606.

Christian Spirit, the third volume of which was left unpublished at the time of his death in 1949.

What was published at the time of his death was the short volume we are now presenting in English translation. Blondel signed off with the publisher for it the day before he died, realizing that he would not be able to have his third volume of *Philosophy and the Christian Spirit* ready for publication. Once again two of his friends persuaded him to publish what he had written twenty years earlier, in anticipation of the trilogies that were to follow. And so he did, thus documenting the essence of his method for doing a philosophy of the Christian spirit in keeping with the rich, living tradition out of which he was operating as a modern philosopher of Christian religion.

The work we are presenting, therefore, is a work of reflection on the method he was to use in what was to be his philosophy of the Christian spirit. It consists of two main essays, the longer one *The Christian Sense*, and the shorter *On Assimilation*, followed by a *Reconsideration and Global View* and an *Appendix: Clarifications and Admonitions* written later in answer to an inquiry about his method. These shorter additions at the end seem to have been included as complements to the two original essays at the time of the decision to publish those two main essays, while the second essay on assimilation, as Blondel explains, grew out of proportion for the place it was originally intended as part of the essay *Christian Sense*. Hence the unity and the seeming disconnectedness of what had originally been conceived as a set of notes for shaping the two systematic trilogies that were to come later.

The main facts of this rearrangement of earlier reflections are given in the original French edition of the work, where we are told that "the text of this work was revised by the author shortly before his death on the first of June, 1949." To understand better how Blondel pulled all these pieces together under a single title of *Philosophical Exigencies*, we must keep in mind that Blondel was concerned with philosophical exigencies from the beginning to the end of his philosophical career, starting from his dissertation on Action, where he had made a case for a hypothetical necessity of a supernatural aid from the Creator or from the necessary Being of Action. Hence the idea of a philosophical exigency, which theology, even of a supernatural religion, has to take into account in its own religious sense, no matter how supernatural. Whereas the dissertation on Action was addressed mainly to philosophers, the final work on *Philosophical Exigencies* was addressed mainly to theologians, or to those who had a supernatural religious sense, without calling into question the existence of the divine, or of God, and of any supernatural aid taken for granted in the *Christian Sense*.

Hence the philosophical centrality of the Christian sense, which Blondel wishes to emphasize, not just for philosophers, but for theologians who start from a belief in God and from a revelation that can come only from God in his total transcendence of anything accessible to human reason. Blondel begins the essay on the *Christian Sense* with a justification for a philosophical study on the Christian spirit with its historical aspect and its intellectual aspect as a permanent unity. He talks about internal proofs and the spiritually vivifying aspect of Catholicism and a method enabling access into the domain where the indissoluble unity of the Christian spirit lives on. He talks about the experience of Catholic unity and the inventions of charity and of the supernatural leading to a destiny offered and imposed on human beings, and the progressive march starting from the generative idea of Christian religion.

In chapter 11 of *Christian Sense*, he examines the conditions for realizing the divine plan of supernaturalization by overcoming the difficulty of a union between two incommensurables, the Creator and the creature. After considering the supernatural under its triple aspect (metaphysical, ascetical, and mystical), he tries to show how the order of grace completes the natural order and forms with it within us a life and a personality that is truly one, in the practical, intellectual, and spiritual orders. From all this there follows a philosophy of sainthood in conjunction with the attributes of catholicity and apostolicity mentioned in the Creed for the Christian sense, or the Church, in this world where we find ourselves as Christians.

On Assimilation grew out of the intellectual aspect of relating the two incommensurables, the natural and the supernatural, that came together in the *Christian Sense*. This essay plays on the term "assimilation" as distinct from the term "analogy." Both terms had been used amply to speak of how the creature relates to the Creator. For Blondel the term "assimilation" spoke more clearly of something supernatural than anything understood only by an analogy between the creature, including the spiritual creature, and the Creator. In other words the term "analogy," though appropriate for understanding the relation of inequality between the Creator and any creature, was not appropriate for indicating anything like a supernatural gift *elevating* a creature into the sphere of something divine, or assimilating it to the divine itself, as Blondel was insisting on doing, without confusing the two orders with one another and without keeping them separate from one another in a truly Christian life, both in the here-and-now and in the hereafter.

Blondel begins by going beyond metaphors that risk masking the true problem. Then he distinguishes a truly vital participation in the divine itself from a merely simple ideal participation, as proposed by certain theologians, which leads him to the irreplaceable role of a "laborious trial of parturition" for the "New Birth," where the paradox of the just suffering comes into view. He speaks of the problem of evil in its most universal form as the highest objection that can be resolved only by an assimilative theogony by way of renunciation and even death, not to oppose a hostile God, but rather to meet the exigencies of divine charity itself.

In the *Reconsideration* and *Clarifications* that follow he speaks of a twofold inspiration in this philosophical inquiry and of a unity of outlooks. He speaks of the objections and contradictions, not as obstacles, but as opening the way for an enlightenment on the problem, and he concludes by showing how philosophical thought can resolve the enigma of a destiny we cannot decline without suffering an eternal damnation.

The entire work we present in this book is an introduction to the third volume of this trilogy *Philosophy and the Christian Spirit* that Blondel was unable to write at the end of life. For a summation of what Blondel had in mind for that volume, based on notes he left behind, see the end of the book on Blondel's life by Oliva Blanchette, *Maurice Blondel: A Philosophical Life* (Eerdmans, 2010).

Finally, a word of explanation for our translation of what Blondel speaks of simply as *christianisme* in the title and throughout the essays by the term "Christian religion" in English. A literal translation of *christianisme* would have been something like "Christianity," but that would not have conveyed, in English, the religious connotation that the term *christianisme* had for Blondel and for the audience he was addressing in twentieth-century France. Blondel was not speaking of Christianity merely as a cultural phenomenon, as other philosophers were willing to do. He was speaking of it as something spiritual that surpasses the merely phenomenal or cultural, in relation to the divine, and to be more explicit, to something supernatural in that relation, as becomes clear in the development of both main essays in this book. The important thing for Blondel is not to confine Christianity as something of this world, but to see it as relating to the transcendent, and even to the strict mystery of something supernatural inaccessible to inquiring reason. This is why he had chosen *Philosophy and the Christian Spirit* as the title of his final trilogy.

Oliva Blanchette
April 17, 2019

1

THE CHRISTIAN SENSE

FOREWORD

Allow me, even before publishing Volume III on *Philosophy and the Christian Spirit*, where the duty of the philosopher in the progression of civilization for the work of supernaturalization of humanity will be studied, to present these meditations on an inexhaustible problem. Dictated almost twenty years ago, more rapid, more direct and accessible to non-professionals in philosophy, they will project a new clarity on the works already published, by helping to grasp better the overall inspiration and the fundamental views of this *opus* which is *ultimum in executione* (last in execution) only because it was *primum in intentione* (first in intention).

The text of this work was revised by the author shortly before his death on June 4, 1949. This foreword and the one that appears before *On Assimilation* were dictated by him on June 1, 1949. (*Editor's note.*)

Introduction

Is it possible, is it legitimate, is it good to study, from the viewpoint of philosophy, the Christian spirit?

Let us consider first the objections that arise against such an endeavor. Is it not to do violence to this spirit to seem to bring it down to theoretical and critical perspectives of a purely human order, with the appearance of assimilating it to other properly rational doctrines, as a history of the Stoic spirit would be? Moreover, doesn't this term, "Christian spirit," create some equivocation between two meanings, one relative to a speculative and dogmatic interpretation (such as an exposé of the Spinozist spirit), the other reduced to applications that proceed from the "genius of Christianity," to repeat Chateaubriand's title? Besides, do we not risk, whether we follow either one of these orientations, breaking up the mysterious unity of a life whose supernatural character seems to depend on the indissoluble unity and solidarity of doctrinal truths and practical precepts?

What makes our scruples worse, is that attempts by historians, exegetes, philosophers to study this Christian spirit from a scientific and rational point of view have given the appearance of denaturing this spirit, at times by trespassing into it to render a false account of the supernatural, and at other times by letting that odor evaporate that Saint Paul says surpasses all human perception. Hence do we not have to leave to those who are "more than man," according to the expression of Descartes, a study that seems justifiable and salutary only from a properly religious or even theological point of view, not to say mystical? Even more so, does not the Gospel warn us that these things remain hidden from the curious to be revealed only to the simple and the little ones?

Finally, we come to an objection that is more actual, more radical still, the one that echoed through a recent Conference of Catholic professors: "There is no Christian spirit; there is the human spirit that is universal, and there is the historical fact of Revelation; there is the person of Christ who commands with authority, whose deep reasons we have no business poking into, because these teachings surpass our human way of knowing just as his action escapes our science and our conscience."

Having many times been questioned myself on the Christian spirit, and especially having been frequently questioned on what Harnack, in his famous book, calls "the essence of Christianity," I have come to observe an extreme diversity, I do not mean just of ignorances and misunderstandings, but even of favorable and learned conceptions and interpretations: everyone who reflects in the least personal way on this problem comes up with a judgment that hardly resembles most of the vague or banal ideas the multitude is satisfied with. Is that another reason to avoid the inquiry that I had undertaken more than forty years ago, since it seems almost impossible to bring the infinite perspectives of Christian thought and life back to a center? Or else, on the contrary, is it one more stimulus to search for clarity, for an ordinance, for a harmonious unity, among so many dissonant conceptions?

None of the objections we have just gone over seems decisive, and it would be possible, with the backing of sacred texts, of the highest authorities and of the most traditional examples, to establish that, without trampling on the supernatural order, it is legitimate, profitable, desirable to examine from three points of view the reasons, the meanings, and the applications of the Christian spirit. For the Christian religion presents itself not as a creation superimposed on nature, but as an elevation, an assumption, a transfiguration, a grace that makes use of normal faculties, fortifies them without destroying them, rests on rational foundations and perfects without suppressing. Moreover, if it is true that the mysteries of faith remain impenetrable to our intellectual insight, just as the life of grace as such remains unconscious, still mysteries and grace bring with them a light that shines in what we know and in our conscience. Saint Thomas, as jealous as he is to maintain the inaccessibility of revealed truths, nevertheless indicates that they are not unthinkable and that meditation on them is *"fructuosissima"* (most fruitful); similarly there are psychological states that, in an anonymous but real and observable way, express (as Cardinal Dechamps remarks) the presence of the divine order in the life of persons and of peoples. And therein lies a very precious study that reveals, in the human species, the divine spirit of Christianity. In the end, there is in us not duality; there is unity of destiny. In the historical and concrete state that is ours, the [First] Vatican Council teaches that there is no separate philosophy, that the problem of religion strikes persons and peoples with an undeniable force; and, by reason of this very universal vocation of humanity, the Council declares Revelation to be necessary for reason: also necessary are the attention Revelation calls for on our part, the examination and the adherence that should result from it. Hence, it is a task that is not merely permitted, but is in a sense required, that consists in applying completely to the study of the Christian spirit this verse of Scripture: *qui elucidant me vitam aeternam habebunt* (those who shed light on me will have eternal life). Rather than discussing diverse objections, we shall see them disappear little by little in the course of a study that is entirely positive and direct.

Might not the difficulties we encounter the moment we try to define the Christian spirit lie in that it is wider than any purely notional definition, than all simply human comprehension? Pascal said: "Contradiction is a bad mark for truth." The twisted sense perpetrated against this text, for being very widespread, is nonetheless certain: Pascal has in mind by it that, in the concrete order and better still in the things of God, it is not enough that two assertions clash to justify excluding one or the other. Antithetical with regard to the understanding, they can be complementary for a higher wisdom, as they are solidary in the deeper life of souls. Has it not often been noted that the Gospel seems to advance precepts opposed to one another, bringing war and peace, gentleness and harshness, mortification and joy? Moreover, to respond to the question: how to understand the Christian spirit, the method that presents itself to us consists in examining antagonistic traits, to see if they can be brought into some accord, to discover the viewpoint that not only gets rid of false superficial oppositions, but manifests the reciprocal dependence of truths and of practices that, far from excluding one another, call for one another, vivify one another and fecundate one another mutually. It is Pascal once more who said: we understand an author, only if we have joined together all the most embarrassing texts in order to reduce them to a coherent and even a single view.

Let us then go back over the theses that at the beginning had been thought of as contradicting one another. First of all, it seemed that there were in tradition itself two interpretations that led us to a dilemma between two conceptions where all too often people have claimed to show incompatibility. From one side, we are told that Christianity perfects nature, that it is rooted deep into its most intimate fibers, that there is, according to the words of Tertullian, in every man "a naturally Christian soul." And in the book *La Clairvoyance de Rome*, one of the authors, who had done most to denounce the naturalist and immanentist error, writes that nature could not have its complete finality without a supernatural crowning that gives it its supreme meaning and its providential significance.—From another side, people have incessantly reminded us that the supernatural order is entirely gratuitous, that God could have created man in the present state, wherein he finds himself, without calling him to a higher vocation, and that any formula appearing to imply a postulate, an exigency of our nature regarding the supernatural undermines a faith that remains essentially a free gift of God.

At the first approach, we do not see any way of uniting these two trends; and, in fact, under the abstract form according to which we have just presented them in isolation from one another, they are incompatible. But there are new efforts attempting more and more usefully to bring together under a wider light these two fragments that an abyss of obscurity seemed to keep separated. It seemed that we could not completely abandon either one or the other of these aspects and that nevertheless we could not see any way of safeguarding both of them. To succeed in that, there had to be a concurrence of many initiatives, historical, philosophical, theological. Abandoned texts had to be explored; it has been shown that, even in Saint Thomas notably, there is a fitting sense that can be attributed to the diverse passages where he treats of the natural desire to see God and of the normal failure of such an aspiration. Little by little the effort of analysis has discerned the bearing of the *desiderium naturale* and of the meaning we must give to the word *frustra* designating the impossibility of the sought after, but metaphysically inaccessible vision, except by grace and by adoption. The critique of texts was thus rejoining with metaphysical and moral investigations in such a way that, through some theological progress, we came to understand finally that the supernatural is neither a creation *ex nihilo*, without any preparation in the aspirations of the spiritual being, nor an arbitrary superimposition, nor at all an exigency the nature of which could be made the object of a sort of congenital right. None of this is true, even though each one of these aspects expresses a specious appearance. What makes the solidity and the beauty of the Catholic thesis on this fundamental point, is this alliance of the two gifts: that of the rational nature, prepared to receive and to taste,—and the gift of supernatural grace coming to fulfill in an unforeseen way the expectation of the spiritual nature, without reason by itself ever being able to discover and to attain the term of a destiny that renders man "*consors divinae naturae.*" That is how far we have to go to unite in infinite charity the oppositions that remain insurmountable as long as we remain in the lower regions of abstraction. Thereby we can also resolve the conflict, so painful to many human consciences, between the liberality and the severity in the divine work of Christian religion. On one side, everything is presented as an effusion of more than maternal goodness, of infinite condescension, of sacrifice going all the way to the cross of Christ. And then, on the other hand, we are shown the terrible reprisals, not just of a justice that punishes faults, but of an inflexible exigency with regard to those who simply refuse liberalities that are entirely gratuitous. So that man seems quite right in being stunned, irritated, as we see so frequently, before a religion that does not allow him to just be himself and that obliges him to accept, to utilize a gift allegedly generously gratuitous and that appears terribly burdensome since one does not have the right to pass it up without becoming blameworthy.

In the study of the Christian spirit perhaps the greatest difficulty to overcome is the one that results from the unreal character, so to speak, that Catholic dogmas have taken even among many of the faithful. By dint of habit that dulls the mind, due to the development of a science that is either too notional or too focused on purely utilitarian applications, contemporary minds have turned away from invisible and concrete truths that generations of solid and practical faith have lived by. Very few *realize* (in the sense Newman gave to this word) the historical and permanent sense of the Christian mysteries; whence a sort of nebulous atmosphere that envelops them, without their being denied, but without anyone looking on them with the attention that gives them depth, that would understand their exigency as that of a presence coming to bear on our adherence and on our action. Very often, among intellectuals, those who call themselves faithful and intend to be faithful, cut their beliefs short in conversations with those who are strangers to their faith: a tacit half-concession makes them avoid literal formulations, formal adherences, the attitude that should result from a truly complete and effective confession of faith regarding the most essential dogmas that are simultaneously the most embarrassing at times for unbelievers, as they were already with the contemporaries of Saint Paul.

Now that is a disposition or, if one prefers, a temptation against which we must above all be on guard. Two dangers threaten us constantly. One consists in looking for idealized meanings, less brutal interpretations, symbolic forms where unbelievers could themselves find charming allegories and as it were enchanting myths. But if one were to let oneself go down this incline, one would slip inevitably into a sublimation that would make evaporate the authentic reality of the only true Christian religion. Nevertheless the other danger, symmetrical to the first, is hardly less deleterious and menacing. In reacting against deleterious idealization, many fall back on a pure and simple literalism or latch on only to the container of the facts, the formulas, the rites, the traditional precepts, as if it were a question of ancestral custom or of a magical practice to be preserved without putting one's soul and all of one's entire life into it.

Between these two deformations of the Christian spirit, what would be the fitting attitude to define and to justify? What is the proper and truly unique mark of Christianity is the coincidence of historical reality and of dogmatic truth. The facts remain posited in the positive order in what is most singular, most personal, most apparently contingent about them; everything is incarnated in accounts that bear on beings of flesh and bones, on events humbly enmeshed in the course of this world that passes. But at the same time these authentic data serve as support or even as substance for divine interventions, for supernaturally and eternally acting causes: the virginal conception, the redemptive value of the cross, the fact of the Resurrection are not parables, and their historical reality, which is a matter of faith, requires not only that they be accepted as facts taken literally like other facts of the phenomenal order, or as symbols analogous to other mythological and moral teachings; they are constitutive of an intrinsic truth whose dogmatic value is absolute. In this sense we can say that the letter of the facts is at once the living spirit, the incarnate reality without which neither the letter nor the spirit would remain what they must be. In short, in the presence of these fundamental dogmas, we must always preserve the most indissoluble union in the twofold belief in the letter of the facts and in the divine spirit of which they are the wrapping, the bearer, and the authentic manifestation. We can therefore conclude that we must take the letter literally, because the true letter is such only by the spirit and the spirit itself remains spirit only if taken absolutely literally.

How far we are then from the fading attitude wherein contemporary thought is satisfied and takes refuge when faced with categorical teachings. We will be able to call ourselves Christians only on this twofold condition: that we accept as historical certitudes certain facts what we can call dogmatic, even where the proofs do not pertain to the critique of texts and testimonies: and, on the other hand, that we try to understand the intimate sense, the vital exigencies, the transfigurative character of these doctrinal truths that never remain in the state of speculative mysteries, but that must pass into us as principles of spiritual vivification and of transformative union.

We shall not examine the questions pertaining to the proofs and to the integration of the facts on which Christian religion is grounded and what is called positive theology. Nor is our role to organize the ensemble of truths to be believed in, nor to go over in the least into the field of dogmatic theology. Our task is altogether different. It must consist in justifying the formula according to which human meditation and the philosophical study of naturally inaccessible mysteries is nevertheless fruitful, very illuminating, quite appropriate for showing the conveniences as well as the speculative and practical coherences of the faith. This is a rational task that calls for intelligence, having recourse as well to the experience built up through the exercise of moral and religious life, as to the concatenation of truths that support one another and call for one another. This is indeed the ensemble, made of nuances and of clarity, of spiritual tact and of intellectual ordinance, that we can call the Christian spirit. It is in fact of a unique character, as are the equilibrium and the coincidences we have just been indicating, unique above all by the more than human origin of its development, for which consequently no purely exterior effort of natural thought can substitute.

Will it ever be possible to restore a truly Christian vitality and to bring back anew one of these epochs like the one Comte called "organic," one of those centuries where some spiritual equilibrium can be found between science and the life of the soul, between the general orientation of mores and the frank and integral profession of religion, in the face of such widespread incredulity even among the faithful who, from their infancy, breathe an atmosphere that evacuates or destroys the vigor of faith? We have to hope so, but above all we must strive to provide this benefit, as desirable for the happiness of individuals and of peoples as it is favorable for the eternal destinies of human persons: but under what form and at what price is such a renovation conceivable, when spirits have become more conscious of critical exigencies, of individual initiatives, of ethnic diversity, of the legitimate originality of traditions and of various civilizations? What can be said is that spiritual unanimity, if it becomes once again possible, will not be as impersonal, as passive, as homogeneous as it may have been in the Middle Ages, when so many of the problems that have since split us apart were not raised nor even suspected. To these new conditions that we cannot suppress must therefore correspond new methods, a more profound and more reflective way of coming to what is necessary in doctrinal unity, to what is free in accidental forms and to what is unifying thanks to a mutual understanding of the diversities that, far from hindering, serve better to enhance and to love union in charity.

With regard to the basic ground of the teaching that is the indispensable principle of Catholic unity, how are we to conceive the possibility of bringing so many spirits who are estranged or hostile to our faith to resume contact with questions that presently seem to them obsolete, chimerical, or even contrary to the ideal of civilization they are pursuing? This is where our task, as difficult as it is, appears possible and salutary. Without this effort to reintegrate this Christian solution into the prevailing concerns and to show that it alone responds to all the exigencies of what has been called modern consciousness and of rational and moral speculation, we would be unable to veritably revivify all these spirits that think themselves in possession of a response to the meaning of life and to the exigencies of thought. What we are therefore looking for principally here, from the philosophical point of view, is the raison d'être for the Catholic solution, by showing the ties through which it relates to all the problems left in suspense by the most robust initiatives of our actual civilization. Regarding the objection according to which there are no more Catholics, or almost none, who are truly conscious of their faith, of the difficulties it presents, of the consequences it entails, we must answer by showing that on the contrary the more we become conscious of these difficulties, of its exigencies, the more we perceive the roots it has in universal reality, in man such as he is, in society such as the most modern discoveries make it, which proceed secretly from the Christian *sursum* itself.

It has been said that in the already long history of humanity there have appeared, intermittently, four or five periods that can be likened to a fever of growth, insofar as transformative inventions of ideas and mores seem to coalesce around some privileged moment of this history. From the prehistoric era, the use of fire, of arms, of metals gave rise to prodigious initiatives where already on many decisive scores the genius of invention makes itself known. More numerous still, discoveries are multiplied at stages we can identify either at the early ages of oriental civilizations, or at the epoch of the Hellenic and the Latin splendor, or at the time of the Renaissance, or during the intense surge of the scientific and industrial transformations of the last century. But it has been remarked also that such periods are ordinarily followed by a sort of concentration, an effort in the renewal of spiritual values more or less upset by changes in the material, political, and social orders that result from inventions seemingly most foreign to the problems of consciences. Perhaps it would be fitting for us, who have come through so many upsetting crises and who remain ever in full and rapid transformations and upheavals, to hope that the hour is coming for us to see come forth, in another order, not only spiritual restorations, but new instaurations: *instaurare*, that is not simply to redo the past, but to keep up the constant progress of life, to sow tradition anew and to realize the ambition that the [First] Vatican Council took from Vincent de Lérins speaking of a growth of truth better and better known and understood, ever the same *in eodem sensu*, but ever susceptible of being explained and practiced more broadly.

In an enterprise such as this, there is no room for modernism of any kind: on the contrary, we want to justify at face value the most positive assertions of Christian dogma. But for these assertions to penetrate consciousnesses such as those formed by our critical sciences, what must be explored are not only the extrinsic arguments, but, if we may say so, the intrinsic meaning of these truths presented for us to adhere to, *rationabile obsequium*, while being careful not to commit against this text the all too frequent counter-interpretation. What Saint Paul means, what he requires, is not submission without illumination, arrived at by a deduction that would impose the fact or the formula to be believed; on the contrary, what the original text entails, is an intelligent assent, a justification that no doubt does not in any way suppress its mysterious and supernatural character, but that gives it a value that is assimilable and nutritive for the spirit no less than for the will. In this sense, all of Christian religion is higher than reason, but nowhere is it contrary to reason; and reason, without transgressing on the mystery of grace, finds in it nevertheless a light in facing certain problems that it can and must raise, but that it cannot and must not resolve itself. For humanity to live more by Christ, it is therefore good to show it ever more to what extent it needs Him. Not that we therefore have to speculate on a state of nature that, in fact, has never existed historically and that is no more than a fictitious entity, possible to be sure, but apart from the authentic conditions wherein the activity of men and of peoples is deployed; we have to take ourselves as we are and to make our belief rest on all the foundations that render it both obligatory and salutary.

If anyone wants an example of the depths thanks to which ancient truth receives a new luster, we could choose this or that dogma, to all appearances quite remote from our human experience and without any roots in our thought, without any influence on our will, as if it were a matter of an x to be admitted without our knowing either its raison d'être or its usefulness for us. In his pragmatism, William James cites as a dogma quite lacking in any philosophical interest, and hence absolutely indifferent in his view, the Trinity or again the Resurrection. But what a profound illusion that is! Through a really penetrating analysis of thought within ourselves and of the life of our spirit, we are led to discover that the very mystery of our intelligence has its origin in this supreme mystery of unity in Trinity, and that the history of the world, from the *fiat lux* all the way to the consummation of the heavenly City, is set in motion, is oriented by what Christian theology and philosophy have said of the creative design: *omnia intendunt assimlari Deo*. To bring all that out radically is therefore to tie nature and man back to their roots and to make them bear their true fruit, which is final union with God; but, on the other hand, it is also to enable us to understand better how the supernatural and quite gratuitous gift of grace has prepared in us the points of insertion, so that, within us, it is not a stranger or an intruder. Regarding this, the many efforts of immanentist doctrines have provoked a more explicit consciousness of the absolute transcendence of the supernatural order, but also of the condescendence with which, without being confused with it, it descends into nature, stimulates it, perfects it: a view that sheds light on the very sore point among many philosophers who are always afraid of repression by religion of the energies and the ascensions of human nature under a yoke that would be truly imposed from the outside and be humiliating for reason and freedom.

Let us take also the fact of the Resurrection, which will allow us to indicate the sorting out to be effected among the ever-numerous affirmations or negations surrounding this dogma, which Saint Paul speaks of as the keystone in the arch of faith. Let us consider first the fact in itself and in its modalities, in order to see afterwards in what precisely it fundamentally concerns our own history, all of our being, present and future.—In the recent debates, some have seen fit to interpret the Resurrection in a spiritual sense, allowing that on the night of Easter the body of the Afflicted One remained in the hands of the disciples, for whom the true sense of the mystery that had taken place was to let it be understood that the victorious Christ henceforth would have as His only and true organism the entire material universe and, better still, all the faithful who would receive in Him the Eucharistic incarnation in their living flesh. That is one of the interpretations against which we have absolutely protested: it is according to the letter that, in order not to lose all the spirit, our faith must take the fact of the glorious arising from the tomb: Christ reappeared living and triumphant *in carne propria*.—But is that to say that we must hold ourselves to this brute fact, to see it only with our eyes of flesh, that it is enough to adhere to what could be called in the modern style an exceptional "incidental fact," and that we are lacking in faith when we examine the new modalities of the life of the Risen One or the characters of the proofs He offers Himself of a physical fact the bearing of which has essentially a supra-sensible character? It has often been remarked that the risen Christ, in letting His material presence be observed, reveals it only to his disciples, intermittently, without allowing anything else to be touched but his wounds, as Pascal notes. Thus it is that the material fact, as real and as consistent as it is as grounding the spiritual sense, calls for being completed, vivified, and recognized in a higher order than that of banal history. Saint Matthew expressly declares that, among the witnesses of the Risen One, some believed and some did not, notwithstanding the evidence for all of the corporal presence of Christ. Thomas Aquinas vigorously takes note of the teaching to be drawn from the verification by Thomas Didymus of the wounds of the Savior: *hominem vidit, Deum credens confessus est.* We can indeed observe humanity in flesh and bones; but to recognize the divinity, that is not something only for the senses, only for animal perception, only for positive science, nor even for reasoning alone, but for concrete intelligence, for rightness of soul, for the religious sense that is the most complete and the highest form of reason.

Yet that is not all. It is not enough, to exhaust the content of the Christian spirit, to join the historical truth to spiritual interpretation, to the ideal value of the facts divinely interpreted; it is necessary also that invisible realities be understood and admitted as having still much more than the force of an example, than the reality of a teaching, than the value of an ideal we would have to adhere to speculatively and conform to practically: to restrict ourselves only to this would be to open the door to an entirely subjective symbolism, to a simple moralism that would at the most deserve the name of Christian religiosity, but would not in any way yet be Catholic realism. What then is this essential element that it is sovereignly important to integrate into the living unity of the Christian spirit?—Quite simply it is the properly supernatural efficaciousness of the divine action, of grace, without which we would believe ourselves only capable, so to speak, of thinking the Christ without living from the very life and the light of Christ. It is not an idealist interpretation or a sentimental effusion—whatever generosity one might otherwise put into it, as we find with so many Protestants—that constitutes this spirit essentially, which is no longer ours except to serve as a docile receptacle, one as it were permeable to the truly supernatural operation, to the truly efficacious and substantial reality of Christ and the Holy Spirit, under the veil of unconsciousness, but with the reality of an effective presence.

With this example—which helps us to understand that Christ cannot be said to be risen except by being something else than a man external to other men, and by being something else than a God external to our present humanity, as a purely transcendent idea would be: we are led to go beyond the objections as well as superficial and timorous interpretations: as we were told earlier, the Risen One has, in some sense, the entire universe, the total humanity as its glorified body; but this must be understood, not as if it were a question of a purely ideal extension that would depend on the imitative activity of believers in it: it is a question literally of the living person of the incarnate Word, who authentically acts in each one of the beings called to form the mystical body that takes its nourishment from His life, His spirit, His charity.

We see thus in what sense the difficulties raised against Christian religion can and must serve to sharpen, to broaden, to increase our intelligence of the riches of the Christian spirit. The difficulties that bother so many of our contemporaries often depend on the incomplete, superficial, falsely literal or falsely spiritual way in which is presented the living and harmonious organism of faith. How then, following these samples that serve to suggest the complexity of this faith, which is still accessible to the simple, must we order the general outline of our study?

I. Establishing the authenticity of the Christian facts

A first task will consist in establishing the authenticity of the Christian facts in what is positively historical about them. This means defining the legitimate role of the critical method, for some eliminate it too much in accepting parasitic facts, without seeing that instead of fortifying they compromise the most indispensable and the most salutary certitudes; others, on the opposite side, have the pretense of restricting the historical certitude of Christian facts only to those that satisfy all the common exigencies of what they call "historicity," without any preoccupation for the exceptional characters, for the experiential and moral confirmations that Christian life and tradition can bring to events overflowing the habitual conditions falling under critical scrutiny. From the very beginning then we have two obstacles to steer between: that of a pious credulity, that of an unjustified exigency with the pretense of reducing the

Christian fact to the purely external side of its appearance in a point of duration and space, by assimilating it to phenomena of the most banal order, which by hypothesis this fact, as Cournot noted, "is not a fact like the others." Fustel de Coulanges once said to me that that is where the historian must beware of being "philosopher"; and as I showed astonishment at this cautionary distinction, the great historian began faulting philosophers for their bad habit of reducing everything to generalities (without any suspicion that there could be a philosophy of the concrete and of the singular); whereas in his eyes the historian must always keep alive in himself what he named the sense of the unique, of what is always different, of what never happens twice. Let us apply to Christian history this excellent golden rule so few have the heroism of conforming themselves to with total impartiality and freedom of spirit.

II. Examining the structure of dogmatic teaching

On the basis of facts, some solidly established, others affirmed from a still historical viewpoint, though still unchecked or impossible to be checked by the customary methods of the historical sciences, we shall then examine the course that makes up dogmatic teaching. There we find in fact a singular mélange of sensible realities, of intellectual conceptions, of moral interpretations, of ritual precepts, of sacramental acts whose progressively developed harmony has to be understood in the very perspective where these many lines, at times apparently divergent, form a combination where some claim to find a composite style, deviations and even contradictions, going as far as to oppose the primitive spirit to what they name the ulterior deformations of the Christian spirit.

A very delicate task, very essential, ever actual, and particularly opportune at a time not only when schism and heresy have broken the unity of the Church, but also when, in the Church itself, there are those who have claimed to find, amid the opposed camps, those they call the better Catholics, whereas there can be only one Catholicism, without any need (as Saint Augustine had said and as Benedict XV has repeated) of any epithet, laudative, restrictive, or reactionary, for designating a spirit whose name already means that it is one and universal. The difficulty to resolve here will then be first to discern the antagonistic tendencies that have more or less clashed over time in the course of Christian history, to look for their origin, their reasons for being, and their risks: at that point we shall be able to arrive more effectively at more than a simple conciliation, at a compromise or at a synthesis, for what is fitting is less a spirit of concession than a sense of unity in diversity itself. Indeed if the different nations within humanity have to justly accept oppositions of interest and of ideal to be realized, while practicing reciprocal mutual aid and affection, how much more, in the family of Christ, must there be room for a beautiful variety that, far from preventing, enriches and makes more meritorious the most profound unanimity.

III. The proofs of credibility

Then, moreover, it will be a matter of scrutinizing the reasons for believing, the proofs of credibility in their widest extension. For our contemporaries this is no longer a question of taking arguments from the physical world and from material realities: these two foundations, which remain solid, need to be strengthened against critical undercutting and completed by other arguments our contemporaries are more attracted to, because they show more attention to and more confidence to human facts, to psychological and social data, to experimental truths and to inductive methods, all things that ancients had no suspicion of or that had no scientific value or objective bearing in their eyes, but that today have more convincing authority and a more decisive influence on spirits. Thus the domain of credibility has been broadened and now takes into account the interior life and properly human data, without falling thereby under the accusation of being variable, arbitrary, subjective, as if our nature were not something regulated, something fundamental, with laws and a solidity we can call objective, inasmuch as the subject itself is indeed something universally valid and substantially true. The Christian spirit penetrates all this; hence it is normal that from it all we would have some light and some nourishing conclusions to draw; that is the field of what has been called the integral apologetic of credibility, the one that brings to light all the rational supports, all the justifications and the verifications of faith, insofar as this faith can be studied in its preambles, in its accompaniments, in its manifestations, and in its consequences visible from outside in the intellectual order.

IV. What remains mysterious and what becomes thereby proof of a new kind

Can the philosophical study of the Christian sense go further without transgressing on the mystery where the supernatural order dwells inviolably, ever inaccessible to the direct view of consciousness?—It does not seem so at first. And yet there has been traditionally a sort of negative study that consists in drawing from the mystery itself something in response to the highest exigencies of the religious sense. How often has it been said that false would be a religion that would entail no mystery and would place God at the disposal of our eyes and of our hands. But perhaps it is possible to go further and to focus, if we can speak thus, on the contours of the mysterious abyss that no look can fathom in itself, but whose edges have discernible lineaments or are like lips serving to proclaim the needs of the soul and the exigencies of the highest truth.

We have in this way been able to examine the states and the life of mystics under an aspect that is still philosophical and thus, thanks to observation as well as to reason, to determine the phases of the spiritual life, the aspirations that serve as supports for the graces of illumination and of union. For the supernatural is not a creation *ex nihilo*; it is an elevation, a transfiguration of our natural faculties under the motion of the gifts of the Holy Spirit; it is therefore legitimate to analyze what in our human faculties is thus elevated, transformable, as a preparation in which we can and must cooperate. De Rémuzat used to say that the habitual exercise of our intelligence is possible only because there are in us "faculties unknown or hardly opened up." Well, that is the field of investigation that offers itself for a study that is still hesitant, no doubt, but that may be instructive and pregnant for the philosopher who takes advantage of the testimonies furnished by the true mystics. Besides, all the study of thought leads us to this conclusion, that, through all the avenues of our intelligence as of our will, we are led to the edge of a real abyss that is not exterior to us, but that resides in our inmost selves, in what some call, with Tauler, the depth of the soul, in what has frequently been called, with Francis de Sales, the fine point of the spirit. Always we are, so to speak, separated within ourselves and from ourselves by this mystery of our origins and our destiny: Saint Augustine used to remark appropriately that to go from ourselves to ourselves, from our apparent ego all the way to our fully possessed reality, we must pass through God. There is no complete philosophy if this problem is masked over; and Dechamps insisted on what he called the philosophical truth par excellence, the affirmation of a question that arises invincibly in every conscience and the inability of reason to define and to resolve this problem of problems.

We see thereby how we have to excavate within ourselves the place where the supernatural solution will come to fill the abyss. Let no one say then that it is ridiculous and useless to put so much effort into indicating such an emptiness, into proving such an abyss: the acknowledgment of this impossibility the philosopher finds himself in of completing himself, of tying thought and life into one another, is on the contrary the highest service reason can render; and the Christian spirit, which has no greater enemy than the false sufficiency of egoistic autonomy, has no better auxiliary than this sense of mystery and of humility. God, says Scripture, loves empty vases in which to pour Himself. And it is already a beautiful role to have to shape and to purify these vases of nature and of man that are to contain the divine presence.

V. Proof drawn from the real union of these apparently heterogeneous elements

At this point, have we not reached all of what we can reasonably say of the Christian mystery and of this accord within it of the most positive proofs with the most repressive and the most negative purifications? No, there remains one last task, the one most rarely undertaken and yet perhaps the most rewarding: the task of showing that so many disparate elements, so many aspects, historical, mystical, intellectual, can cohere, unite in one truly simple life that surpasses all justification and remains accessible to the most humble, even to the most ignorant. There are not in man many floors, and the Christian in man does not dwell on a terrace that would leave the natural affairs and faculties in their free state on the lower floors. The Scholastics said with good reason that there are not, in a composite being, however diverse its faculties, many substantial forms: there is only the highest form that somehow digests all the others by penetrating them with its unique vitality.

That is the dominant trait, the incomparable beauty of the Christian spirit, in that, without setting aside, without mutilating the most diverse powers of the "human composite," it animates the whole man, body and soul, with an inspiration everywhere supernatural and that is thereby only more humanizing. This is one of the points on which it is important to redress many erroneous judgments. Too readily do we accept the caricature some "saintly folks" paint of the Christian spirit, as if, by having more we could dispense with what is less. To be sure, sanctity can do without genius, and subtleties of the divine spirit often do without polite conventions; but, as Newman said, Christians, who are often treated as the rejects of humanity and find themselves among the lesser folks, are nonetheless, according to his emphatic English expression, *gentlemen*, each in their social status, which means that the refinements of conscience are reflected in acts and in words even among the most rough-hewn and least educated. The complete study of the Christian spirit from the philosophical viewpoint that must be ours to its end will therefore strive to trace what there is that is common among all the souls that really live of this spirit and are ready to commune in a charity that is not make-believe and that manages to love in those who appear the most coarse the highest culture of the human soul.

In Christian language, this center where human knowledge never penetrates directly is often called "the heart," as in the hymn of Pentecost in which the Holy Spirit is called *lumen cordium* [light of hearts]; and in the Office of the Sacred Heart, the first words that designated the newly instituted Mass are these: *cogitationes cordis* [thoughts of the heart]. It is important to note that this is not about an affective life, a simple sensibility, the intuition of the soul warmed by love; it is about a secret presence of the divine gifts that, invisible in themselves, are illuminating without ever being illuminated; and in the word *heart*, we must understand what remains hidden between the folds of the soul, where our personal gaze and egoistic affections have no access. In *La Penseé*, we saw that in effect, we could not by any avenue of knowledge or will arrive at interior unity; there remains in us a place accessible and destined only for God. If God is not admitted by us to occupy this center and to make unity in us, then we have damnation, with disunion of parts, the intestinal discord that divides being like fire disintegrates bodies.

CHAPTER 1

The Historical Aspect
What Is Specific about It in Christian Religion

Without doubt positive religions have all claimed they were founded on real data, lived histories, and divine revelations. But none has realized these characteristics like Catholicism. Prepared by a long tradition, it appeared at an epoch of civilization where the controls of its contemporaries already had a truly critical and certain validity. In vain have some fanciful adversaries maintained Christ never existed, or that the fermentation of oriental ideas in conflict with the Helleno-Latin culture had spawned this solar myth: birth at the winter solstice, Passion at the spring equinox, glorification at the summer solstice, etc. But such interpretations are only paradoxes that will never prevail against the documents and especially against the most authentic traditions and monuments. Moreover it is remarkable on the other hand that after a phase of destructive boldness, critical studies should have restored many of the certitudes that its first temerity had shaken or denied. The intelligent quality of the first witnesses has generally grown in the estimation of people, and people have become more aware that at all times there have been men no less informed, with as realistic a sense, with as vigilant prudence as that which our contemporaries themselves give proof of. The most recent discoveries of Christian archaeology have fully confirmed traditions that fifty or eighty years ago were thought to be purely legendary. Thus it is on solid history that the Church rests and not on an idealization of a few facts transfigured by a fervor without discernment.

But our role is not to describe the Christian origins, to nail down the points that have been definitely established or the properly historical foundations. All we have to do is take into account this truly unique character: behold the most supernatural of religions that at the same time is found the most rooted in the natural order of events in keeping with its civic state, its complicity with the political world and with official institutions, in short a coincidence between the empirical data and the transcendent teachings, conferring upon the facts a meaning that leaves them in the domain of history at the same time as they are penetrated with meaning that is ideal and of universal value.

This coincidence is so extraordinary that instead of seeing in it a reinforcing proof it has often been objected: if such accords exist it is that they were invented after the fact; hence what is to be drawn from them is not an argument but an objection, by maintaining that most of the narratives that carry the double historical and doctrinal meaning were constituted from scratch. But such a criticism, besides being arbitrary and even vicious by supposing what is called into question, is undermined by a new aspect, no less historical, of the Christian fact. For this reality to which faith adheres is not only in the past and subject to erudite research, which supposedly would be the judge of last recourse with regard to it: it remains living and constantly verified by an intellectual and practical tradition, which itself serves as an experience and as a control by manifesting the ever-present, ever-resourceful perpetuity of the Christian spirit through the successive generations. Saint Augustine had already long ago noted this ever-varied, ever-identical character of Christian history that unfolds in complementary aspects: the apostles, he says, saw Christ and had to believe in the future Church; whereas we see the Church and have to believe in Christ. And it is always one and the same faith that inserts under the visible, a certitude of the invisible, a conviction at once reasonable and mystical. Thus, as the [First] Vatican Council teaches, echoing the quite profound work of Cardinal Dechamps, the fact of the Church is of itself a historical proof, a permanent revelation, a supernatural manifestation; so that this fact by itself is sufficient to ground the Catholic faith and render it coextensive with the whole Christian past as well as with its whole future.

We see thereby what we must understand when we speak of the original, unique, and specific character to confer on Catholicism an absolutely transcendent value with respect to all other positive religions: for in no other is historicity as sweeping, and as allied to a doctrinal validity no less than to a perpetuity of life throughout souls and societies.

What results from this privilege, when it is a question of resolving objections to the Christian faith, is the right of having recourse to a method that goes from the whole to the parts, from the ensemble to the details. Most criticisms have to do with particular points, with isolated difficulties that can surely be multiplied and tied to one another as well. Far be it from us to think of misunderstanding the duty of probity that imposes on us a rigorous examination and at times a necessary transparency. But what must not be lost sight of is the concrete unity of Christian history starting from the fundamental facts and following the orientations of the ensemble that trace the line according to which the life of the Church develops. Heresies are always a departure from this rule: they presuppose an abstraction, the excess of an idea, the abusive preference of a tendency, something unilateral, partisan, or partial, over against the equilibrium and the mass that follows the impulse constantly maintained by a sort of acquired momentum and continuous action. Moreover, we count on even the most useful controversies less than on the global force of tradition, of which the Magisterium is the authorized interpreter, whose decisions the past has always finally consecrated. That is another aspect, and perhaps the most prodigious one, of this historic unity of the Church, which has never had to reverse its judgment. It has always remained higher than the intellectual genius; for even among the great doctors we find parts that are obsolete; but the work of this historical Magisterium is such that nothing has fallen away from it, and its continuous effort gives at once the impression of a fidelity, an initiative, an unpredictability such that in what passes and seems to change an immutability and a kind of eternity is manifested. And isn't that what in fact touches the substantial depth of beings, since, as Aristotle already remarked, what enters into reality through human action remains forever as something of an atemporal order, so much so that unlike future contingents, what has once been posited by history is such that henceforth is impossible that it could no longer not have been? Catholicism is a proof against this awesome thought; it alone persists, fundamentally coherent with itself and gathering, so to speak, all its successive states, all the lives it has vivified, in an essential solidity that makes of it a unique body, a substance in comparison to which all the variations of banal history appear as fluctuating images.

We get thereby an idea of history and of tradition that singularly surpasses the banal conceptions we too often limit ourselves to. We readily parcel out succession, as if beings and events were outside of one another, rendering thereby an ontological value to the abstract concepts of space and time. Positive science and metaphysics have already purged themselves of this anthropomorphic way of representing the relations of the real order: in truth, we should not isolate the phases of a life, and according to the saying of Bossuet, it is on the whole that judgment must come to bear. The Catholic spirit participates in the vision of eternity; it is in no hurry to come to conclusions at each moment of duration, at each point of extension: it alone therefore gives us the full sense of creation and looks over the centuries to bring them all back to a single perspective. It is this feeling of continuity that is expressed by Tradition, in the strong sense of this term: it does not designate only transmitted customs, oral remembrances; otherwise Tradition would be variable, it would be erased with time or disappear along with the literary means that put writing in the place of remembering perpetuated by the confiding that goes on among successive generations. But not so: Tradition has taken hold of what dominates all ages, all the variable details; it is the voice of eternity in time itself; and far from being a retrograde and stabilizing force, it is a perpetual renovator, because it draws the truth that it transmits from the inexhaustible source.

Do we not see thereby what doctrinal value, what religious significance the historical aspect of Christianity contains? Even before studying the intellectual content of its doctrine, the mere examination of the framework in which it is proposed, of the vehicle that brings it to us constantly, it seems, is already enough to make a profound impression on any soul capable of the least reflection. One last feature deserves to be indicated. It is the one that without doubt causes irritation for many, but it is also the one that shows the seriousness of our destiny and the exigencies of divine charity. For this entire history that we have just examined in its essential traits is not far from each one of us: it is imposed on each one, so to speak, at all the crossroads of our journey. As the Constitution *De fide* [*catholica*] [of the First Vatican Council] remarks, the Church is a reality that physically strikes all gazes and all hands; she is importunate to all those who do not see in her their mother; hence she serves as a sign of contradiction raised among people and peoples; impossible to steal away from this contact, from this urgency, from this indeclinable summons. All other parts of history can be relegated, ignored, forgotten. But in due course the fact of the Church must be brought before all as a direct blow that forces the secret of hearts to be revealed; and that is why the Church is missionary, wishing to fulfill this precept of reaching all souls visibly by making its historical reality visible to spread its spiritual life, which is that of its divine Founder really present in all His members.

But other objections press down on us and it is necessary to answer them, not just to refute them, but to draw from them new confirmations. Let us not fear to present them with all possible force. How can Catholicism present itself as historically universal when so many people have been ignorant of it or have misconstrued it? Do not more and more human throngs turn away from it, and is there not some theological or chimerical paradox in saying that its jurisdiction extends without exception to all epochs as much as to all human beings?—This is where we see better still the sense we would claim to be substantial and universal of its historical character. For even those who will not have had an explicit knowledge of its existence or those who will have claimed to escape its exigencies remain under the influence of the invisible action of prevenient graces: no one escapes, for either salvation, or for condemnation, the solicitations of the invisible soul of the Church. Even if it is not accessible to empirical supervision, this extension of the reign of Redemption is no less a reality that history will only have to ratify on the day of Judgment, of which it has been said that it is the summary of the whole life of humanity.

We have said that the state of pure nature, as possible as it may be, in the view of theologians, cannot be realized in the present condition of the earthly trial. It has been said that it can be realized in what convention calls "limbo," although many theologians today think that the option is made possible for every soul and that no one could be deprived, except by one's own fault, of supernatural life, inasmuch as it is true that the mystery of Christ cannot have any limits. Whatever the case may be, what constitutes natural happiness in this lower state still proceeds from a special grace that, like any grace, is due to Christ as mediator and savior. In this way we can maintain in its most exact sense the truth of the entirely historical character, and without any exception, of Catholicism, according to the etymological and literal meaning of this word, since neither in heaven nor in damnation nor even in "limbo," nothing escapes the supreme and eternal reign of the Christ.

Through these views we see perhaps the way of getting around one of the objections that in recent times have stood in the way of the better part of cultured spirits. You speak, we are told, of the one thing necessary, of Catholicism, as of an immense fact that, in the quite empirical order, is imposed on all eyes, on all reflections; but look on the contrary at what a little thing it is, in comparison to the awesome antiquity of life, even in this narrow corner of the earth; see especially under what minimal and negligible traits have occurred events ignored or scorned by contemporaries, whose importance some have tried to exaggerate without succeeding in drawing, from diverse facts that occurred some centuries ago at one point of space and time and under totally contingent or almost childish forms, a truth of absolute, necessary, universal value.—This objection, implied in the incredulity or the resistances of many minds who see themselves enlightened with a critical sense, manifest on the contrary a narrowness and a lack of comprehension of history. History always appears formed of little facts whose bearing has not been seen by their contemporaries; and it is always under contingent and almost imperceptible traits that the great movements of humanity come to form a coherent sequence, far removed from the official appearances that deceive the masses and mask the secret reality of decisive events. History is not just phenomena that can be recorded on film or on disc. As Leonardo de Vinci says, it is something mental; what is most historical is spiritual significance, the invisible reality, the concrete unity that takes shape underneath the superficial play of appearances. That is where lies the truth of Catholicism, in spite of fluctuations among which it often seems ready to fall apart, as if its role and its benefits had been definitely relegated to a dead past and to a bygone order of things.

Thus our first look at Catholicism and its historical aspect brings us to a problem quite different from the one where the erudite, the critical, enclose themselves, always ready to separate doctrine from facts and to bring all things back to what they call the problem of historicity, as if it were only a matter of checking upon what may have been noted, recorded, described in the domain of sensible facts or of contemporary judgments on the events themselves: such witnesses are indispensable to be sure, and we have insisted on this character of the Christian fact always incarnate in perceptible data; but to keep ourselves to this is to forcefully cut history off from what is most divine in it, which goes without saying, but also from what is most human, most real about it. We are thus brought to our second part: the spiritual contribution, the philosophical aspect of Catholic doctrine, the intrinsic significance it inserts into the facts themselves is the soul that vivifies the body of which it is historically clothed. Only this examination, it seems, will reveal to us whether there is truly an intelligible coherence, a real unity, in spite of interpretations and transformations whose multiplicity has served as an objection against the Church, accused of having disfigured the original message, of having survived from expediencies, and of having practiced, even in its dogma, a politics of success. No objection is more serious, no critique hurts the faith more, since the distinctive sign Christianity gives of itself is of course not that it is immobile, but that it is immutable, perfectly consistent with itself through all renewals, one with itself in all places and at all times, as the seamless garment that we could not tear without killing the very life it harbors and expresses. Everywhere therefore we find this indissolubility of history and doctrine, which is summed up in the idea of living tradition, throughout the prodigious diversity of times, of races, and of civilizations. Will we be able to discover, under this complexity, a permanent simplicity, a directive idea, an action ever identical to itself and nevertheless constantly creative?

CHAPTER 2

The Intellectual Aspect and the Permanent Unity of the Christian Spirit

Catholicism is so much a doctrine that it is under this aspect that most look upon it spontaneously, either to admit and to love its dogma, or to accuse it of falsifying life and of oppressing reason with a set of ideas and beliefs incompatible with science and philosophy. There is therefore a great debate to institute, and we must first mark off the edge of the precipices that our path must avoid. An initial danger would be to transform Catholicism into a sort of metaphysics or of gnosis, as if the concrete facts, after having served as starting and leveraging points, could and even had to be left aside or kicked away by foot, like a ladder that after having served to climb up to a summit is thrown off as henceforth useless. How many minds there are who are persuaded that they rise to the Christian heights by speculating on the theological formulas and by leaving aside humble devotions! Do we not find an interpreter of Saint John of the Cross deploring that this great contemplative did not abandon all religious imagery in favor of a purely noetic interpretation, or an ontology stripped of historical forms and even of determinate conceptions! Do we not know that Saint Theresa had to protest against spiritual counselors who thought of the humanity of Christ dangerous as an obstacle to perfect union with God? Therefore, from the start, let us maintain that the most ideal sense of Catholicism must always remain tied to the most humble realities of history, of common experience, of a humble and down-to-earth practice. Therein lies the incomparable grandeur, the singular mark of a religion that, according to the words of Pascal, clings to all there is between the two and whose order of charity is also and first of all an order of abasement and humility.—But, on the other hand, if we must remain always tied to the most concrete facts, to the realities most sensitive to the heart, it is no less necessary to find implied in these positive facts a spiritual meaning, and this doctrinal sense is no less essential and inexhaustible than historical truth under its most contingent forms.

The danger nevertheless here again would be to deploy two parallel series each of which would have its independence, as was proposed recently in opposing history and dogma, positive theology and speculative theology. There is constant interaction between the factual data and the dogmatic ideas; and the sealed compartments that, under the pretext of methodology, have often been maintained between critical erudition and intellectual speculation are false and lethal. In establishing the facts themselves we cannot with impunity abstract from doctrines that are really incarnate in them. And conversely, for the development of Christian dogmas, we could not legitimately and with impunity close ourselves up in a sort of intellectual dialectic and systematic deduction. Between these two orders, in constant solidarity with one another, tradition inserts itself, at once ideal and experimental as it composes the unity of belief and the fixity of practice into one and the same life, ever supple and moving no doubt, but ever conformed to the precept: *crescite in eodem sensu, in eadem caritate* [you must grow always in the same sense and in the same charity].

Thanks to this mixture of plasticity and firmness, the Christian spirit realizes the ambition that in the human order is chimerical and always disappointed, in spite of the recurring dream of a fountain of youth: Catholicism is on the contrary a threefold source of eternal youth, first because the history by which it lives, inexhaustively, in the liturgy and in the secrecy of souls who prolong and complete the work and the passion of Christ; second because the dogmas that generate faith, as an ever-fecund seed, are susceptible of being illuminated, adapted, opened up in every generation as in every country, without ever giving out the plenitude of their riches; finally because piety and mysticism, without needing any innovation, acquire through the ages and according to the changing needs of humanity, a savor, a vigor that are impervious to decline, like the manna that had all tastes and that, while seeming the most perishable of goods because it rotted at noon each day, only to reappear more abundantly and more fresh every morning.

These remarks bring out truths we must never lose sight of and respect for: in the facts, in the ideas, in the sacraments that constitute the functional unity of Christian religion, there is a real presence, the very body and spirit of Christ: that is what we have to think and to live as much as possible, by a meditation and by an experience that realize the twofold program of Saint Denis retrieved and taken over by Saint Thomas: the Christian is one who acts and bears divine gifts, *non solum discens, sed agens et patiens divina* [not only learning, but acting and accepting divine gifts].

It was necessary to indicate, from the start, this organic unity; and now with the benefit of these cautions, we can come to the analysis of the integral elements that abstraction can legitimately and usefully discern in this reality without analogue that constitutes Catholicism in the full sense of the word. Quite naturally our philosophical inquiry focuses on the aspect that we can call reasonable or even rational in Christian belief and life. It is a matter of tradition that submission to the Church is justified in fact, and justifiable by right, and that in each one of the faithful, be it in a form that is partial and imperfect, there are reasons of credibility to confer on faith an intellectual and moral character. Let us look first therefore at the widest possible extension of this role of a reason keen on uprightness, light, and cohesion. We will have to determine what the apologetics of credibility entails, what it can offer, what it ultimately leaves to be desired. It has often been restrained in an excessive way; it has also been stretched beyond measure by overstating its bearing and exaggerating its domain. If it were a matter only of theoretical controversy that does not affect the purity and the vitality arrived at through imperfect methods, we could ignore that kind of inquiry. But we should note that the insufficiencies or the errors of the method seriously compromise the Christian spirit itself. Hence, in order to define it or to propagate it, we have to rectify these deviations, bring precision to the natural preambles, concomitants, and developments of the faith.

Our first task will consist in forestalling disconnections that, for being frequent and almost habitual, are no less faulty and perilous. There has often been a tendency to isolate arguments or even the different spheres where many claim to find justification sufficient for belief. Let us quickly pass in review some of these attempts at fragmentation, in order to arm ourselves against the risk of becoming exclusive ourselves or too soon satisfied.

For some, apologetics is restricted to a science of Christian origins: it is a matter, Fremont used to say, of establishing the testimonies that will make of us the contemporaries of the evangelical events, and their certitude can be established with a scientific precision that leaves no more room for doubt: Christian religion is founded on facts and by facts; the true method of demonstration is therefore entirely historical. But this is to betray the very nature of religious faith and also the teaching of the Gospel: in order to believe it is not enough to see or to hear with the eyes or the ears of the flesh. Hence the warning so often repeated to pay attention to the interpretation of the witnesses, to the labor of their soul, to their internal experience, to their moral uplifting, as the Precursor did and as Christ said over and over again many times talking about ears that have to be opened up to other meanings than those that only echo the noise of the spoken words: *Qui habet aures audiendi, audiat* [Let him who has ears for hearing, hear]. If so many witnesses of the life and the miracles of the Savior remain closed and incredulous, it is because awakening to faith is not simply the consequence of a purely sensible observation.

Other apologists base their demonstration, not on the facts, but on a chain of ideas they think is strong enough, close-knit enough to produce deductively a totally intellectual conviction that only bad faith will turn down. It has recently been maintained that there is thus a *scientific faith* deductively established sufficient for educated minds; such that the supernaturalization of this conviction turns credibility into supernatural faith by the ever-unconscious intervention of grace without having to add anything human to the rational certitude. It has even been added that the learned thus have a demonstration in itself that is absolutely valid for them, whereas most of the faithful, incapable of such a scientific faith, have only to believe on the word of masters and to be content with subjective supplements that leave ample room for feelings and the will. These theses, however, though defended with show, are doubly unacceptable. The more learned need as much as the more humble need something else than a science in order to believe, and the more humble as much as the more learned need proofs addressed to their reason. To be sure, the reasons of faith are of unequal value; but for all, there is a union of clarity and obscurity, the concurrence of a reasonable adherence and even of rational elements with dispositions of the will, and even an effort of generosity always required to correspond with the invisible solicitations of grace, with the partial lights of intelligence.

Already here we have to note that the labor of conversion should not be isolated from the labor of Christian demonstration. During the controversies of the past century, some tried to radically separate, as did abbé Gayraud for one, apologetics from religious psychology or from spiritual direction. Of course, those are realms of action that are formally different. There should be no question here of interfering with the work of the director [of conscience] or of the casuist. But in the interest of credibility itself, it is important to show that, among rational arguments, there should be room for satisfying the intelligence from the role even of good will and of good faith in the preparation and the justification for faith itself. Many objections arise from the fact that too often apologists limit themselves to what they call external proofs and objective arguments, as if these were supposed to suffice in themselves and as if they make possible by themselves access to faith. Since there is no such thing, apologetics has therefore to take into account complements, the concurrences it is normal to provide, to describe methodically, and to instill in souls.

Conversely, it would be abusive to keep separate these internal proofs, these dispositions, which are necessary, but by no means sufficient for a faith in possession of itself. Due to a misunderstanding that has gone on for a long time, certain Catholic apologists have been saddled with the unsustainable pretense of replacing historical, rational, and objective apologetics with a demonstration based only on subjective life, on the aspirations of the heart, on the disposition of the will, and they had no trouble in showing that, left to its own resources, such an apologetic is nothing of the sort at all: it would let evaporate all the support of facts, of reasons, of dogmas, of precepts, of Catholic practices, only to be left with what has been called, by an arrogated name that already bears within itself its own condemnation, neo-christianism, a sort of religiosity that is neither new nor, truth to tell, Christian.

Thus forewarned against mutilations of the Christian spirit, betrayed at times by its own defenders, we must now indicate how and why all the arguments that contribute to arousing and justifying Catholic belief have to be united in one stream of light.

There is a first idea to be enunciated emphatically from the start. The diverse proofs are not, in fact, required by all, and often even the support of faith by reason is extremely weak. But we must say also that the diverse proofs are not independent, interchangeable, or supernumerary. Hence, on the one hand, we must maintain that faith is an affair of common sense, a largely and simply reasonable adherence, without anything technically rational, without recourse to learned research in history, philosophy, or criticism. On the other hand, we must show that, for minds capable of systematic reflection, an integral apologetic can and must effectively group together the ensemble of proofs whose beauty and strength it is good to manifest. Hence it is wrong to consider apologetics a juxtaposition of expedients, variable in accordance with times and people, a sort of parade of ideas, that come in or go out, or, as has been said, a sort of self-styled sacred "pantology," but that is reminiscent of the Tower of Babel rather than the Ark of the Covenant.

This being said, to constitute a homogenous science of apologetics, it is opportune to determine the specific form that will assure its unity, its specificity, and its efficaciousness within limits where it can have a legitimate influence, be it to repulse the objections of the non-believer, to support a budding adherence, or to promote a deeper knowledge and fecundity of the truths of faith. For it would be a mistake to think that such a study would have no benefit for believers themselves: we all have to convert ourselves more without cease by penetrating ever more into the Christian spirit: we do not communicate it if we do nothing but pass it on from outside, like an object from which we are detached as from an old acquaintance; the faith is not contagious except by staying always fresh and alive, compassionate with incredulities, inclusive of doubts, inexhaustible in its aspirations.

Dechamps used to say that all told there are only two facts to take note of: one outside of ourselves, who is Christ and the Church; the other within ourselves, which is our wretchedness, our grandeur, our aspirations, our weaknesses, our invincible hopes, notwithstanding the obscurities that even the most integral philosophy cannot but acknowledge without dispelling them; these two facts call for one another, answer to one another, and interpenetrate one another; and, he used to add, of these two facts, both immense and constant, the witness and the agent is ourselves, with all that is at stake in the mystery of our destiny and the urgency of our responsibilities. Yet the relation between these two facts is not a parallelism: the internal fact is less what is seen than what makes us see, which leads to receiving eyes [to see] from God Himself. But this level can serve as a framework for what we can call an integral apologetics, quite in keeping with what Dechamps called, in an expressive phrase, "the method of Providence." This method finds corresponding models in Holy Scripture, in the Fathers, notably in Saint Augustine, in Pascal and Newman (we could add many other names, Savonarola, Lacordaire, Möhler, etc.). It opens the way to all the anticipations of grace, *multiformae viae Dei* [the multifarious ways of God], all the powers of man, and this in the unity of a dominant point of view: the encounter of the soul with divine grace.

How does this encounter come about? What can we know of it? To what extent is it possible to foster it, to discern it, to support it? Therein lies the formal aspect that constitutes the proper object of apologetics. In other words, through apologetics we are looking for all that can be known and done by man for inserting and making fertile within oneself the Christian spirit, insofar as our reason, without trampling into the mystery, can shed light on it in some way. We will therefore have to show not only the luminous sides [of the encounter], the strictly intellectual arguments; for, since it is at once reasonable and divine that there be obscure aspects in it, supernatural concurrences, we shall have to make room for those exigencies that, indirectly but quite really, enter into the framework of justifications for the faith. To be sure, we shall not study these mysteries of Christian life in themselves, nor as Revelation makes them known to us, behind the veil of analogy;[1] but we will take their existence into account as a condition that makes possible Christian faith and practice. In this regard, rational apologetics extends to what is suprarational, and the objective study legitimately takes into consideration the indispensable role of subjective dispositions as well as divine aids. In short, an apologetics is not truly integral, one, specifically grounded as a formal science, unless, under the rational aspect, it studies the complete organism of credibility; and what makes Catholicism believable, is not only its rational aspect but also all that is added to it of moral, mys-

---

1. We have tried elsewhere to pursue a study or rather a meditation on these great mysteries (cf. Tomes I and II of *Philosophy and the Christian Spirit*).

tical, and properly supernatural elements. In this regard, the extent of apologetics is much wider than one may imagine, without thereby having to go out of its framework or violating the reservations imposed by theology.

Still, let us not be mistaken about the nature of our task: there cannot be a question here of a treaty in apologetics; our aim is quite other than to enumerate the multiple proofs, to repel objections, and to fortify Catholic demonstration. There is only a question [here] of analyzing the Christian spirit and, in this part of our study, to look into what, in the intellectual apparatus with which it supports itself before reason, contributes to vivify it or to compromise it. This is an aspect that is at times little noted, little examined, but that is nevertheless of prime importance. We shall see in effect that certain arguments, valid in themselves, run the risk of upsetting the balance and of causing religious thought to deviate, however true these arguments may be and however indispensable they remain for the harmony of the whole. Dechamps had a keen sense of the uselessness at times dangerous of an abstract apologetic, noting that it is ordinarily ineffective, but not always without disadvantages either for those it satisfies after they have the faith, or for those it repels leaving them disappointed in their incredulity. The question, obviously, is worth examining fundamentally, since paradoxically albeit it all too really, with the best of intentions in the world and with well-grounded arguments, we run the risk of causing the Christian spirit to deviate or of stifling its diffusion.

Will we be accused of discrediting the proofs of long standing in tradition for doing this? That would be beside the point; for, far from intending to weaken these proofs, we are seeking to maintain their precise meaning, their proper function, their maximal value. The only thing we are criticizing is a way of proceeding by abstraction of fairly recent origin that does not in any way correspond to the habits of mind or the expressly affirmed doctrines of the Church Fathers and doctors, always concerned with what Eusebius called, in the particular and in its entirety, "the evangelical demonstration." What Dechamps called "the apologetics of academic courses," only to criticize it, is not in any way the expression of Tradition; it is the product of certain manual writers and subsequently the translation into an abstractive language of modern forms in an analytical and often disintegrating pedagogy. On his side,

Newman had criticized these procedures that he dubbed "notional," by bringing out that believers really base their faith on reasons quite other than the abstract arguments they seem to be content with when they have to expose or to justify their faith. According to him, proofs of this nature are only helpers, presumptions, probabilities, without any real certitude coming from these isolated arguments. He then had recourse to his celebrated theory of a convergence of cumulative proofs that determine a moral certitude and that thus serves as a sufficient basis for a reasonable acceptance of the Christian truths, so that this "assent" will have only to be supernaturalized by grace to constitute the virtue of faith.

It does not seem that we should concede to Newman or even to Dechamps the weakness of proofs seen from the partial aspect under which the philosophical mind of analysis and abstraction considers them. Far from compromising the force of properly rational arguments, we should maintain that they have a permanent rigor, that we must consequently avoid weakening confidence in them at the same time as we indicate the danger there is in isolating them and in being satisfied with them. Let us take for example the classical proofs for the existence of God, starting from sensible realities, using the rational principle of causality: the misuse people have perpetrated of such arguments does not legitimize an abandonment of them we might be tempted to do as we take other points of departure and other methods of demonstration. These proofs, venerable by reason of their antiquity, endorsed by the highest authorities, recommended because they are useful regarding many intelligences more taken in by these proofs that seem to them more precise, more tangible, more commanding than all others. They have to be integrated into an ensemble where they will always serve, for all, as an invisible structure, as the skeleton does to support the more free and supple play of a life that covers it but that has contributed in producing it and has to continue to nourish and to rejuvenate it. The criticisms that have been rightly leveled at our ideas on matter and on causality should not tend to suppress the affirmation of sensible reality nor of the necessity of a first cause: that we should purify these affirmations is well and good; but there remain, in these data of nature and of reason and in the cosmological and metaphysical proof of God, a consistency we cannot do away with, a primordial force that resists all efforts of negation and that assures victory and security for all ulterior proofs, in their moments of trouble and of internal panic; like an army backed up against a wall, and which can neither go back any further nor fear any surprise from its rear, keeps the élan and the confidence that push it on to triumph.

This being said, we are now freer to approach the perilous criticism of the method that consists in grounding faith on this or that argument, as if one alone taken by itself could be enough to shed light on the Christian spirit and nourish it. Yet there is nothing more insufficient, at times more denaturing, than a presumptuous confidence that fails to acknowledge the complexities, the exigencies, the mysteries of the doctrine a Catholic has to be impregnated with and live by, if he does not wish to risk falling short of his duty, becoming an obstacle to the faith of others, or giving the impression of superficial, trenchant, or inconsequential thought. How much harm have some done to religion, whom we are not in a position judge in their interior forum, but who have lowered the profession of Catholicism to all sorts of intellectual, moral, or social wretchedness! To be sure, imperfections are not an argument for opposing the truth or the efficaciousness of faith and of grace. Nevertheless, there should not be narrow-mindedness and harshness coming from shortsighted and too absolute ideas on which certain minds rest their convictions, often more penetrated, unbeknownst to themselves, with passion than with a religious sense.

Something new, at least under a systematized form: some have claimed to completely isolate rational apologetics and even theological science from any moral element, as if it were an issue of demonstrating a theorem and not a concern of the soul, a question where intelligence needs all the spirit of finesse and of uprightness in coming to bear on what is in fact, according to the words of Bossuet, the whole of life and the highest meaning of one's destiny. Dechamps insisted strongly on the fact that one never arrives at faith unless one has, along with the desire for light, the need for a more pure and a more generous life. And in the encyclical for the [sixth] centenary of the canonization of Saint Thomas [*Studiorum ducem*], Pius XI bases all his praise and all his teaching on the constant solidarity of science and virtue that support one another indissolubly and complement one another necessarily in the labor of wisdom as for the propagation of the Christian spirit.

To finish fine-tuning this reciprocal causality, Dechamps had deliberately reversed the usual order of apologetics: instead of scaling his argument by starting with establishing deism, thereby justifying Christian religion in general, then finally Catholicism in what is proper and more decisive about it, he maintained that such a process, which seems in conformity with discursive understanding, has going for it only a clear logic, but one that is dead, inert, and without appeal for souls. In fact, I was told one day by a missionary of Saint Francis de Sales, who had spent his life preaching missions and preparing the way for thousands of conversions, that he had never witnessed a single return, or a single movement toward God brought on by such an artificial, such a languishing demonstration so foreign to the needs of a soul aroused by the sense of its misery and by the grace of God. Indeed, he added, deism, difficult to establish in contemporary minds when it is made the first goal in isolation, runs the risk of coming to a halt for those attracted by abstractly speculative proofs, and, after much waste of time and effort to have the God of philosophers accepted, one would often cause obstacles to arise and to harden on the way that leads to the God of Christians. Hence Dechamps wanted us to proceed, not from the parts to the whole, but from the total unity, and to propose, from the start, the fullness of the Catholic organism with the Church and Christ: that is what he called the Catholic demonstration of Christian truth and of religion, established on the most incontestable facts most immediately accessible for all to see.

Let us then take note of the method of Providence as truly generative of the Christian spirit: but let us also always keep in mind that under the cover of this unitive method, we are by no means dismissing any of the rational arguments, any of the partial justifications, any of the intellectual and moral confirmations, which require only to be coordinated, hierarchized, and vivified by this holistic inspiration that we are trying to define precisely under this single designation of Christian spirit. The word *catholic* on which the Fathers of the Church have already so much insisted implies in effect many meanings that all converge on unity and universality: the Church that bears this name and, as Saint Augustine remarks, will always remain the only one to desire it and to have it attributed to itself, as it reunites at once the totality of its proofs and the totality of its members. There is one light that shines. One life that flows through the indefinite multiplicity and variety of its beliefs and its faithful; and it is this unanimity, at once spiritual and corporeal, that we must never break up by any analyses, or by any gut dissension. Hence even regarding the justifications having to do with the rational side and with the credibility of faith, the true outlook is the one that aims constantly at the integrity of the demonstration without being satisfied with partial aspects.

The danger to avoid here and that is not chimerical is to run the chance of having minds canonize isolated arguments that, far from giving the truly Catholic sense, run the risk of denaturing it by reducing it to Scholastic partialities or to personal preferences. Indeed, because Catholic certitude is a whole and takes on an absolute character, many ascribe a sort of infallibility and of exclusionism to their peremptory views, to their individual perspectives and even to their passions. Hence this trait, often noted, but that applies only against a perversion of the religious sense: Catholics, it has been said, are incapable of understanding one another, of cooperating in a disciplined way, because each one holds to his own ideas as if their own judgment took the form of universality and of sovereign authority. And that is true not only of practical or social questions, where divergences are so numerous by reason of the complexity and the incessant renewal of perspectives, but also in what concerns doctrinal attitudes where unity should prevail on all that is essential. What results is that, with each one wanting to make himself the center and judge, we tend to see the most authoritarian become the most rebellious and even the most anarchic of men, when their ideas are contradicted, and they come to that in the very name of reason and of the principles of order that are reduced to the conception each one likes to fabricate of them. Hence it is very important to form minds to a wider, more comprehensive notion of Catholic unity and in particular of the role of reason and of historical and intellectual evidences in the service of the Church. More often than not an incomplete culture, but one that thinks itself sufficient misconstrues unwittingly the essential conditions of credibility and of what theologians call the preambles, the concomitants, and the assistants of faith. Moreover, to assure an equilibrium of consciences and to prevent partialities and narrowness no less harmful to truth than to Christian charity, it is necessary to expose the harmonious organism of the proofs that reason can and must bring to bear at the service of the *rationabile obsequium* [reasonable obedience].

One first risk would be to believe that what is rational here is only what can be positively established in the order of ideas by speculative reason itself. That is why argumentation has often been limited to proving the existence of a personal God, the immortality of the human soul, the truth of a natural religion, and the obligation to obey supernatural revelation based on Omnipotence and on miracles meant to accredit the imperious message of the divine authority. All that, which is literally truthful and which will remain implied in faith, is nevertheless not the direct vehicle that brings minds to face decisive options. With this remote preparation we do not in fact account for the interior movement of man toward religious truth that is not imposed on him only from the outside, nor for the conscious and unconscious causes that make universally obligatory and possible the adherence of intelligence and will to a truth that is not only a command resounding externally and not reaching all ears, nor for the reasons why, even in ignorance of Revelation, salvation remains obligatory and possible, nor for the supra-conscious conditions of the realized union between the good will of man and the gift of God; all things that, without being accessible to intellectual analysis, are nevertheless consequent with one another and even in conformity with the idea that reflection must have of true religion in spirit and in truth. So that where we might risk seeing only obscure difficulties repugnant to rationalism, we discover satisfactions for a living and concrete reason that, far from being stuck in the analysis of partial proofs, considers the ensemble of correlations and even of exigencies for a perfect religion.

Undoubtedly, it is by supposing the religious problem resolved so to speak that we determine the "requisites" (according to the words of Leibniz) of faith; but, although these requisites cannot be directly illuminated or verified, they are nonetheless illuminating, reasonably admissible, or better still they bring, as if by reflection from an invisible source, a satisfaction that is still of an eminently intellectual order. Saint Francis de Sales admirably described this relief that this supposition brings to the spirit of a truth too profound or too high for sight to attain, but that, when it is revealed to us, makes us say interiorly: that is what I was looking for then without finding it and what I am finding without knowing it enough, but with a feeling of ease and a kind of warmth of the soul that is worth more and gives more light than all proofs of the understanding.

It has often been asked whether, in faith itself, which always remains obscure under its veil that nothing in this world can completely push aside (cf. the constitution *De fide* [*catholica*] from [the First] Vatican Council), we can nevertheless, without self-contradiction and without violating the mystery, speak of the lights of faith, of an interior witnessing that makes an increased credibility come up from faith itself. Let us carefully distinguish between the false idea of a clarity penetrating into the proper object of supernatural faith or the unconscious action of grace, and on the other hand what we could call the halo of clarity and of warmth that radiates around the invisible source. Regarding *fides ex auditu* [faith from hearing], it is not a question of hearing the intrinsic secret, but of perceiving the formulated teaching that leaves room for the necessary interpretation of the well-disposed soul: in one sense then it remains true that the formal object of faith cannot be believed and seen at the same time, it remains *argumentum non apparentium* [an argument of things that do not appear]; in another sense, faith, which does not see, makes us see, not its object, but what must be believed about it, which gives us new reasons, a kind of "knowability" and connaturality such that the formulas of faith do not remain empty words, things unthought and unthinkable, for upon meditating on them we find a fruitful nourishment, a savoring that surpasses all feeling, because it is the fruit, in nature itself, of supernatural Wisdom (*sapit* [savors]).

One can surmise thereby that, in this richness of proofs ever united in a living faith, human analysis can find, according to tastes and temperaments, diverse ways of satisfying itself. There is only one Christian spirit quite simple and quite straightforward; and yet there is infinite diversity, each soul having, as it is said in the Apocalypse, its single name, proper to it and secret. From that also comes the felicitous variety of spiritual families among religious institutes, which providential governance uses not so much, as it has been said at times, to encourage more liberty and flexibility against absolutist and exclusive tendencies, but rather to enrich the heavenly city with more abundant colors and works, as if to remedy all the indigences of the earthly city. Under the safeguard of unity, all the particularities of the saints, who have often shown great originality, are, if not imitable, for we have only Christ to imitate, at least admirable, because in the end the simplicity of perfection is all the more close to God by containing more internal richness in the domain of souls.

CHAPTER 3

The Internal Proofs and the Spiritually Vivifying Aspect of Catholicism

Credentity and the Intaking of the Supernatural Life

Based on historical facts,[1] supported by intellectual arguments, Christian religion is nevertheless neither something simply contingent given from the past, nor a pure idea that reasons of a speculative order could accredit in a sufficient manner. Even as it is at once fact and truth, it is still a spiritual life and nourishment. Just as the liturgy celebrates the triple birth of Christ, birth in time in the crib, eternal birth through generation from the heavenly Father, birth in souls by a mysterious, but real extension of the Emmanuel in the most intimate heart of the faithful, so also does the Christian spirit call for a triple study: we have already looked into what are its manifestations in history, we have seen the reasons that militate in favor of its credibility and tend to impose it on our reflected assent, on our voluntary consent; but there remains an aspect, and not the

---

1. Translator's note: The term "credentity," in the heading, was used in theology to designate truths that had to be believed, or were *credenda*, on the basis of grace, as distinct from truths arrived at as believable or "credible" through human reason alone. Some theologians saw credentity as totally separate from credibility. We shall see how Blondel maintains the distinction between the two as a philosopher, while integrating both into a perspective that is properly supernatural, without separating itself from the natural as a new creation.

least one, to be examined for understanding better its fullness, its obligatory character, the conditions that render it not only believable but also something having to be believed and susceptible of being incorporated in our human life by an intussusception that would make of it at once the nourishment of our soul and the divine transformation of supernaturalized man.

Already we had, from the rational point of view, indicated that this mysterious operation is hypothetically in conformity with the requirements of religious thought, when its exigencies are presented to us in the name of dogma. To be sure, we could not have foreseen them, invented them, verified them; but when they are proposed to faith, they become for a rigorous spirit much less an objection than they are a satisfaction and a speculative confirmation: "If it were true, we should say, that is quite the way it should be!" From this comes a subtle new objection and a new problem: "It is too beautiful to be true," it is replied, "and this marvelous arrangement of Christian faith and practice proves only a slow idealization, a secular romanticizing of sacred emotions." And it is then added: "What puts us on our guard against this splendid dream of the sacred genius, is the impossibility of conceiving the effective union of two orders, of two lives, we are told are radically incommensurable with one another: the assimilation of man and of God, under the conditions where it is claimed and where it is proclaimed is, as Aristotle had noted, something radically absurd, out of place, even culpable of that sacrilegious ambition the ancients called ὕβρις [pride] and became susceptible of the vengeance of the gods, νέμεσις: the vengeance that for moderns translates into the all too ordinary breakdown of the pretensions Christians have of being better than others, even though they are pressed down by the same miseries; so that, far from proving the presence of divine action, their life often shows only the illusion of an ambitious credulity."

These grievances that have echoed in many souls raise a problem that has not been noted much, perhaps quite subtle, but quite real, quite capable of blocking the way for penetrating intelligences. And since in order to resolve it we must go into a rather profound examination, and one perhaps of novel appearance for many, it is good to pay close attention to it: resolving it, in effect, will bring to light one of the essential aspects of the Christian spirit. In recent controversies people on both sides have often been mistaken about what it is agreed to call internal proofs and about the method that has been equivocally named "method of immanence." It is good to clarify such misunderstandings and mistakes, by making more precise the true problems, the orientation of the research, and the conclusions to be reached.

Let us first dispel a false conception: many have claimed that this so-called internal apologetic could stand by itself, furnish isolated and sufficient arguments, even offer knowledge of what the facts of history, expressly revealed dogmas, and the official teaching of the Magisterium present as constitutive of Catholicism. Nothing could be more contrary to what is intended. Just as the objective arguments for credibility should not be taken in isolation and form only one link in the thread of the one total demonstration, so also the internal proofs should not be taken apart from the others nor could they supply what only the other proofs can teach us and make us accept.

Nevertheless, it might be said, if the internal proofs cannot get along without objective arguments, are not the latter traditionally considered capable by themselves of justifying faith and of furnishing the intellectual material that grace, ever unconscious, has only to secretly inform in order to supernaturalize our natural conclusions? Therein lies the illusion to be unmasked. The objective arguments, as it is implied in the constitution *De fide* [*catholica*] of the [First] Vatican [Council], absolutely valid in themselves, become valid in us and for us only on a twofold condition: the help of grace, *interna auxilia* [internal aids], and, simultaneously, but indispensably, a conscious and voluntary disposition that corresponds interiorly to these aids, themselves also both at once interior and higher.

However, it may be replied, these internal dispositions, in the subjective order, are they not infinitely variable, individual accidents, matters of direction and casuistic, but not of science and of an impersonal method? Yet another error and misapprehension that is quite compromising; for, in such serious questions, to settle for something incomplete or even to deviate ever so little is to risk diminishing its hold on intelligences and its vitality in souls. For, the object in studying subjective dispositions is no less real, no less regulated, no less useful to know than the facts said to be external. To suppress the sense of our moral responsibility, the necessity of a personal education for us in the work of our religious formation is to unduly give way to false subjectivity, to affectivity, to arbitrariness, to partiality, even to capriciousness, in the emotions on this level that, more than on any other, needs moderation as mature and as learned as possible.

Still, the objection continues, in giving the internal proofs a decisive value, do we not run the risk of confusing divine supports and human efforts, to the point of losing sight of the properly transcendent character of the divine operation and of falling thus into the confused error of immanentism that has been quite rightly condemned, because, under the guise of pious emotions, sentimental aspirations, spiritual levitations, and even mystical élans, such teaching reverses the roles or rather radically suppresses the intervention of grace in favor of all too human effusions and illusions? Here again the fear of abuses should not make us put aside the legitimate and even indispensable salutary truths. The use of internal arguments is grounded at once on an authorized teaching, on profound experience, on a need that it is useful and indispensable to satisfy. The importance of these points is such that we must bring to bear on them all possible precision, even at the cost of some overbearing developments.

In order to form a true unity of life, of nature, and of grace, in such a way that Christians honor their human dignity, as Pope Saint Leo used to call for, it is not enough to juxtapose two existences, one according to the world of positive science and of common reason, the other according to an ideal nurtured in a glass bubble! The supernature is not a creation *ex nihilo*, a tacked-on superimposition; it is an elevation of our faculties, a vital and vitalizing compenetration, without confusion, but without duality. This supernatural is not made for remaining in itself, as if it were a sort of distinct being or a receptacle for sucking us up by making us come out of our human nature. On the contrary it is made to be in us, *in nobis*; and the admirable and touching sense of the Emmanuel is precisely to have come to dwell among us, for us, in us, at once by his carnal birth, by his Eucharistic gift, by his mystical life that mixes together two absolutely inconfusable, but entirely united lives. Hence the problem is not to underscore distances, which are indelible, not to prevent promiscuities, which are not to be feared since the supernatural is absolutely unnaturalizable, no matter how humbly it comes down and hides within us; the question is quite the contrary: how does this assimilative convergence become so close to unity, where Aristotle said that it would be scandalous and indecent to speak of love between God and man, so infinite is the disproportion? Do we not see then how much the interior preparations, the moral ascensions, the spiritual preparations are necessary to confer a human sense, a moral value to this rapprochement that should not be purely and simply a juxtaposition between heterogeneous entities? As unconscious as grace may be as such, it has to find in nature some support, some nourishment, some expression for its secret flame. Hence, to give the impression that the methodical attention given to our internal dispositions matter little, is to open the way to those two-faced accounts of conscience that become one of the most stressing spectacles, one of the most painful objections to absorb, the most difficult to refute, when unbelievers declare that they would willingly admit all of Catholicism if it were not for the Catholics themselves who make them doubt about its truth and its efficaciousness.

Far be from us the thought of confirming such a reproach, whose profound injustice we shall try to show later on: for it is not the Christian spirit, but the lack, the deviance, or the denaturation thereof that leads to such misrepresentations. Still it is nonetheless true that Newman's desire is not always realized and that great human faults are compatible with a sincere confession of Catholicism. The fact is that the unconsciousness of the supernatural order, even as it is vitalizing within us, allows the insufficiencies of nature and of the will to hide from witnesses, or even and especially from the most pious of the faithful, the divine operation that leaves one or keeps him in humility. This has always been the way Providence has recruited Christians in large part from those who seem contemptible in the eyes of the world, of this world that admires more willingly the *splendida vitia* [splendid vices] than those virtues that Nietzsche and many others before him despise as base, puerile, even as vile.

There is a more profound explanation of such a paradox, which has often served as an objection against the Catholic spirit accused of debasing persons and peoples, to be found in the doctrine that is summed up in the disconcerting word of the Gospel: I thank you, Father, for having hidden these things from the learned to reveal them to the little ones. Human reason is naturally inclined to situate the grandeurs of God on high and to attribute the most desired and the most elevated value to the religious speculations and the noble virtues of a will analogous to that of the Stoics. Divine wisdom goes so to speak in the opposite direction. God, Corneille says, does not lower Himself toward souls so high in their own estimation. And Pascal is right in saying that it is from below through humiliations that we offer ourselves best to inspirations and to divine union. Let us pursue this analysis, using, for such hidden ways, images quite accessible by their metaphorical character: we readily figure that God can come to us only from the outside and so to speak from the celestial heights, as if it were on the condition of being transcendent in space itself that He remains properly supernatural, inaccessible in His mystery. Now is it not the contrary that is true: the transcendent is so to speak more intimate than what is in us in our most profound soul; and it is this transcendence hidden in what psychologists and metaphysicians call our immanence that carries within us best the hidden life of God, the unconscious presence of grace, the humble charity that does not even know itself.

Many illusions could have been avoided during the controversies about immanence, if people had fortified themselves against the false and tyrannical ideas that the term "transcendent" understood spatially evokes, when it comes to discerning the interior transcendence, not only compatible with the gratuitous and supernatural character of grace within us, but that precisely has such a character only to the extent that transcendence passes, so to speak, underneath the soul, through its most interior recesses. For at the same time, all that comes from the outside can serve as a revealing warning and as a vehicle, but always it is by the intimate operation that is consummated the supernatural vivification. It is in this precise sense that the evangelical word must be heard, in accord with the masters of the spiritual life, unanimous on this point: *regnum Dei intra vos est* [the kingdom of God is within you]. It is better and better understood that the study of the internal proofs and of the immanent aspect of the Christian spirit is at the antipode of the short-sighted idea many are satisfied with, either to approve of it, or to condemn it, or even to keep it in reserve as a useful argument at times to lead us from the rational preambles to the threshold of the temple, but without letting us see into the sanctuary. Here we have to dissipate two misunderstandings that the preceding analyses enable us to define and to avoid.

To begin with, the study of what are called the internal proofs does not in any way try to make the Christian truths simply plausible to the extent that they would only correspond to the aspirations of our nature, as if the virtues of the philosopher or of the sage according to the world were already part of the divine justification and adoption. What we have to maintain, as it is the most formal of teachings, is that all this preparation, as praiseworthy or as indirectly useful as it may be, does not constitute in any way, nor even begin the work of salvation; there must be a reversal of perspectives, a new birth, a conversion in the strong sense of the term; and it is surprising that certain people about whom a lot has been said as if they were already saints—be they otherwise deprived of the sacraments—have claimed that they have always kept their initial spirit before as well as after their conversion, as if that were a matter of changing an object, and not a spirit, and as if they persisted in glorifying their own rectitude and infallibility throughout their successive professions of faith.

What brings the manifestation of such a misunderstanding of the Christian immanence, that is, of the life of the Emmanuel within us, to completion is this complementary elucidation. The study of true immanence does not lead to affirming an interior plenitude, to justify our moral conquests, to define dogmas and acquisitions; it consists on the contrary in giving evidence of our incurable spiritual indigence and misery. Far from any pretense of filling an emptiness through the deployment of our nature, it deepens the emptiness that only the supernatural can fill, but that we cannot even discern or measure by ourselves.

We see in this the supreme injustice there would be in accusing such research of trampling on the mystery of grace, of naturalizing the supernatural, of inventing truths and virtues specifically reserved to the action of the Holy Spirit. Here two shoals are to be avoided. On one side, we must not in any way belittle the efforts of good faith and of good will; we must act in a word as if, in one sense, everything depended on us. But, on the other side, we must expect everything from God, because for the salutary work that has to take place in us, literally nothing depends on us alone.

It does not take much to accuse this study of the conditions of divine immanence within us of falling fatally into the vice that is most contrary to the virtue of religion, the pride that pretends to deify itself by itself, like a Prometheus, or a Lucifer. Yet we have just shown that the final outcome of such a study is the quite absolute and grounded negation of such a monstrous aberration; if there is some aberration or some lacuna here, it is where we might think that we could legitimately and with impunity do without a philosophical inquiry concerning the limits of man as he faces the problem of his destiny: without such an investigation, the apologetics richest in arguments runs the risk of finding or even of forming spirits full of themselves, truly closed off from the paths of access to divine grace, which does not enter in through the rational certitudes and moral satisfactions of spirits satisfied with their own knowledge. What is definitive and we could even say canonical in the work of Dechamps is to have shown that the more philosophy and the more human virtue are developed and perfected according to their natural measure, the more they feel their deficiency, their impossibility of limiting themselves to what they attain by themselves. Now this result, without which minds remain rebellious against the Christian mysteries and practices, could not be obtained without the help of an internal apologetic. Such an apologetic is therefore not apart from the pale of the normal demonstration, it is an essential part of it. We have never failed to have recourse to it at least implicitly, albeit under the cover of individual direction of consciences. But it is extremely important to methodically and explicitly raise this essential part of the Catholic conscience to the level of a science that is universal and communicable. And that is not only useful for the good of souls to be enlightened and moved, each in its own singularity; it is salutary to enable onlookers, whether well disposed or hostile to Catholicism, to understand more deeply and to judge more equitably of what Harnack called, not without denaturing it in so many respects, "the essence of Christianity."

Clearly, the psychological and moral aspect and all that relates to the internal proof and the immanent conditions of the Christian spirit is more complex, more nuanced, more penetrating, more essential than is ordinarily supposed; what is at stake is an objective study with a scientific and universal character that is not in any way reducible to a simple individual direction of consciences or to a method of conversion. When we were talking about what there is that is conscious, subconscious, unconscious, intra- and supra-conscious in this question of the intimate bonds of Christian religion in our life and in our thought, some may have thought that we were abusing words and juggling paradoxes and obscurities; perhaps now it may be conceded that such is not the case. There are indeed moral preparations that are conscious and have to be voluntary. There are more profound dispositions that, before or after the illuminated zone, constitute habits, in the Scholastic sense of *habitus*, that is, states of soul of which we are not directly conscious even though they often result from acquirements for which we are partially responsible, as it is said of the hardening of the heart, of the obnubilation of the spirit, or conversely of the redressing of the will and the purification of the soul. And underneath this subconsciousness there is also an unconsciousness that comes entirely from the impossibility either of perceiving the motions of grace or the aids of a supernatural order, *interna auxilia* [internal aids] or of knowing the depths of our nature, of our heredity, our personal worthiness, since no one knows whether he is worthy of hate, according to the word of Holy Scripture. We must also add that this unconscious is, we could say, infra- and supra-conscious, in accordance with how it can become an ulterior object of natural knowledge (as when Bossuet says, following Saint Paul, that the supreme judgment will not have to change the sinner, but only reveal his malice to him, so much so that hell is the sin and nothing else than the sin, but made conscious of its ugliness and its culpability), or else we can say that it is an issue of revelation and of remuneration that adds to one's consciousness laid bare before itself an added perfection, a new work of God to bring his creature to completion, not just according to its merits, but beyond all proportion to those very merits: to those who already have more will be added; and the sufferings of this world are infinitely surpassed by the effusion of charity: *non condignae passiones hujus temporis* [lacking in dignity are the sufferings of this world]. . . .

It is of this ensemble of experiences, of inferences, of hopes that the Christian lives, of whom Newman used to say that, amid the spectacles of this world, he beholds always a sort of vision that is at once underlying, interior, and dominating, according to the text from Saint Paul, *rerum substantia sperandarum* [the substance of things to be hoped for]: a contemplation that always accompanies us like a *beata pacis visio* [a joyful vision of peace], even though aridity and distress can often hide this joy, but without ever destroying this peace, which is the legacy of Christ to his faithful and the terrestrial name of Christian joy.

But, it will be said, all this presupposes that we already have faith, while our study of the Christian spirit should convey an idea of it that does not depend on this heroic confidence, which may be only a mirage or, as modern psychologists say, an autosuggestion. For this objection, there are many responses that corroborate one another. First, we are not proposing an apologetic and we are not aiming directly at a conversion of souls: that is not our task as philosophers. Second, we are trying to give an account of the state of soul that constitutes the Christian spirit in its fullness; and we have already shown that this sprit is not just an idea, a theory to be defined speculatively, as if it could be it known completely from the outside, but rather a total disposition of the spiritual being insofar as it knows, it senses, it acts, it hopes, it loves; hence even for those who do not have the personal experience of this reality lived integrally, it is good to call upon some sympathy that would allow them to imagine hypothetically something of this mysterious state responding to the invitation: *vide quam suavis est Dominus* [see how sweet is the Lord]. Finally, let us not forget that, to set aside certain objections that tended to declare impossible for man assimilation to a more than human life, it had become necessary to turn this objection into a more decisive argument. For, far from ignoring this difficulty, we have to take advantage of it to overcome the superficial scandal of minds that are obfuscated by the dogma according to which *Deus dat quod jubet* [God gives what he commands], which is to say that only prevenient grace makes possible what would in fact be impossible for man, so that in rewarding our good will, it is still his own gift that he is crowning: the profound coherence of all this teaching, based at once on our experience, on our powerlessness, on divine liberality, is therefore a proof quite superior to the objections that served to make us propose it and to make it count.

To complete this study of the psychological and moral aspects of the Christian spirit or even of the human part in the ascetical and mystical preparations, there remains an important point to be brought to light. Regarding the rational aspects or the credibility of faith, we had to guard against the temptation to isolate and to exaggerate diverse proofs, as if each one was valid by itself to ground and even to require a faith of science; we had even insisted on the danger of such an abstraction that at times backfires against the intention of the defenders of the Christian religion. In an analogous way we have to question and to prevent an abuse of the internal proofs that is no less perilous: they too must not be isolated neither from the rational proofs nor from one another. What has been called credentity [belief resulting from grace, as distinct from pure human reason] is not to be separated from credibility;[2] both require integration into a coherent and harmonious demonstration, and this demonstration itself has to preserve the place and the role of grace without which neither intelligence nor will could arrive at faith—the faith that is always part science, part good will, and in its totality a supernaturalizing grace.

If we were to isolate the diverse internal proofs, as has unfortunately often been done or understood in recent times, we would be liable to denature the Christian synthesis and would rightly incur all the severities deployed against immanentism. Let us suppose, for example, that we insist only on subjective dispositions and on morally religious aspirations; we would end up directly in the Modernist theses according to which Christian religion itself is only a progressive expansion of the primordial inclinations of reason and freedom, only a response to the initial gift of a God of goodness who offers us his friendship in exchange—on equal footing—for our love for Him, having given us so to speak to ourselves for us to have the merit and the joy of restoring ourselves, of elevating ourselves, of uniting ourselves personally to Him: what is at issue in Christian life is quite another drama and an infinitely higher destiny, one more paradoxical and more truly supernatural. Conversely, if we

---

2. Translator's footnote: We see here the important point Blondel had in mind in allowing for credentity on the basis of grace as distinct from credibility on the basis of reason alone, but without separation between the two. Just as there is nothing supernatural without something natural, so also there is no credentity without some credibility, and to leave out one side from the other side is to lose sight of all there is to work with in the human spirit that has taken in Christian faith and grace.

Blondel was trying to overcome the weakness of one-sidedness, not just in the natural sciences, including philosophy, as he states at the beginning of this paragraph, but also in the relation between rational credibility and grace-based credentity. Only in this way can we appreciate the internalization of the supernatural into the natural, in a "faith that is always part science, part good will, and in its totality a supernaturalizing grace."

insisted in a more dominant or even exclusive fashion on the transcendence of the end God assigns us, on our incommensurability with Him, on a sort of theocentrism interpreted in the sense of a divine egoism that would turn everything back to his glory, then we would be giving a caricature of the Good News; we would render this supposed goodness revolting in looking only for servile courtiers, we would be giving the lie to this mystery of charity: *non dixi vos servos, sed amicos et filios* [I did not call you servants, but friends and sons].

In a more compensatory way, if we confront and compose all these apparently divergent and even contradictory views one with the other, then, by a more penetrating light than that of an abstract logic or of a speciously superficial logic, we discover that these opposed aspects compensate one another, complete one another, come to one accord in a unity of thought and life. Then everything can and must be reintegrated into this unity that is more than a synthesis, since a synthesis implies elements that can be decomposed and be really separated, whereas here all the ingredients are themselves only by their mutual relations and their effective symbiosis. That is how we can meld together the two paradoxes of Tertullian, who has often been accused of passionate incoherence, whereas at bottom it is a case of two aspects of one and the same truth in spite of the opposition of the two sides of this solid medal: *homo naturaliter Christianus* [naturally Christian man]. This testimony on the soul as naturally Christian has often been cited in fact, not without some embarrassment at times, as a term that, taken literally, would convey a naturalism destructive of Catholicism, but that conveys an excellent sense; *credo quia absurdum* [I believe because it is absurd], faith has as its reason for being in seeming to go against reason: a thesis antithetic to the preceding one, and that we must not be too quick to approve without some explanation or to condemn without reservation. In fact both assertions can be associated with one another and compenetrate one another, if we are willing, as we have shown, to comprehend on the one hand that the most fundamental aspirations of human nature are oriented toward the God of our repose and felicity, and comprehend on the other hand that there are in our creaturely infirmity, and in our fallen nature, not only resistances and repugnances, but also that the divine mystery essentially surpasses and disconcerts our discursive thought, or even our contemplative intelligence that does not know how to scrutinize the Trinity without being overcome, blinded and as it were annihilated by this glory more deadly to our poor human wisdom than the sun is when stared at in the face by our sickly eyes of flesh.

Once, in private conferences, there was an apologist who maintained that the one and only true proof for Christian truth is that it turns reason upside down, and is revolting for human will; if it subsists, it has to be then that this truth has a supernatural force to tone down such resistances. Well, even in this attitude there is something to be kept in mind, a remedy for a contrary exaggeration, a caution against an apologetic that stops short, which would show only the attractive sides, the optimistic forms, the facile promises that are heaped on the beginner, but that are so often different from the vital experience and from the necessary purifications. For we have seen that, among the internal proofs, the one that sums, redresses, and surpasses all the others is the admission of our insurmountable indigence, of our profound nothingness, of our salutary renunciation. A Christianity that would not incorporate this supreme attitude would no longer be the religion of the Gospel, of Calvary, and of the saints. "You are the one who is not," Catherine of Sienna used to hear it said to her; and in order to bring this radical infirmity all the way to the divine Being, there is only, as we shall see better later on, the abnegation prescribed to every true disciple: *abnega temetipsum* [deny yourself]. The negation of a negation, it has been said, is the strongest affirmation: the renunciation of its nothingness by nothingness to give itself to God is the true and only way of arriving at a divine realization.

Of course, in this summary sketch, we have suggested the importance of what has been called the integration of a single apologetic in a balanced ensemble. It is not that each of the faithful should need to know expressly all this weighing of proofs; but for science to constitute itself, it needs to have as universal and as comprehensive a character as possible. We should even add that in this endeavor there is not only a scientific interest, not any more than there is a more perfected instrument of conversion. For non-believers and even more still for believers themselves, it is an issue of offering a more precise and a more resourceful view of Christian religion in its integrality. Already we have let it be understood, religious practice often suffers from a lack of knowledge, a partiality where the human and the deficient limit too much the influence of the divine and of the superabundant of grace. The [First] Vatican

Council solemnly proclaims that the vitality of the Church at each moment of its terrestrial existence must be a decisive proof of its divinity, and that it could well be, for all, the sufficient proof. How important is it then that the thought and the life of the faithful should confer on this argument all the power and all the efficaciousness it has! The advances of the Catholic diffusion are measured by the very intensity and the purity of this radiance; and that is why it is so desirable that we render the Catholic spirit fully conscious of its riches, of its duties, of its resourcefulness. From the very beginning the spectacle of Christians was given as the argument par excellence; but still each one must as much as possible observe and justify the precept: *agnosce, o christiane, dignitatem tuam; filius lucis esto* [acknowledge, o Christian, your dignity: be a son of light].

Leo XIII has many times insisted on the causes that have too often hindered the most generous efforts because they were poorly enlightened, tarnished with partiality, incapable of adapting to changes allowed by providence; and he would conclude that "the imprudence of good people has hindered more than the cleverness and the ardor of bad people." If we suppose, he would add, that of the one hundred causes of our difficulties, ninety-nine come from unjust efforts of adversaries and one from Christians, that is the one that we must make disappear, first because that is the only one that depends directly on us, but also because it is the one that lends a hold and efficacy to all the other attacks. Hence we will be pardoned for pointing out one thing that seems reformable to us: not that we should ignore either the many injustices of which Christians are victims or their proper merits, but rather that we should, it would seem, remain in accord with tradition by rehearsing and practicing the precept: *noli vinci a malo sed vince in bono malum* [do not be overcome by evil, but overcome evil in doing good]. Those who care less about resisting evil in a defensive and even an aggressive attitude than about doing something positive by making "the sun shine on bad people as well as on good people," are accused of "submissivism," and even of treason. The study of the Christian spirit must therefore understand and justify this attitude that is so contrary to the spirit of the world, of the world that boasts and believes itself to be in the "right frame of mind" or that even esteems it is alone to be in the right frame of mind and in the right frame of action by its very intransigence.

All the foregoing reflections thus converge toward this assertion: the Christian spirit cannot be reduced by analysis to elements really separable and independent of one another; it is only under this aspect of unity that it remains itself, and it is not prudent to isolate partial arguments, however valid they may be in the eyes of the most critical spirit, if they are not always brought back to the perspective of a single center. Such is the admission made more or less explicitly by so many Christians, who, when questioned on their reasons for believing, answer that they need no particular argument, because they have the security of a whole they no longer need to analyze and that seems to them more solid, more luminous than any other assurance. "I am more certain of my faith than of myself," Saint Augustine used to say, notwithstanding the paradox he has been reproached with in this regard, and that Malebranche took upon himself with regard to Revelation and the Sacred Scriptures to assure the reality of the sensory world; even though Malebranche's argumentation does not correspond to the attitude taken by his master, Augustine, who does not use faith to support a subalternate belief: all Augustine finds in faith is an intrinsic justification of faith itself that leaves nothing out of itself that could be opposed to it or serve as a pretext for doubting.

Out of fear of the vagueness of internal proofs drawn from conscience and that by themselves could not lead us beyond a very liberal moralism or Protestantism, do we have to say that the only solid, precise, commanding arguments are those based on facts and that the historian is equipped to produce and to justify? Do we have to add that, in and of themselves, these historical proofs can suffice and become decisive or even binding? There are confusions there that must be dissipated while keeping the part of truth that explains the attitude frequently found among people more gifted for the study of positive facts than of spiritual realities, which are besides no less positive than historical events. The facts by themselves cannot suffice for the evangelical demonstration. Just as the supernatural escapes psychological consciousness, so also it escapes historical empiricism. It is a matter of faith that some effort of the soul and some help of grace are indispensable to derive from facts, even the most miraculous, the divine sense faith finds in them. It is not that faith places in them a meaning that would not be really there; but the simple view of external realities could not provide the supernatural element that we have to believe in and that supposes an effort at interpretation on our part and an act of good will. Hence, regarding a first point, the thesis enunciated goes beyond moderation; it is dangerous to offer as absolutely conclusive, sufficient and even exclusive, proofs that are not such, that should not be such and that, if we think we can be content with them, refer secretly to other intellectual and moral dispositions. We can even add that, to the extent that we would be willing to stand by such arguments alone, we would risk denaturing the faith we have arrived at by other complementary and unconscious ways: the attitude of those Christians who think they have a right to require of everyone a formal adherence to arguments of fact and to binding deductions, is no longer inspired by the evangelical spirit nor by the respect with which even God, according to Sacred Scripture, treats the human soul, seeking only a free and spiritual adherence.

But there is a more radical difficulty to be brought against the pretensions of apologists by way of fact and of deduction. For the idea of having recourse to fact to sustain and as if to incarnate the religious ideas is one of the most irritating points for certain consciences. That was the objection I encountered most often at the École Normale: is it conceivable that absolute truth should convey itself in phenomena that are always contingent and relative? How can the eternal life of spirits be tied to such insignificant and such unknown events for the greater part of the human race and that, if they were happening today in a time of great publicity, would not even be mentioned among the "diverse facts" in our newspapers? There is then a preliminary question to be resolved, precisely that of the entirely singular and concrete incarnation of universal and eternal truths that, starting from a point in time and space, such as the crib of Bethlehem or Calvary, reach out to all that has gone before it, to all that have ignored it, to all that will subsist forever in the history of the world and of humanity. Therein is the legitimate question that goes before and dominates proofs from fact, which in spite of it all seem to provoke objections and repugnances rather than to provide light and satisfaction to many minds. Now to answer such a difficulty it is necessary for us to bring in considerations that rise above the simple historicity of events. If indeed one of the most original grandeurs of Catholicism is never to leave ideas up in the air and truths in suspense, but rather to realize them in beings, in acts that have at once an existence accessible to direct observation and have an invisible and universal bearing, there is no way of isolating either one of these facts from the other nor of being content with either speculative arguments, or empirical data.

Moreover the method indicated by Father Pinard de Laboulaye supposes a progression of analytical proofs; as if the combination of the fragments of demonstration could add up to a synthetic certitude. That is how he wants to pile up historicity, then messianity, then the divinity of Christ, as if each one of these stages had of itself a solidity established independently of the fact that crowns them, or especially as if the infinite weight of the highest conclusion could be borne, without crushing them, by the lower arguments. Hence for most minds who, not without reason, go straight to the conclusion, these initial building blocks give the impression of artificial props and of on command arguments that resemble begging the question. How much more right is the method of Dechamps, the method he called that of Providence and that is also the one of true science, that consists in presenting from the start the whole of Catholic faith in its unity, by showing that the convergences lead from all sides to this unique reality, which is not obtained by bits and pieces! We do not begin by being deists, then Christian, then Protestant, then Catholic, as if we had to pass through human stages and through analytical steps, when it is a matter of saying yes or no to the question that arises at the bottom of all consciences and in the whole history of humanity.

What we have just said about a so-called scientific and historical demonstration through facts should be repeated, *mutatis mutandis* [having changed what has to be changed], of a demonstration pretending to be based on ideas, on intellectual proofs, on metaphysical arguments. All of that must be made part of the ensemble of justifications; in fact none of this could be isolated or considered sufficient with impunity, even in the order of proofs of simple credibility. The objections against Catholicism taken from its incarnation in singular realities have their analogue in the opposition of many metaphysical minds to the idea of a living and entirely personal truth: to them it seems an abstract or ideal interpretation is infinitely higher or even the only one possible, when it is a question of the absolute. There is then in this a first obstacle, a stubborn and specious error to be eliminated from intelligences that esteem themselves the highest and the most clear-sighted. Thus the defense of Christian religion cannot be satisfied with what used to be called the rational preambles of faith if we do not begin by knocking down the specious illusion of immanentism or of idealist pantheism. But we could not succeed in this without bringing into this task something else than dialectical speculations; and it is indeed one of the most urgent albeit most difficult tasks to bring to light the secret sophistry of these doctrines, supposedly fascinated with coherence and intelligibility, but that falsify the very data of the problem and are unable, in spite of their contortions, to remain consistent with themselves or, thereby, remain intelligible in keeping with their own intent.

If in fact many converts, many believers are persuaded that the arguments based on facts or ideas have given them satisfaction and brought them certitude in the faith, it is because unbeknownst to them they completed their explicit arguments with a tacit recourse to premises from common sense. For ordinarily no believer has recourse practically to the totality of the Christian demonstration; certain aspects satisfy one and rightly so, but only because this one virtually admits all the others. We should not however misconstrue these other proofs, which it is good and necessary to bring into a balanced science of the justifications of faith; and we can even add that knowledge of this equilibrium is very desirable in the interest of the Christian spirit itself, made up of harmony, breadth, and peace. From this arises a new question, a central problem to be raised. Inasmuch as the Christian spirit is this unity of certitude embracing all of being, rallies all it knows, vivifies all its attitudes, how are we to define this unique and total principle? We speak of the Christian spirit and of the Christian sense in the singular, as if it were everywhere homogenous and identical with itself; is it not important to define this essence able to spread itself as a perfume, as a soul, throughout the extreme diversity of its manifestations?—That is the point we must now examine.

CHAPTER 4

Is It Possible to Define the Christian Spirit by Reducing It to a Principle of Essential Unity?

It has often been objected that, like all realities of history, Christian religion has incessantly evolved, to the point that it seems to end up in contradiction with its primordial *élan*. Some claim to go back to its original pure state; yet others praise its indefinite plasticity and its fidelity to a tradition that perpetuates itself only by adapting itself to ever-changing needs; others still pay tribute to the Church for having corrected by its realist sense the dreams of its early ages and the illusion of a *parousia*: a millenarism that keeps reappearing at all epochs, as if waiting for a temporal kingdom in this world. Thus there arises a difficulty from the start: if there has been change, can we still maintain with Vincent of Lerins, quoted in the [First] Vatican Council, that these renewals have always been done *in eodem sensu et in eadem sententia* [in the same sense and in the same pronouncement]? This assertion already makes us set aside the idea of some immobility that would freeze Christian religion in the abstract, in the unreal, in the dead past: this is not about a static unity; what we have to look into is whether there is really a dynamic unity, a continuity of orientation, a moving fixity, in keeping with the ancient formula: *motus fundatur in immobili* [movement is founded on the immobile].

Brought to precision in these terms, the problem already presents itself to us in a way that is more clear, but that remains embarrassing because of the difficulty of comprehending how a guiding idea can be

Is It Possible to Define the Christian Spirit? 63

at once immobile and moving. To this first hesitation a second one is immediately added: if this is about a living idea that has to assimilate foreign influences without losing its originality, what in Christian religion can the dominant conception be, under which all the other conquests of thought, all the enrichments of history, come to be aggregated and united? It should not come as a surprise if, in the presence of such problems, we discover that in fact divergent responses have been offered and that judgments have varied singularly on what biologists would call the dominant trait of this immense living being that is centuries-old Catholicism.

If we consider over the course of ages the principal types under which the Christian synthesis has been classified according to the historical elements that seem to have contributed to its formation, we find three fundamental themes to harmonize. There is nothing more instructive than to determine these notes, of diverse origins, that have served in composing the Christian symphony. Let us begin by listening to these themes separately, these melodies that some have tried to bring into concert with one another as the most learned composers make use of counterpoint and of all the richness of musical polyphony.

Diverse types of synthesis

(1) By Reduction to the Idea of a God of Power

One theme to begin with, transmitted to us by the Hebraic tradition, is that of an almighty God, sovereign Lord and creator of all things, inaccessible in His mystery, God of fear and of majesty whom we cannot name by His true name nor represent under any trait invented by human thought.

(2) By Reduction to the Idea of a God of Truth

The effort of philosophy, especially as it concerns Hellenic philosophy, offers us another theme that also spread profoundly into the Christian soul: a God of intelligibility, a transcendent principle of truth and wisdom, a Logos, by whom all things were made with weight, number, and measure. And this divine Word, uncreated light, is the source of all spirits, who participate in His light, have to penetrate themselves with His life and return to Him, the one and only Mediator and Savior.

(3) By Reduction to the Idea of a God of Charity

But, alongside these two powerful harmonies, there resounds an even newer, more exalting chant, the one that sounds like the Good News par excellence. We knew that God is power; we knew that God is truth and intelligence; but dared we to believe that God is charity, not a Good that would be like something neutral, like the radiating of heat analogous to the nature of fire, which is to burn, but an infinitely generous goodness, a love giving the lie to the frigid wisdom of the ancient philosophers for whom the very idea that God could love man was scandalous? If Christian religion has anything original to offer, is that not where it is to be found? Surely, it has been said, rightly, that the miracle of the Jewish people was to preserve, amid the deluge of idolatries, an intransigent monotheist affirmation of the divine omnipotence and of its pure transcendence. Surely it has been said, also, that the Greek miracle is to have conceived the spirit, pure thought, supreme reason as the divine intelligence ordaining the whole, even as philosophy was never able to rise to the idea of creation and of the divine incommensurability. But what is truly unheard of, is the teaching, or rather more, is the appearance of incarnate love going to the length of love and giving its life for man.

Will we therefore find ourselves facing three conceptions more or less irreducible to one another, or should we hope to make of these three themes one and the same harmony without each one ceasing to be heard in an inspiration that surpasses them and transforms them? That is the problem we have to solve and that is perhaps not as simple as it seems at first sight. We are so used to uniting these diverse conceptions of diverse origins that we would readily believe them to be spontaneously attuned. Nevertheless, let us not be deceived. The study of history shows us that, time and again, each one of these fundamental themes has tried to dominate; that, in keeping with the prevailing idea, the subordinated themes and the harmony of the whole take on a different aspect; that consequently we find ourselves really in the presence of tendencies difficult to reconcile, and at times even of discordances. Let us scrutinize the variations on one and the same doctrine and see one after the other the ways Christian religion has appeared according to how the accent was put on one or another of the themes we have just enumerated. Perhaps this critical analysis will prepare us to see better the true unity, the incomparable originality of the Christian spirit that must blend into itself all nuances, allow for all diversities and yet remain animated with one life that none of the elements of which it seems to be constituted can claim to sustain by itself alone.

It has been said, in comparing talent and genius, that the former excels in grouping together scattered ideas in the atmosphere where it deploys its reflective art of ingenious synthesis: whence the often rapid acceptance of a work where contemporaries recognize one another and that shows them the many facets of truths most in fashion. The latter on the contrary, even as it assimilates ancient and new factors, brings with it an unheard-of principle, an inspiration that, according to the very etymology of the word, breathes a new life into materials that until then were dispersed or even unknown. The question we must deal with now is the problem raised by interpreters who tend to make of Christian religion either a mixture of tradition and of ideas coming from the most diverse corners of the East or of the West, of Jewish, Greek, and Roman thought, or a theological and philosophical construction systematically made up of systematically ordered notions, as certain intellectuals claim (of whom someone at one time said that the *Summa* [*theologiae* of Aquinas] dispenses us with having recourse to the Gospel and that the thirteenth century represents the *terminus ad quem* [the final end] of the Catholic synthesis), or make of it a sedimentation formed and constantly accrued by the flow of life more than of thought, or of Christian morality more than dogmatic speculation. As different as these interpretations may be, do they not misconstrue the Christian genius, which, more than any work of the most creative human art, expresses the divine unity of its origin and of its entire development?

In order to better justify this second alternative it will be instructive to pass over in review the interpretations that, speculatively or practically, make of Christian religion a juxtaposition or, as the Alexandrians said, a syncretism wherein dominate alternatively several of the associated tendencies and of the heterogeneous ideas that seem to compose the Catholic religion as some great river where we recognize by their color the water coming from diverse tributaries. To be sure, none of the three ingredients we have previously discerned could be lacking without the Christian religion disappearing; and in this sense it is only by abstraction that we can distinguish them. Nevertheless the role we attribute to the one component or the other in their combination can differ very much, and we should see in fact that, depending on which one of these elements is taken as active and dominating principle, we find ourselves facing syntheses that do not resemble one another. That will explain the paradoxical fact of an ever-more complete and bitter opposition among Catholic factions that has scandalized many spirits in recent times as they witnessed an ever-more complete and disrupting opposition among Catholic camps; so much so that, where understanding, cooperation, and at least mutual support should seem easy, as well as obligatory and salutary, contentions have arisen in a way that is very painful, very tenacious, and very disturbing. This is not only a theoretical question to be elucidated; it is an issue of a practical coordination of efforts or, better still, of "the unity of spirits in truth, of the union of hearts in charity" in keeping with the ardent prayer of Father Peruet.

I. First Form of a Catholic synthesis starting from the fundamental idea of the God of power

For certain minds, full of zeal, fixed on the rights of God, preoccupied with order and authority, the guiding idea, the primordial inspiration, the sovereign intention must be respect for the almighty power, the majesty and the exigencies of a God who cannot but relate all things in the end back to Himself. Sublime adoration that prostrates the nothingness we are before absolute infinitude and perfection; deep sense of religion that is in effect *"initium sapientiae timor Domini"* [the beginning of wisdom is the fear of the Lord].

If this thought becomes the principal one as much as it is the initial one, under what aspect will the other elements of the Christian synthesis appear? The God of majesty and of fear also appears as the God of truth and justice. But this truth is mainly that of what has been called absolute theocentrism and divine egoism. From this point of view there is no attempt to comprehend, in what has to do with providential design, anything but the very incomprehensibility of the decrees of omnipotence. What God wills and does, that is the true, the just, the good; and so, from the top of theology down to the least details of political and religious discipline, everything is explained only by this willing that is one with the science and the wisdom of the Master and Creator.

Already we can also guess with what nuance the doctrine of charity will be colored here: if the good is what God wills, our love, as it enters into the divine predestinations and outlooks, latches onto and reserves itself for those that divine mercy has drawn out of the mass of perdition, and our zeal is inflamed against those who resist grace, to the point that compassion toward natural miseries or supernatural indigences is taken as debilitating for resistance to evil; it shows submissiveness and false liberalism; it amounts to crossing over into the enemy camp and already to half betraying the holy cause that requires what Tertullian calls the "venging flame."

Undoubtedly, we are exaggerating certain features in order to bring out the danger in a slope where certain minds tend to slide all too logically, where a sincerity more ardent than enlightened tends to call the fire from heaven down on the enemies of God. An exaggeration, we have just said; and yet are there not innumerable cases of such impassioned violence that had already deserved the reproach of Christ to his own apostles?: "You do not know of what spirit you are." Here already we can take note of the major disadvantage there is in abstracting principles from which we ratiocinate, at the risk of shrinking the Catholic spirit. At any rate it does not seem that we should make the equilibrium of Christian thought rest only on the idea of such a theocentrism, and we must now see if we shall fare better by examining another form of composition.

II. Can the dominating principle of the Catholic Synthesis be taken from the idea of the God of truth and of a pure intellectualism?

Starting from the name of its divine founder, Christian religion seems to have its center in this eternal Word, adequate image of the Father, sole and supreme mediator between God and the created order (cf. the development given in *La Philosophie et L'Esprit chrétien*. I), the total truth from which proceeds the Holy Spirit. In this conception, of which Gnosticism has given a caricature, the Hellenic idea of the Logos has come as a commentary and an explicitation of the evangelical teaching and especially of the texts from Saint John on the light with which the mystical sense is identified with the sense of truth itself, the principle at once of life and of light. Similarly again, borrowing from Aristotle the word and the idea of a pure contemplation that eternalizes man by allowing him, as in a flash of light, to see a glimmer of the immutable, some have transposed this speculative synthesis into a mysticism where the notion of a vision becomes dominant: even in this world the act of intelligence is the highest degree attained by aristocratized spirits and in the future life it is contemplation that constitutes the highest and beatifying end.

Coming under this inspiration, what becomes of the other ideas that seemed to us indispensably included in the Christian synthesis? The divine power is intimately linked to intelligence, which is its essential law. God sees Himself and sees in Himself all possibles, all essences, all the intelligible natures; willing is included in this light as the expression of an infinite wisdom, and truth is not a creature, it is the Creator Himself. The motto that dominates everything, that is put in the first place, is the key word: *Veritas*. Whence the tendency to subordinate the governance of everything to a discipline based on science, according to the repeated formula, *sapientis est ordinare* [to order pertains to the wise]; and, if this wisdom contains elements that do not at first sight seem to be of a theoretical order, little by little a secret dialectic leads to the enunciation of a thesis and of a practice according to which wisdom itself ends up considered as a pure science and pure theory.

What becomes of the idea of charity finally in this deliberately intellectualist synthesis? The divine essence is considered as diffusing the good by nature just as fire naturally diffuses heat: *Bonum est diffusivum sui* [the Good is diffusive of itself], the old adage goes, using the neuter as if to emphasize better that there is in this something constitutive, intelligible, and so to speak impersonal. Whence finally this other formula: *ens, verum, bonum et unum convertuntur* [being, the true, the good, and the one convert into one another], which is to say that being, the good, and unity are identified with truth and in truth itself. From this then comes the imperturbable serenity of the Christian who, having demonstrated the reasons that provide him with a faith of science, posits the doctrine, without any interest in questions pertaining to persons or any regard for those who err or are ignorant. A man speaking from the heart about a philosopher troubled by doubt and whose fate I was bemoaning once said to me: we must not be bothered with individual accidents; in our perspective only truth counts; we never take persons into consideration; there is charity only in truth: it is enough therefore to show the light; so much the worse for those who cannot or who do not will to see it. Once in a conference given at the Sorbonne, before the Society for the Study of New Ideas, the following thesis was upheld: the modern world goes a way of its own, the Church goes its own way: so much the better for those upon whom grace has fallen; we have only to let others follow their own way. It is with a logic such as this that the role of "atheistic Catholics" is justified, as certain faithless defenders of the faith have been called: we cannot, it was said, have anything against them if they have not received the grace of believing; and we must all the more appreciate the services they render to truth through the human aspects of truth they discover and through the tactics their faithlessness allows them to use where religious scruples might encumber the boldness of believers. In a famous letter to Albert de Mun, Louis Veuillot once declared that a well-placed blow with a saber can be the best of charities. Without going that [far] into the paradox, many are the spirits who have subordinated the extension of their charity to their conception of the truth, a truth they often reduce to their own conception, to their spirit, to the perspective of a clan, a hermetic devotion, a caste, a tradition or a personal interest. As great and as necessary as it may be, the idea of truth has the risk then of denaturing the properly Catholic conception and of reaching the point of making of the name itself a partisan sign, when what matters above all is to recall the saying: *Deus vult omnes salvos fieri* [God wills all to be saved]: Christ died for all, and we love Him, we imitate Him only by including all men, even the most unworthy, in an infinitely charitable solicitude. Will we not have to say then that if there is an overarching idea, an original principle, a unique soul in the Christian inspiration, it is this affirmation of Saint John: *Deus caritas est* [God is charity]?

III. Is it the point about charity that can be taken as the dominant and unifying principle of the Christian spirit?

It has often been said: God is love; it is by love that we recognize the disciples of the one who promulgated this new commandment, this greatest commandment of all, as He has said Himself: the one who has the love of God and of neighbor has accomplished all of the law; everything else disappears, only charity does not perish and subsists eternally.

Nevertheless, let us examine the consequences that a certain abstract and, so to speak, logical way of looking at charity sometimes entails, when we do not apply rightly the injunction: *ama et fac quod vis* [love and do what you will]. This wonderful saying from Saint Augustine (which entails the highest of meaning in the perspective in which its author understood it) has the risk nevertheless of causing the Christian spirit to deviate; and we have seen in diverse times in history the danger of a doctrine placing all the accent only on charity: thus Joachim of Flores in the twelfth century claimed that after the reign of the Father and the Son, of power and of intelligence, was to come and had to come the advent of the free Spirit of love; thus many illusions of heterodox mystics have germinated across the ages in heated imaginations and in hearts more ardent than enlightened and pure; and it could be that, in our time, we could discover traces of a generous fervor that, under the guise of exalting the divine goodness, misconstrue the salutary rigors of Christian ascetics.

In all of this, what do we make of the idea of divine power, of majesty and transcendence, which places an abyss of incommensurability between the Creator and the nothingness He calls into existence? Of this power as such we hold on only to the notion that there is nothing impossible for the inventions and the condescensions of the infinite love. We conclude that, from the start, God has given us to ourselves so that we may have the merit and the joy of restoring ourselves to Him who gives Himself to us in exchange for this restoration itself; then all distance disappears, in a familiarity that inclines certain modern *Origens* to fall finally into the same error as this great speculative figure of the Orient did: God is so good that He will not condemn anyone, and hell is only the threat we oppose to children to make them more behaved for fear of the boogeyman.

What becomes of the idea of essential truth and of fundamental intelligibility in this combination whose idea of charity becomes the guiding or even the exclusive principle? One refuses more and more to ground the Christian order on an ensemble of necessary truths; one resists, not without some good reason, the notion of a God identified with an Essence, source of all other essences, but that remains transcendent to all of created nature. One is unwilling to stop at this difficulty: how can there be union of charity where there is incommensurability of nature? One is inclined to stifle this question into the domain of abstractions and of false ontology, which used to discuss beings of reason and entities as if they were the most positive of existences. Also condemned en masse as though they were remains of idolatry are all assertions relative to the distinction of human nature and of the pure spirit that God is, in whom being and essence are only one, whereas in creatures subsists an indelible difference between nature and concrete existence. And when we try to call back to mind this metaphysically indestructible heterogeneity, people get irritated as if we were stuck in pure verbalisms, instead of seeing in God only a Father Whom nothing could separate from His children. This is a serious consequence coming from this superficial optimism that levels all unevenness and every obstacle, but which thereby, as we shall soon see more clearly, lowers God instead of elevating man, and hence also drags down human destiny by not recognizing the supreme exigencies of divine charity.

Later on we shall have to make it better understood how much this so-called charity—that is being pushed to the forefront as if to facilitate access to it and to extend its reach—is cruelly deceptive and lethal in the eyes of divine Goodness, which has for us infinitely more ambition than these knightly servants of a human charity, reduced to the measure of our personality. We had to denounce this distortion at this point, in order to let this negative conclusion be understood to which we have finally been brought and which opens the way for us toward a more comprehensive intelligence of the Catholic unity.

What is in effect implied in the analyses we have just made use of in this rapid sketch is that our discursive reflection succeeds only in decomposing and recomposing the Christian spirit, as it is found in the souls where it lives mysteriously. But in this there is a false presupposition. It can be said that, to the extent that one has claimed to dissect the Christian sense, to undo its organs, to redo its synthesis in an explicit cognition, one has killed it instead of vivifying it. It is not that such analyses should be set aside, but they are useful and salutary only in another perspective than the one in which people too frequently present them and in which we have just laid them out. It has often been noted that what touches and illuminates souls, is much less a long elaboration of erudition, of logic, of eloquence than it is a spiritual contact, the approach of sanctity: it has even been added at times that the spark from which faith wells up is produced outside of or above all the laboriously accumulated materials in view of preparing the illumination and lighting the fire. This is to say that we have not yet come to the true terrain on which the sacred flame catches fire, warms up, and blazes forth. We have still to make the most considerable effort, the one that puts us on our guard against insufficiency, the false starts Dechamps called the powerless science of scholarly demonstrations.

But, it will be said, is it possible, is it permissible to enter, without encroaching on it, into this profoundly obscure domain, reserved in saintly fashion for the soul and God to meet? Is not the Catholic Spirit a living mystery, inaccessible to the learned, that opens itself up only for the simple and the humble, be they the most knowledgeable of men, because we become believers only by letting go of indiscrete curiosities and by accepting to enter under the veil, there where Denis the Areopagite said that we would be able to find only impenetrable shadows and "the great Dark-ness"? That is what we must now explore, even if we were led to conclude that in effect we could encounter only obscurity. Let us hope nevertheless that even there still we will be able to justify and practice the *rationabile obsequium* [reasonable obedience].

CHAPTER 5

On the Enabling Method for Acceding to the Domain Where Lives the Indissoluble Unity of the Christian Spirit

If it seems cumbersome to define the Christian spirit, could it not be because we are using an insufficient and imperfectly adapted method regarding its object? What has gone before could have or even was intended to leave an impression of worrisome ambiguity: undoubtedly there is a legitimate and providential variety in the Catholic unity, *in dubiis libertas et multiformes viae Dei diversa quoque dona spiritus* [in doubts there is liberty and the ways of God take many forms as do also diverse gifts of the spirit]; this variety, however, must not lead to a radical diversity, much less to a visceral contrariety. *In necessariis unitas* [in matters of necessity unity]; and if we must add to this adage falsely attributed to Saint Augustine, *in omnibus caritas* [in all things charity], this charity should not consist in closing our eyes to better open our hearts: in granting open credit and humble receptivity toward all, charity must tend all the more energetically toward the fundamental and definite unity of souls in the light as in the love of Christ; otherwise Christian religion would be no more than a sign stuck on a caravansary of ideas, as it has sometimes been unjustly reproached with being. Let us not then blame those who never compromise regarding doctrinal exigencies. Pascal said: truth is not truth without charity; it is necessary to add as a compensatory assertion: charity is not charity without truth scrupulously sought and served.

To account for the hesitations and the conflicts that sometimes trouble the Christian conscience and stop many nonbelievers on the road of return or of access to faith, let us therefore examine in what can consist the methodological inconsistencies that prevented us, in our prior approach, from yet arriving at this unity of perspective, from which, according to the word of Bossuet, everything becomes clear in the eyes of the soul on the confusing stage of the world. Three principal causes seem to explain the relative failure of attempts often made to determine, from the philosophical or apologetic point of view, the inner nature of Catholicism, to which is applied still the witnessing of the Precursor regarding Christ: there is one among you whom you do not know: people believe they know and even judge Him, because they are in day-to-day contact; but these constant encounters do not reveal his secret or they even contribute to make him unknown, just as psychologists have noted the paradoxical fact that the inhabitants of a house are often more unable to describe it from memory than a visitor with newer and more vivid impressions. But let us leave these accessory details aside that could be multiplied not just in the purely psychological order, but also in the moral order; and let us examine the causes that hide, even from the most attentive and the most impartial of witnesses and critics, the most essential basis of Christian thought.

To begin with, people are all too ready to reason about the Catholic spirit as if it were entirely reducible to analysis. We have become so taken with the scientific habit of splitting difficulties in the Cartesian manner, of dissolving solid bodies, of dissecting living beings, of peering into the subconscious or the unconscious down to the most infinitesimal dimensions, that our presumptuous ambition is to attain thereby the finest of the fine, the base of the base of everything, even of the spiritual secrets, the divine operations, the mystical states, and the supernatural union. Whence that curiosity that today inclines so many analysts, believing and non-believing, to probings from which we hope to draw out the key to the mystery. Yet, even in the study of nature, this all too exclusively analytical method inevitably remains incomplete: it fails to catch the spark without which no synthesis is possible; and to the extent that analysis, which never captures this spark in its test tubes or under its scalpel, abstracts from it (without forasmuch keeping itself from affirming that it is exhaustive of the total reality), it becomes mutilating, deceiving, murderous. All the more so, when there is a question, no longer of lower nature, but of operations that, by hypothesis supposedly, imply some divine intervention, such analytical procedures are fatally bound to misunderstand the very object they are supposed to grasp in its intimate and indivisible unity.

A second cause, connected with the foregoing, accounts more clearly still for the semi-failures we have alluded to. We had sought earlier to bring together the diverse sources from which the Christian spirit came historically and doctrinally. To do that we took advantage of analyses bearing on facts, on ideas, on states of consciousness, and transforming all these data into notions as distinct as possible, we had asked ourselves how such conceptions, formed apart from one another and more or less disparate, could group themselves in a living organism. Nothing could be more chimerical than such a pretense, and yet it is so ordinary to do so that we do not even notice it has already destroyed what we would like to explain and justify. If the Christian religion were susceptible of such a method, it would not be a religion, being neither one nor religious: it would be a syncretism of beliefs and speculations mixed in with facts; it would not proceed from a principle higher than the disparate phenomena of a subalternate and moving character.

Third cause and another consequence of the methodological errors we have just indicated (and it is with this point that we shall see better already the remedy to be applied to such prejudicial deficiencies): if Christian religion had in effect been formed out of elements put forth by analysis and by grouping elaborate notions together abstractly, it would result entirely from accommodations, from adaptations; it would have come forth after the fact, as a complement for a life already constituted, out of a spontaneity on which it would be imposed in an extrinsic fashion, without taking any of its sap from the natural and rational order. That is how it has too often been considered as an added burden, worse still, as a repressive intrusion, as a troublemaker, as an arbitrarily and gratuitously onerous mortification. Among the objections that turn cultivated minds away, none is more tenacious and more harmful than this charge: the Christian religion presents itself as an accident in the normal life of humanity: historically, it is made up of bits and pieces; philosophically, it is repugnant to principles now established by science and metaphysics; morally, it shapes passive and submissive characters, without true virility, without initiative, without nobility of soul. And I once encountered in the notebook of an undergraduate the following formula, which, it turned out, came in fact from the professor: the state of holiness is an immoral state—we see then from this synoptic sketch the seriousness and the convergence of charges that a bad method of exposition can quite unjustly accumulate against the Christian spirit. It is for us then to take precisely the opposite of such a conception and of a method so disintegrating.

From the viewpoint we shall take, we shall show that the objections enumerated above will on the contrary be changed into illuminating proofs: what seemed to contradict itself will call for completion. This is true even for the metaphysical order and the preambles of faith; it will be even more true for the properly Christian truths and for the unity of revealed doctrine. In other words, where some thought they saw disparate data and surging conflicts, there will appear convergences, better still, implications, aspects of a unity that no analysis could really tear apart. How often, in keeping with our human ways of thinking and speaking, we oppose the divine attributes to one another, as if they got in one another's way and limited themselves mutually. And yet reason as well as faith must raise us above these anthropomorphic discourses, if not to make us understand entirely, at least to make us glimpse and affirm the essential simplicity and the perfect unity of God. What is truthful from the viewpoint of metaphysics, could that not be recognized better still in the order of supernatural wisdom where the power, the science, and the goodness, whose factious oppositions we saw, are at bottom one and the same Providence?

But how are we to approach this perspective that seems to surpass our human mode of knowing and teaching? For it is not enough to acknowledge the insufficiencies of our thought and of our speech, nor even to denounce the shortcomings that result from them: *in divinis, multum deficit omnis cognitio humana* [regarding the divine, all human cognition falls far short], according to the Scholastic adage. This is a matter of knowing, in spite of these deficiencies and above them, whether we can place ourselves, in a way that is positive and legitimate, if not at the divine center of unity, at least, thanks to the concurrence of reason and Revelation, at a point of view where the discordances and the oppositions giving rise to the fundamental objections against the Christian religion disappear.

To do that, it is necessary to go over the entire problem of human destiny in its most basic sense. Yes or no, can man, as he is in fact, be self-sufficient and give his thought, his personal and social life, his higher inclinations, his religious aspirations, a satisfying solution? Or else, from the lowest to the highest of secular experience and of the most rigorous analysis, does lucidity and probity require that we recognize a radical and incurable insufficiency? And if this last affirmation is the only one that matches our historical state as well as our philosophical inquiry, is it possible to go beyond a brute admission? Is it legitimate, in the face of this emptiness, to examine the edges of the abyss, to peer into it with a gaze, to draw from such a shortcoming, from such a defect, from such an emptiness that seemed at first entirely negative, some positive teaching? Indeed, let it be well noted: this emptiness is called such only in contrast to the apparent and false plenitude of experiences that fall short and that should themselves be called more negative than saturating, *vanitas vanitatum* [vanity of vanities]. Hence apart from this emptiness of which we were speaking not being fictitious since it is posited as the end-state of all the reality we experience, we must add that it represents paradoxically the very contrary of what has seemed vain, inconsistent, faulty. From that we can therefore say that, in spite of the mystery and the indetermination wherein it appears, such an abyss of obscurity is invincibly conceived as containing the maximum of being, the goal of our aspirations, the only plenitude that is not disappointing.

We have just taken up, in a purely experiential and rational way, the very experiences and the teaching of one John of the Cross in searching and in seeking to find being only by the dark night of the soul and by nothingness. But still we shall have to be on guard against the temptation into which have fallen so many metaphysicians and pseudo-mystics by leaving this highest goal of speculation in absolute indetermination. This is where we shall have to insert the precise data of history and of Revelation and justify the attitude of Saint Theresa as she protested with sovereign energy against all those who, in trying to attain "the God without form," would want to set the humanity of Christ aside as a means henceforth obsolete. The Christian spirit would disappear to the very extent that it would end up as a sort of gnosis and as a sort of idealism detached from incarnate realities. It is therefore more necessary than ever not just to show that the supernatural faith supposes and completes the entire edifice of nature and of reason that serve as substructure (just as the human composite serves as a support for the spirit in this world and in the future life too), but also to constantly tie the highest Christian speculation to the concrete data of history, to the experiences of popular piety, to the most humble devotions, to the love of details in which was incarnated the life of Christ, of the Virgin, and of the saints. Some think they are rising by detaching themselves from these presumed "childhoods" of Christian religion; in truth they lose the Catholic sense, without forasmuch gaining the philosophical sense or the human sense, quite to the contrary.

Thus little by little we shall see falling into one and the same plan the most opposed elements at first sight, the highest philosophical speculation and the devotion of an ignorant little girl, the secret of all of creation and the appearing in one point of space and time of a fact that seems minute and quite disproportionate to this immensity of centuries, of generations, and of worlds. Much more still, in the moral order as in the philosophical and historical order, the contrasts will have to be molded into one and the same light and the rigors of the divine exigencies will have to appear, according to Dante's word, as born of the first and incomparable love. Only on this condition can we hope to accede to the unique and incomparable spirit of authentic Christian religion. But, as is clear to be seen, the task required by the method sketched here is in fact immense, and we can do no more than lay out a few strands, meant to orient the inquiries in the direction that the Catholic tradition has always taken to resolve, sometimes without stopping to discuss them, the many objections nagging at it as it goes forth.

This synthesis cannot, it is true, be brought together for us here below in the perfect unity that remains a wish, a promise for the heavenly Jerusalem. But, as Newman said, it is good, amid the very infirmity of our earthly thoughts, to always know and even to have already a bit of the presence of the blessed vision of peace and unity. We would not be participating in the Christian spirit, we would not be able to speak of it in any way, if we did not have some sense of this definitive accord of nature, of reason, of faith, and of the union of grace: it is to sketching this harmony of the whole ensemble that we would now like to devote the sixth part of this study, in anticipation of the conclusions that will result from a glimpse, partial and from afar, of what Saint Augustine spoke of as "The City of God."

CHAPTER 6

The Catholic Unity

Catholicism is nothing if it is not everything, and its name, which means "universality," would be deceptive if a single point were missing in its plan, uniquely providential. This affirmation indicates by itself the full extent to be embraced; it dispatches absolutely the idea, so commonly widespread, of a religion that would have its moments, its domain restricted, without impregnating all the atmosphere we breathe, all forms of activity. Many, without being fully conscious of doing so, live and reason as if nature, science, public life were outside the solicitudes of Christ, and as if the only true Catholics made up the group of those called "the professionals of the confessional question." We will have to justify an attitude quite contrary to that. If the philosophical problem is the one that expresses most completely the ensemble of inquiries into nature, life, being, and the meaning of things, all of philosophy then has to bear witness and show that thought, like action, should come finally to attest in favor of the answers that Christian religion offers to the disquietudes of conscience.

Without going over the work laid out in the three books on *Thought*, *Action*, and *Being and Beings*, it would be helpful here to condense the results of these inquiries, undertaken without bias or begging the question, but spontaneously converging toward this one center of perspectives, where the lines of their aim converge. On the one hand, we will have to show the kind of preparation without which Christian religion could only appear as an overload. But on the other hand, we will have all the more to safeguard its irreducible originality and let it be known that, as prepared as it may be, it is an absolute novelty, with a wholly gratuitous character on the part of God, while being obligatory for man who has no other destiny than the supernatural vocation, from which he could not hold back with impunity.

I.

The first track to follow in the effort to align Christian thought with thought pure and simple, consists precisely in reverting back to the most distant origins of the history of spirit, in observing what Bohn calls "the birth of intelligence," and in showing that this genesis implies needs, successive advances, partial successes, but also insufficiencies and even failures for which there is no accounting without coming to the disposition of spirit that has rightly been called "religious expectation." If then it is consistent with itself, without illusion regarding its strengths and weaknesses, always attentive not to sin against the light, not to be discouraged nor to overrate itself, it normally surpasses the sensible world, the scientific order, metaphysical speculations, moral satisfactions, in order to make us face up to a disquietude that is not merely congenital and transitory, but final and naturally incurable.

On the whole, the typical state of humanity is found to be realized in two facts, historically defined. First, there was the original promise, the messianic expectation, the message of which the Jewish people were the recipients par excellence, but which, in diverse degrees, has resounded more or less throughout the ages, among all peoples, in all souls. Some may say that legend situates the golden age far back: this partial truth does not stand in the way of the yet more profound and more universal certitude of a higher reality toward which the looks and the hopes of humanity rise, ever in quest of a *ripa ulterior* [further shore]. This disquietude that, in spite of its disappointments, revives with an invincible confidence is one of those facts that cannot be ignored or denied without lying to one's conscience. And the question is precisely to inventory all that this fact implies, to discover the spring of this incoercible movement, to explain how human thought, always pushed forward, perpetually surpasses itself. The second typical state that history presents us with is no longer this messianic expectation, however obscure and anonymous it may be, but precisely the state of Catholic security, as if therein alone thought had finally found the word of its enigma, the secret of its destiny, and that homeland of truth that, according to the Scholastic expression, marks the center of its election, its true *ubi* [whereunto]; for, as was said in the Middle Ages, each thing has its place, its point of equilibrium, and its proper act, its *ubi*.—Now these two states correspond to one another, and apart from this calling and from this perfectly adapted response, everything is but difficulty, incomprehensibility, errant going about or resting in the night, like that anguish of travelers that Plotinus describes by the seashore in a darkness without stars.

In the work on *Thought*,[1] there is exposed in a detailed and coherent way this continuity that goes from the most inorganic world all the way to the summit of contemplation: the intent of this study is to make evident the ensemble of necessary conditions for the appearance of consciousness and of the spiritual life, but also the inevitable limits we find imposed on every finite intelligence. The primitive wish of thought is the perfect unity of what it is and of what is, in the image of the perfect union of the Father and of the Word. But this divine unity is the inaccessible privilege of God Himself and, though reason takes its light from the uncreated light, it remains nevertheless profoundly inadequate to pure Thought. To be sure, it could be that this inadequacy would remain the natural state of every being. As Saint Thomas says, the desire to see and to possess God, which is the object to which intelligence aspires, cannot be brought to completion naturally; and reason itself cannot but recognize its own limits, without having to incriminate the author of such an order that leaves unsatisfied and vain a natural aspiration, but one that is not reasonable in spite of the spontaneous wish of the intelligent nature. If then Revelation proposes for us through grace the possibility of surpassing this inaccessibility and of becoming, as Saint John says, "children of God" and participants in the divine light, to the point of seeing Him finally *sicuti est et facie ad faciem* [as He is, and face-to-face],

---

1. Cf. the two volumes of this work published in 1934: the Presses Universitaires de France, who took over and continue the editions of the Alcan publishers, have reedited volume 1 and will shortly reissue volume 2, now almost sold out.

then Christian religion, as unforeseen as it is, as gratuitous and as unrequired as it may seem, is no longer at the most something overbearing, an intrusion, a repression, a subjugation, a diminution, or a vilification of man; quite to the contrary: it breaks forth before our eyes as something we did not dare to hope for, something we would have wished being able to expect, something that crowns and consummates the entire edifice of nature and of thought.

Do we not conceive now already how justified is the name given to the Gospel, the Good News? It is new, with an inexpressible newness; and yet it is what there is that is most profoundly in conformity with all the élan, *ab origine mundi* [from the origin of the world], with all the ascensions that mark the biblical work of the six days, with all the profound effort of science, of art, of philosophy, of true civilization. Thus are reconciled the characters that seemed at first incompatible: the absolute transcendence and the immanent preparation of Christian religion at the most profound depth of the universe.

Let us reflect still more on this problem of thought, in order to better understand how the Christian dispensation, though absolutely free and gratuitous on the part of God, is nevertheless the most integral, the most substantial truth that can be conceived. Already on this point we can justify, as we shall do better still later on, the liturgical adage: *nihil debuit, plus non potuit* [more He did not have to do, more He could not do]. God owed nothing and creation, like the elevation of man, remained pure liberality; but there is nothing greater He could have done, nothing better than what He has realized; and it is in this sense that creation is worthy of Him, as incommensurably as it remains beneath Him, and while His essential glory remains above the external glory that the entire order of creatures and even their supernaturalized life procure Him.

Indeed, if we meditate on what thought is in itself and on the immense difficulty of raising created beings to the faculty of thinking, we remain in wonderment over this marvel. To think is, absolutely speaking, the intimate life of the holy Trinity where unity is consummated in the reverberated light from the Father to the Son in the reciprocity of love of the Spirit. *Lumen de lumine, spiritus, lumen et vita* [Light from light, spirit, light, and life]. The Father is spirit, the Son is spirit, the Spirit is the kiss of the Father and the Son. Apart from that there is only darkness. How then is it conceivable that a light be lit outside of this glow?

Let it not be thought indeed that there would be any other brightness than the divine light of God: nothingness does not exist; let us set aside any image that would let us suppose that outside of absolute Being there is room for something else, eternal essences, possibilities or impossibilities, in the way Leibniz figures there are divine fulgurations as a fatal production of an infinite intelligence, stained with pantheism. It would be better to imagine that, to produce creatures and especially spiritual beings able to know and to love, God, according to the expression of Saint Paul (*Philippians* 2, 4), made room in Himself, *se ipsum exinanivit* [emptied Himself], in order to allow these beings to reconstitute in Him, to resurrect, so to speak, His own life, His own thought. But in order for these beings to remain themselves and to enjoy this reconstituted divinity, it is exactly necessary that they not be confounded in this immensity by a return that is absorbing, like a spark that falls back and gets lost in the glow from which it has sprung. Thus the divine love and power are in accord to produce and to limit at once thinking beings who at once participate in the divine light and distinguish themselves from it by limitations that are the very conditions of a personal life, of a beatitude of one's own, of a new extension of the reign and of the very glory of God.

Thus the problem of thought examined as freely and as fundamentally as possible by a philosophy concerned with rendering intelligible the genesis of spirit comes to conclusions in keeping with the exigencies of Catholic theology. These exigencies can be summed up, from the rational viewpoint, in three propositions.—There is no other light than that of God and of His Word; this is the light that illumines everyone coming into this world and that is at once shining and living.—But this divine thought cannot be naturally and completely participated in by any creature; it is through analogy, through a thousand deficiencies, that the created intelligence aims at, without attaining it, this unity of being and of truth, as a sun that cannot be looked at frontally; intelligence is as it were blinded, before the infinite, by a central scotoma, and, as Bossuet puts it, the spirit can only draw near to this inaccessible light as if in a "stunned flight" and by "fluttering about it."—Nevertheless, if thinking, in the fullness of this word and of this act, is possible only for God whose ancient wisdom already knew how to speak as from pure Act, from the Thought of thought, through grace there can be infusion of its light, participation in the divine spirit. Hence the Christian religion is indeed what renders to our natural darkness something else than an illusion, something else than a mortification and a darkening of reason: it brings us, if we will receive it, "the power to become children of God" and to commune with the eternal Word incarnate in our nature, incarnate in each one of Its faithful and mysteriously dwelling at this center of the soul, which, without it, would remain empty and dark, but which is destined for it, and which, through it and with it, becomes the principle of illumination and of divine life in us. The entire thought of creatures is in fact oriented toward the divine for such a solution; but this end remains naturally inaccessible; hence it is entirely gratuitous on the part of God. And thereby comes the conciliation of the double character that is always recognized in the Christian religion: it is in conformity with the essential wish of intelligence that invincibly and ineffectively aspires to see, to possess God, yet it could be withheld without injustice; there is no necessity to make God debtor to this creature, and the supernatural gift, which constitutes our thought in intimate union with the Word, remains therefore pure liberality, sublime invention, charitable initiative.

II.

No less than the problem of thought, the problem of taking action [*agir*] leads us to analogous conclusions that must also be exposed, in order to push aside so many obstacles and to orient this human will toward its end, equally inaccessible and infinitely desirable. This problem of taking action, in what does it consist, if not to make us understand the difficulty in conceiving and in realizing a secondary cause that would nevertheless be deemed worthy to be thought of as taking action. But is there, for a created being, a possibility of absolute initiative? This is the point that, through the examination we must make of it down to its depth, will reveal better still the most secret spirit of the grandeur of the divine plan as Catholicism makes it known to us.

For there to truly be *taking action* [*agir*] in the proper and total sense of the word, it seems indispensable that the initiative proceed form the agent; otherwise it would be, according to the expression of Malebranche, only some being acted on [*qu'un agi*]; and that is quite the way on the whole that Malebranche, even Leibniz, and all the more so Spinoza, present our role to us: we are moved, even as we believe ourselves to be moving. This appears to be so necessary that the most hardy speculative minds have ended up suppressing God's pure act to make way for becoming, for the obscure but sovereign élan of man, as post-Kantian metaphysicians and the immanentist philosophers of recent years have done. That is how much the concept of acting seems to imply an absolute beginning and how much thought itself, to be active, that is, to be intelligible, seems to call for some creation that is at least partial or started. How then, from the Christian point of view, can philosophy make way for exigencies such as cannot be ignored which we cannot but think that they seem imperious and, in certain respects, well founded?

Let us begin by observing that we invincibly have the sense of being cause and, according to the expression of Aristotle, of having paternity of our acts with greater certitude than the paternity of our children; yet we are led by analyses that we cannot doubt to recognize that in most of our actions we undergo multiple influences: we find ourselves torn between the evidence of our constant passivity and the conviction of having in spite of it all an initiative of our own without which we would not have the consciousness of being active, nor even the consciousness of being passive, nor finally the consciousness of being conscious beings. The study of action consists essentially in resolving this difficulty: to give passion its due by unpacking everything that weighs on our apparent decisions, on our actualized operations, on the consequences so often unforeseen of our resolutions and then, if there remains anything for us, to give activity worthy of that name its due.

The problem is so fearsome that it has often been concealed or that people limit themselves to outlining the desirable terms for a solution, without rendering distinctly conceivable the very relation of these terms: it is what Bossuet called "holding on to the two ends of the chain, without seeing or grasping the in-between." Of course, it is already a good deal to formulate the indispensable proportions to be maintained even when we leave them in their blunt state, like seeds that contain the invisible kernel in its alimentary sheath. It is to the credit of Thomistic teaching to have intrepidly affirmed, along with divine premotion, the freedom of the rational creature, even as it left hardly comprehensible this assertion that God wills and makes humanly free our volitions and actions for which He alone provides the possibility and the realization. Nevertheless, would it not be desirable still to explain better the sense of their cooperation, of which we are told implicitly that it is a double action (*agir*)? Saint Bernard, in a formula marvelous for its descriptive precision, had specified that each one of the two cooperators is, in a sense, author of the entire act. What we would like is that this description could become an explanation; and this is what a methodical and complete study of human acting can alone and must finally aim at and provide.

Now, what such a study of action aims to establish is this: freedom, of which we necessarily have the idea, the use of and the responsibility for, does not consist in partial, subordinate options independent of one another; all these fragmentary decisions that in fact come from our deciding do not take part in freedom except insofar as they are tied to the supreme alternative where our destiny is at stake and for which each act can become the wages and the toll. If the best objects, sometimes under childish ways, can serve as vehicle for the total option, it is always insofar as these occasions bring into question our profound attitude toward the good, duty, fidelity to our light and to our calling. Rather than treating of freedom and of acting with regard to these occasional engagements, we must raise the problem where it truly resides in its integrity; the question of freedom and of action places us inevitably before the dilemma: participate in the divine initiative by identifying our wiling with the very willing of the first cause, or else try in an egoistic autonomy to constitute ourselves in the *non serviam* [I shall not serve]. Thereby philosophy succeeds in raising, from below, the problem in the very terms where Christian religion presents it from above. We see thereby at what depth rational inquiry and religious requirements encounter one another. This convergence, about which there is nothing accidental, arbitrary, or even avoidable, manifests the profoundly realistic character of Christian religion, because all the highways of philosophy, methodically explored to their fullest extent, converge on this central roundabout where we are trying to settle our observation point without yet having reached it.

We have not succeeded in doing so, because in fact, despite seeing more clearly than before the terms to be united, we do not yet perceive why this cooperation of two activities is required, nor especially how the union will be accomplished that will allow man to have the dignity of being a cause, the possibility of a quasi-divine acting (*agir*) and the merit open to being the receptacle of beatitude itself. But it is only by entering into the religious perspective that, further on, we shall give some answer to these questions. For the moment we would like to follow another way, so as to show how the problem of being, like that of thinking and of action, leads philosophy, through an entirely intuitive process, to solutions that, so to speak, propose in depth precisely what Christian religion offers us as a plenitude fulfilling and infinitely surpassing the aspirations, the foretastes, the solicitations of every reasonable and religious expectation.

III.

The problem of being that ancient philosophy had broached from the beginning turned out to be so profound that the moderns have often avoided it only to latch onto the problem of knowledge, as if the critique of our faculties were enough for philosophy and caused ontological curiosity to fade away. Most think that our intelligence attains only phenomena, relations, becoming, subjective states, an immanent activity; consequently Being in itself, and even being in us, far from being apt to be studied as a mysterious reality, is reduced to the history of positive science and to efforts of the spirit in the production of this edifice of universal relativity.

But undermining a problem is not to resolve it. The study of thought and action has itself shown the subterfuge perpetuated by relativism, which claims to know relations while ignoring the terms purportedly brought together. From diverse quarters there arises a neo-realism; and the problem of God, far from having disappeared, imposes itself on the attention of the most liberal and the most critical minds. That such a question is obscure is not a reason for suppressing or even for avoiding it, so that the ancient difficulty reemerges: is there absolute Being? and if there is, how can we conceive along with it, in it, other beings? Must we, with Spinoza, absorb into the one Substance all that subsists, and is absolute Being the unique and total being or else, if there are really beings that deserve this name of beings, how do they fit in with the plenitude of Being in and for itself? In vain have some taken the way of imagining nothingness as a real emptiness where secondary causes would be lodged; but this materializing image is nothing but a false expediency: the thought of nothingness, it has rightly been said, is a nothingness of thought; we cannot suppose that divine being, in a sort of Manicheanism, would have before it something that, without yet being, could nevertheless furnish an available place, a *chôra* [space], according to the expression of Plato, who reduces to this word the idea of prime matter eternally placed at the disposition of the demiurge.

If then there are beings, the problem of their reality is no less difficult and necessary to resolve than that of the first cause and the divine absolute, the double enigma for which philosophy has withal not ceased looking for the answer; and here again the most intrepid enquiry has to lead to proposing a welcome for Christian revelation. Being in itself, it tells us, is not merely a blunt substance without thought, a pure thought without foundation and without love: it is the very unity of this Trinity of persons making up but one indivisible substance. And notwithstanding the entire sufficiency of this perfect life ever in act, the providential plan has freely, out of goodness, without necessity of any kind, called created beings to a participation in infinite beatitude. Assuredly, such beings could not be posited in themselves as immediately solved equations; in them, being could not make itself from the start equal to thought nor could knowledge be equal to the end that is only glimpsed and coveted. This congenital inadequation that highlights the necessary distinction of the Creator from any conceivable creature still does not prevent a progressive assimilation, a meritorious cooperation, a union that, without ever being a confusion of natures, can become a filial adoption and, according to the theological expression, fruition and enjoyment of the divine beatitude itself. In this way beings have both a subsistence that remains proper to them and an inviolable dependence on their sole and sovereign cause: they owe nothing to any other being than God, who in a sense is all in all, without there being any need for invoking the false concept of a nothingness from which to derive; and still this being of creatures is so real that, for spirits endowed with freedom, their existence can separate itself from the divine life, to the point that it would be better for them not to have been born; but that separation is their deed; it is possible only because for the union to be good supposes a voluntary option and a free use of the divine grace.

We see here just how far we must go to give the problem of being an irreducible significance: it melds neither with the problem of thought nor with the problem of acting: indeed it is because our thoughts cannot equal their object, because our actions cannot attain their total end that being in us is not reducible either to the idealist aspect or to the pragmatist aspect. There is, if we may so speak, between the consciousness we have of ourselves and the end of our aspirations, a naturally incurable disproportion; that is why the problem keeps its originality: being within us is never only what we know nor what we realize, it lies at this mysterious center that no natural good, no light of reason could illuminate or fulfill in its depth. Saint Bernard, following Augustine, had the most vivid sense of what he calls the abyss of our being, capable of absorbing everything without coming to any solid bottom. It is not surprising then that philosophy, unable to solve this problem, should have often turned away from it; and yet it is its strict duty to bring us face-to-face with what the Areopagite also called the abyssal depths of every created being.

Hence, through all the avenues that a courageous philosophy must follow to the end of its reach, we succeed in manifesting positive emptinesses, so to speak, real holes whose existence we cannot deny and whose depths we cannot fill; and thereby we understand the philosophical sense of the assertion where the Thomist doctrine has been summed up in saying that if the spirit sums up in itself all of nature, it is because it is itself essentially "capable of God," *capax Dei*, and because our reason is made for being in all the variety and plenitude of senses for that word.

It will be objected that, for us to describe thus all the demands of philosophy as far as they will extend, we must be secretly inspired by the Christian revelation. This is true in a sense: a philosophy that goes without deviating, without collapsing, without coming to a halt too soon, all the way to the legitimate and complete terms of its normal development, is, Fénelon used to say, a fiction of philosophy. But why should we not find for ourselves a more vivid light where already some diffuse enlightening has not been denied us? Let us distinguish then between what can, what should be accessible to a well directed reason, and what could only be the revelation of naturally inaccessible truths. A comparison will make us hearken to this teaching that excessive scruples have often led to misunderstand. The lyrics of a chant escape us and even as we hear the voices we do not get the sense of the words. Once the libretto is brought before our eyes, immediately we have no difficulty discerning the train of the text being sung. Will it be said that the libretto is what creates our hearing, the only or the principal revealer of the words finally grasped? No, because we were already hearing notes and without that hearing the written text would not have brought the joy, at once musical and literary, that make up the beauty of the chant. So it is for those many truths of which Saint Thomas says that revelation confirms, sharpens, purifies, universalizes, without their being in themselves above all rational capacity.

However, it may be added, do you not risk presenting the Christian religion in this way as the mere complement of a philosophy that would through its demands be the grounds and the framework, so to speak, of the supernatural order, which should remain unanticipated, gratuitous, and incommensurable to all that has been given naturally? This objection, well worth being taken into consideration, brings us in fact to a new problem, that of the specifically Christian elements or, in other words, the problem of the original contribution that no human speculation could foresee and that has deserved for that reason to be called, with all the force of the term, the Gospel, that is, the new par excellence, the Good News, a newness that is so great that it remains unknown even to those who have made themselves familiar with it, and that deserves that this word of the Precursor should be said of it: "There is one among whom you do not know." We will thus surpass the criticism that all of our prior effort might have suggested: for we seemed perhaps to be preparing the way for the Christian spirit so much through the human spirit that we were running the risk of provoking a double-edged reproach: either you are trying, through the immanent study of our human nature, to prove the conformity of reason and grace: or else you are suspending nature so much from the supernatural that we can no longer understand how it would be possible to remain purely in the human realm; so that you are oscillating from the abuse of some immanence to the abuse of some transcendence, both equally ruinous for the equilibrium of Catholicism.

Coming to the end of this part devoted to the philosophical preparation, it is therefore necessary to insist most energetically on these two conclusions: (1) The solutions that philosophy can and must propose, not only leave an open field for Christian teaching, but they show in it an unhoped for response, a marvelous congruence, and that without allowing for any presumptuous exigency to result from such a correspondence, because human speculation, far from claiming to provide itself the answer and the means, recognizes spontaneously its powerlessness and its indigence.—(2) Notwithstanding such deficiencies, the natural order could subsist without there being any necessity, any justice, any goodness to render impossible this imperfect, but viable, equilibrium. Hence let no one accuse us of falling from Charybdis into Scylla. The role of philosophy here is of course delicate and very perilous; all the more reason not to evade a task that is forbidding only because it has to be beneficial.

We shall now then change our outlook and place ourselves in a perspective that is quite the opposite to the one we have just examined. We shall consider the divine message and, by the light of Revelation, glimpse what Sacred Scriptures call the inventions of divine charity in the work of the supernatural vocation, reparation, and elevation of man, in the multiform unity of the providential plan of the universe.

CHAPTER 7

The Inventions of Charity and the Supernatural

In what precisely does the unexpected news brought by Revelation consist? It surpasses, according to the teaching of the Church, all that man could have foreseen, desired, obtained. Try as we will, through philosophical analysis, to search into human aspirations and needs, to wish upon a happiness we do not know how to define and that we would will to be infinite: none of these demands can come close to presaging the supernatural gift, which is disconcerting for reason, to the point of having seemed "scandal" and "folly" to the Jews and to the pagans who were the first to receive testimony of it. Moreover, even among us, many hear the sound of the words, repeat the formulas of the Christian message, but very few truly "realize" its bearing and its true content. Dare I say that, before the categorical pronouncement of our destiny in terms stripped of its routine formulas, some educated believers, some professors of theology, some prelates have shown a surprise and almost a certain indignation?

What then literally is this promise of the Gospel? It is the insertion of man into the divine life, the positive adoption, the vital assimilation that mortifies man only for a new birth that makes us *consortes naturae divinae* [sharers of the divine nature]. Those are not, as a wise preacher once said, "pious exaggerations of Our Lord," but it is nevertheless all very difficult to understand humanly; it is of such a gift that the Apostles themselves received the announcement as a disquieting shock: *durus est hic sermo* [this is a hard saying]. How is it that greatness of such goodness can appear hard, provoke fear and flight? How is such prodigy conceivable and realizable? That is what appears to us indispensable to look into if we wish to finally glimpse something of the intimacy and penetrate into the secret of the Christian spirit.

Let us note first then that all prior preparations, however useful they may have been, henceforth seem like scaffoldings, meant to be removed for the splendor of the edifice to reveal itself freely. Such is the testimony of converts: the veil has fallen, and all the arguments that were drawn on this curtain seem to them henceforth erased and excessive: without having an intuition into the truth of faith, they have the evidence of their faith itself, however obscure remain the objects. This sense of certitude higher than any other is a common experience, and it is fully justified from the standpoint of faith itself, which rests, not on arguments, but on the inner testimony that God gives of Himself within us through the gift of the grace without which there would be only human credibility and presumption.

Let us try to give a glimpse of the difficulty God, if we dare to say, has had to resolve in order to have participate in his life creatures essentially different from Him by the incommensurable abyss that seems to render incommunicable the absolute perfection of Being in itself and of itself. From the standpoint of metaphysics, the necessity of such a separation cannot be ignored. From that follows all that the Bible calls to mind of inviolable majesty, of the law of fear, of inflexible justice, of rigorous sanctions: far from hindering the order of charity, this order of necessity, as we shall see presently, is the inescapable condition, but also and above all the very means used by sovereign Goodness. In any case the law of grace does not in any way nullify the law of truth, and the Good News does not derogate in any way from the constitutive order that holds up all of creation.

If it is not in this metaphysical perspective that we must look for the secret of the divine inventions, where else can it be located? We have seen that no created thought, no secondary cause, no derivative being could entertain the adequation that is the privilege of the Trinity, where, according to the teaching of the Magisterium, God is his own being, his own essence, his own spirit, without any distinction of persons standing in any way whatsoever of the absolute unity of substance. Would not the supernatural gift consist in suppressing within us the inadequation that subsists inevitably between our thought, our action, our being?—No, for this inadequation that the Thomists call "the real distinction of essence and existence" and of which they like to make the fundamental truth of their doctrine, is something impossible to be suppressed, because realizing a perfect unity would suppress all differentiation of creatures among themselves and of creatures from God. Here again there subsists an insurmountable barrier. And it is not just a radical impossibility of such a unity that is imposed upon us, it is, even more still, the very exigency of charity that maintains this essential distinction. For, without such a separation, beings, absorbed into the divine unity, would cease to be themselves, and losing all reality conscious of itself, would no longer be beatified as such, children of God; they would be extinguished like sparks in a glow, by ceasing to belong to themselves to enjoy their union. In other words, there is not, for creatures, any beatitude or subsistence of one's own, except by voluntary communion. Unity is not union; and spiritual union can become transformative, but without thereby suppressing the feeling of distances, the grateful humility, the chant about mercies and the infinite élan, ever capable of new discoveries even at the heart of the most assured and the most complete possession.

From these views, there results a more precise conception of the supernatural. The moment has come to set aside certain confused images, certain insufficient uses of the word and of the idea that sums up in a technical term the original contribution of Catholicism. The supernatural is in fact that which, as truth, as life, as end, is infused, that is, given by God without any human effort being able to uncover the presence or procure the action of this element, of this ferment, at once inaccessible and inserted in what is most intimate of ourselves. Leaving aside the vitiated or subalternate meanings of this word or even its aspects relative to the modes of the divine action, let us try to define in what consists what theologians call the supernatural in itself, the absolute supernatural.

Implicitly people are often content with the idea that the supernatural is what, in God, escapes our rational knowledge, what consequently requires a revelation to be known by us, such as the mystery of the Trinity. It would follow that Revelation would reside in the promulgation of a speculative truth, as if we had to conjure up two parts in the knowledge of God. Through one we would naturally attain one piece, if we may speak thus, one aspect of divinity. The rest would be reserved for a communiqué coming from on high and having to do with reserved aspects.—Such a notion of the supernatural seems insufficient and even without consequence. In God, there are no separable aspects, and all our knowledge remains, according to the expression of Saint Thomas, *multum deficiens in divinis* [much deficient regarding divine things]. Besides, how could the revelatory words suggest truths incommensurable with all our ideas and all our human experiences? Finally and above all the supernatural, as we have seen above, is essentially union, assimilation, beatification: everything that does not go to charity and does not come from it, Dechamps used to say is not, in the strict sense, of the Christian supernatural. Hence the conception to hang on to here is without doubt that of a new knowledge, but that proceeds from the spirit of adoption and that tends to communicate to us, according to the wonderful expression of Saint Anselm, the divine mores.

The coherence of these diverse analyses is one more confirmation of the character, in one sense fully rational, in another sense divinely harmonious, of Christian dogmatics: on the one hand, none of the exigencies of metaphysics is misapprehended or violated; but on the other hand, the entirely gratuitous liberality of God is made manifest without being chained to any other convenience than that of its love.

We are touching now on one of the most sensitive points of human conscience: the Christian spirit, it has been said, is revolting, because it makes of a gratuitous gift a rigorous obligation under pain of eternal death; how are we to understand and admit that goodness is imposed and can turn into vengeful rigor, as if it were a question of a susceptible and jealous master, measuring the offense, not according to the infirmity of the offender, but according to the dignity of the one offended, and reviling his courtiers even in the way he distributes his favors at the price of restitution? —This specious objection is no more than sophistical: yet it is important to discuss it thoroughly, and this examination will help us to enter better still into the innermost of the Christian perspectives, by preparing us thereby to understand what means God has used to realize the adoption of his creatures, the true end of the entire economy of this world, according to the historical order that is, in fact, the one in which we have to live, to think, and to act.

Let us look immediately to the extreme paradox that we shall have to justify. Can God deny Himself or, if we may say, commit suicide by renouncing His being, His beatitude, His love for Himself, which in no way resembles an egoism because it is made of the reciprocal love of the three equally divine persons? No, this hypothesis is bereft of reason and even monstrous. Being is so fundamentally good that it cannot but will itself, and that with all intelligibility, with all liberty. Now let us suppose that God deposits in His creature something of His own life, a possibility of participation in His being: must we not say that this presence, this divine aspiration remains without repentance, unable to falsify itself, to misappropriate the excellence of such a gift, the free willing of this existence of which nothing could prevent intelligence and heart from remaining enamored? Even if one makes ill use of this gift of being, one cannot incriminate it; and that is what mystics like Tauler, Julienne of Norwich, and so many others take note of, when they declare that even among the most perverted, the damned, there persists a fundamental good, an indelible attachment to being, without which besides the punishment and the eternal survival would not even be understood. Hence the force of our destiny remains, in any case, tied, supported, activated by the love of a being for itself, insofar as it is analogous to, or even further, insofar as it is partially identical with and participating in the love of the absolute Being for his own being.

Upon this radical dynamism, everything is built up and ordained; and it is in this deepest sense that we must interpret the great theological truth that Dante echoed in the inscription he placed at the entrance to hell itself, which is also itself, like everything else, "the work of the first Love." Once one grasps this secret, one no longer thinks of being surprised at the exigencies that, as rigorous as they are, result inevitably from a maximum of generous goodness. It could not be otherwise without the economy of the supernatural vocation being ruined, without all the divine elevation of humanity being impossible or unreal. It is not in word alone or by only some slight of hand that God wants to unite us to his perfection and to his felicity, it is entirely in reality and at the most just cost, without which we would be only copies, reflections, not living members of Christ living in us.

Hence we find definitively set aside the following objection, tied to an illusion: the Christian is someone like anyone else with a few more duties, a few beliefs, or a few practices added on in order to obtain, through a sort of life insurance on the next life, an honorable retirement. How many people, without going as far as this conception that at one time would have been called prosaic, bourgeois, and reasonable, still have the idea that the Christian religion is a comfortable wisdom and that all excesses are equally repugnant to its spirit of conservatism, of equilibrium, of stabilizing authority! Even among the adversaries of Christian faith many imagine that it is at times tied to the protection of an established order on earth, at times menacing to the human virtues most dear to our dignity, to our independence, to our spirit of social progress and of scientific initiative. Often it has even been claimed that these two different aspects are in concert with one another and confer on Christian religion more and more this twofold characteristic of a slave morality and an autocratic regime.

To dissipate such prejudices—to which some facts and some doctrines have at times given the appearance of lending credit—we have not to attenuate, but surpass the banal idea people too often have of Christian religion under the pretext of praising its civilizing role and its human beneficence. The point is not to organize, in it and through it, a happiness at the measure of man and of temporal societies; the point is, through the risks and the challenges that assail good people as well as bad people, to the scandal of too earthly spirits, to realize a divine ambition. Nothing counts, in the eyes of supernatural charity, except the sublime end assigned to us and that, as we have just shown, is at work invincibly in us as the expression of the spirit placed in us to have us opt between salvation or the loss of God.

No doubt this alternative is disconcerting to moralists, thinkers who limit themselves to obvious considerations; one would like, according to the words of de Musset, to be able to follow to one side a more gentle path. But this road that one would believe to be more human, more pleasant, more certain, would in reality be a deception, a path that would lose itself without reaching any of the coveted aims. And it is not just the authoritarian commandment of God that imposes another solution on us, one apparently more onerous, in reality more loving and more happy; it is the profound movement of our nature itself joined to the solicitations and stimulations of supernatural grace.

Whereas ancient wisdom suggested precepts of moderation, of holding back and almost of abdication: *"ne quid nimis* [nothing in excess]! Mortal, beware of immortal hopes; finite being, avoid infinite ambitions!," Christian wisdom prescribes quite the contrary: *"duc in altum* [lead on high]! the measure for loving God is to love without measure"; and the word wherein the Gospel serves up the new law it promulgates is the word of excess, *excessus*: God going out of Himself so to speak and asking us to go out of ourselves to the end of the possible or even, Christ says, of the impossible, wisdom that in effect, according to the word of Saint John, goes *"in finem* [unto the end]" and that prevents humanity from legitimately being able to belong to itself. That is the great scandal, the principle of repugnances and of hostilities, the terrible stroke and the only solution still in conformity with what there is in our nature that is most generous, most receptive of the preveniences and of the gentle violences of grace.

It may be thought that theoretically this analysis of the Christian spirit, in showing the summit to which it leads us, lets fall into the lower regions and brushes away into the shadows many misconceptions, many false susceptibilities, many pretenses lacking in nobility and in outlook. But does not a sketch such as this still remain up in the air as it were, without hanging from a solid wall? and do we not have to show that what is at stake is something other than a painting, than an outlook? It is easy to sketch prodigious architectures; the difficult point is to make them stand upright with solid and heavy materials. We are told incessantly of our assimilation to God, of a supernatural vocation, of the price to pay in order to transform the loan of grace into an acquired wealth. But is not all that, which is easy to speak of, a fiction, something unreal, even an impossibility? We have had to show the metaphysical obstacles; are there not also moral obstacles to bar the road to what is called the adoption of man by God? and must we not bring this expression from the holy Books down to a parable, to one of those oriental formulations where exaggeration plays so to speak a constant and normal part?

For us to arbitrate these different views among the theologians themselves who have diversely interpreted the doctrine of our deiformity, it is necessary to examine more deeply the means at our disposal to make this sort of deification possible that makes of supernaturalized man a new being: one's activity becomes as it were passive and one's passivity becomes as it were active in this cooperation that we can call "theandric" and that corresponds to a state such as the one for which

Saint Paul gives us the formula: *vivo, jam, non ego, vivit autem in me Christus . . . mihi vivere, Christus est* [I live, now not I, but Christ lives in me . . . for me to live is Christ]. How is that realized? The divine inventions, we have been saying, have an abyss to cross: the moment has come to scrutinize these abysses and to see what bridges can be thrown across them. That will be the purpose of our eighth part.

CHAPTER 8

The Destiny Offered and Imposed on Man

Little by little we have sought to understand in what consists the destiny that is at once offered and imposed on us, imposed in the sense that, even in missing it, we cannot but fall under its reprisals, offered in the sense that our acceptance and our cooperation are required for the imposed gift to produce its liberating and beatifying effects. Those are difficult passes to negotiate, it will be said, for thought trying to discern the ways of God and the movements of human nature. But how much more difficult still is the intelligence and the realization of the means leading to such a goal! We should even say that we could not even become really aware of this goal if we do not know the roads to follow, the means to employ or to undergo to actually attain the end assigned to us.

With all the effort already employed to bring out the enormity of a solution that takes man away from himself and, so to speak, from the entire order of creation in order to insert him into divine life itself, have we truly grasped, otherwise than in just words and images, the tremendous truth of this transfiguration? It is not a matter of a spiritual alchemy that would change man without man into a celestial being; it is a matter of a voluntary renunciation, an immolation consented to, a radical mortification; and here is why. We are naturally attached to the already marvelous being that constitutes our sensory life, our aesthetic, our spiritual life, with all that it affords us of enjoyment, power, excellence: and we are right in admiring this human nature adorned with marvelous gifts. And that is precisely what must serve as the price for the exchange, the cash to spend to gain another life that presents itself to us at first only as insensible, unconscious, unimaginable, even frightening, as Scripture declares in reminding us that the master is exacting and tough, that he wants to harvest where he has not sown, and even that there will be taken away from those who do not have enough ... How is all this compatible with the doctrine of charity? And is that the Good News that gives joy to avid hearts?

We have still to hear of yet more penetrating requirements and more onerous exigencies. The thesis about redeeming (*redemptio*), also the one about the purchase that procures salvation and the precious pearl at the cost of an abnegation of man restoring his natural gifts to God, is but a parable, quite captivating to be sure, quite authenticated by Sacred Scripture and the patristic tradition, quite useful always to jolt our spirits, caught up in the realities of this world; but that is not the complete word for the enigma, not the sufficient explanation. This allegory, which besides corresponds to a literally exact truth, needs to be interpreted, rectified, completed.—Interpreted first, because this deal, which seems to bring together two adversaries for a barter to be negotiated, would send a false idea of divine generosity and human infirmity. It is not for Himself that God wants to buy us or redeem us, as if we were not already his servants and his debtors: but it is for us and to make us participants in his kingdom: *propter nos homines et propter nostram salutem; non dixi vos servos, sed amicos* [for us men and for our salvation; I did not call you servants, but friends].—Rectified, because this comparison would allow us to suppose that we have something of ourselves and belonging to us to offer in payment, as if we had not received everything and as if there were commensurability between the value of the good to be sacrificed and the good to be received: we are told that Christ came unto his own in coming to us, *in propria, in sua venit* [he comes in what is properly his own], and that there is an infinite disproportion between what we give and suffer and the grace or the glory accorded to us, destined for us, *non sunt condignae passiones hujus temporis* [the sufferings of this time are not of equal dignity] in the face of *pondus aeternum gloriae* [the eternal weight of glory].—Completed, because this mercantile parable, analogous to Pascal's wager, suggests less an idea of generous and loving élan than a subtle and cunning calculation, which is more than just a lacuna, since the verdict of salvation, as foretold by Christ, implies that the elect will often have ignored, in advance, the divine meaning of their generosity, as has also been noted by mystics forgetting themselves in order to obey the repeated precepts of the interior Master: "Think of me and I will think of you. *Jacta cogitatum tuum in Domino et ipse enutriet te* [Cast your thought in the Lord and he will nourish you Himself]."

This theory of the commerce between man and God was taken up at one time with the pretense of giving it a completely moral sense. God, without having to redo his first work to supernaturalize it, supposedly would have given us to ourselves from the start, for us to have something to show Him our own generosity by a restoration that would enable us to recover and more, all that we would have provisionally sacrificed. In this way the entire mystery of our divine genesis would be reduced to a struggle between egoism and generosity; and it would be enough to understand how much love of self is false, unintelligent, narrowing, for us to realize, through a will illumined and aided by God, this spiritual transformation for which the moral life is the toll that gives access to the eternal and beatifying union.—An explanation such as this has even more inconveniences than the commercial parable, about which we readily feel that it is an image rather than an exact truth: its danger would be to let us believe that union of man with God is a simple relation of friendship, analogous to those realities of affection that bind through free choice two human beings, but that leaves them external to one another and without real communion. Moreover, this criticism remains insufficient, because among men, be they the most strangers of the world, one same blood, one same origin, one same rational nature allows a true compenetration, whereas between God and man there is nothing of the sort originally; and yet it is toward this union, both substantial and carnal, so to speak, that Christian life tends: hence it is to misconceive both the obstacles to be surmounted and the intimate union to be realized, to limit ourselves to that metaphysical moralism, which does not give us any precise idea of our vital and deifying incorporation into Christ our chief, and through Him, through his Spirit, by his real presence, to the indwelling in us of the divine Persons.

To gloss over what is deficient about this bargaining with God, a theory of buying man back from the devil has been proposed. But prescinding from other serious shortcomings and unacceptable consequences, this explanation, that has been tied to certain metaphors taken literally and exclusively, has the disadvantage of subordinating everything to the "redemption" from sin, without alluding to the "buying" of the precious stone and to the cost for the divine life. It has contributed to narrowing down and deviating the doctrine of the supernatural elevation.

Moreover, the interpretations we have just laid out and criticized, however useful they may be for introducing certain minds into the lobby of Christian religion without opening the doors of the sanctuary, set aside or even misrepresent and eliminate (as in the case of the last one mentioned) an element that seems at once essential and disconcerting: what we can call the intrusion of God into man; for it is not a question of remaining oneself before Him, or even to tend to conquer Him as one would the Titans; it is a question of coming to comprehend, from the standpoint of charity itself, an invasion that takes us out of ourselves for better or for worse and that does not allow for any uniquely and purely human equilibrium. For it is not enough to present Christian religion as an offer of pure goodness; it is much more than that; it is a question of coming to an understanding of how this goodness itself imposes a seeming exigency that could at first be termed paradoxical, tyrannical, and even unjust and revolting. I have been given a nature and I do not have the right to remain simply faithful to this rational nature by forgoing an ulterior offer that I am told is gratuitous and that, moreover, cannot be accepted, used, and justified except on the condition that I surpass, deny, sacrifice this human nature given for me to possess: is there any reason for such an intrusion? and is the only recourse that which is advanced more often than not, the consideration that God is the absolute master over creatures and that, being power and justice in itself, He can impose on them anything He thinks good from the standpoint of his sovereignty; so that therefore any complaint would be a crime of lèse-majesté, an attempted robbery prejudicial to the domain of God, sole creator and lord of all things.

Far be it from us to echo these charges, but if it remains true that, according to the comparison of Saint Paul, the clay does not rebel against the potter who shapes it as he wills, we still have to justify docility on our part otherwise than as a constraint under force; and we have even to search in the goodness itself for the key to the enigma and the secret of exigencies that seem more rigorous only to express a love that is more helpful. Indeed, the intrusion that has so often occasioned obfuscations is not that of a jealous egoism calling for a blindly passive submission; it is that of a charity that is not content, for us, for our good, for our dignity and for our beatitude, with a semi-elevation, with a distant participation in infinite beatitude. For many, it seems that in making Himself man the Word has willed to lower Himself to our measure and to reduce his generosity to some wholly human exchange. But that is to denature the sense of the Scriptures, the entire experience of sainthood. It is not according to our measure that God willed to proportion and reduce his gifts; He became man, as Augustine says, only to make us god, to dilate us infinitely; and the whole sense of the test we have to submit to is to configure us to the divine life, not by making our human limitations disappear, but by making them recede. From this standpoint, the most incomprehensible suffering, at first, when we try to explain them either as a simple penitential expiation or as a purely moral merit, take on a new and triumphant life: *oportuit pati et ita intrare in gloriam* [he had to suffer and so to enter into glory]; a necessity, not from fatality or repression, but on the contrary from a need to procure for man that transformation that renders Him all the more capable of union as he has been pressed down, torn apart, more aggrandized by passive purifications. In a sense we should even say that this union entails an intimacy all the more complete as souls have been first seemingly cut off from joys, and, to forestall all confusion, are left with stigmata of the present sufferings as glorious and protective marks; so that, absorption having been rendered impossible by the sufferings whose luminous traits eternity will never erase, the union will be able to be all the more penetrating for the rigors having been all the more implacable.

The aspect under which we have just been considering the law of putting to the test shows us already that this test is not merely expiatory; for in any event the words *oportuit pati* [he had to suffer] come to be justified by reasons of this double purpose: prevent the union of man with God from appearing as a simple goodwill exchange that would leave each one to his own nature, and prevent a more intimate assimilation from becoming an absorption. Hence it is understood already that the entire economy of the Christian religion and the entire supernatural elevation of man would be impossible to explain or to realize if there were not a toll to pay as it were and a transformation to be worked out. So that the irritation of what convention calls, for no good reason by the way, "modern thought" at the seemingly harsh and humiliating exigencies of Christian religion follows from a profound misapprehension of its true spirit. It is not a question, in Christian religion, of pressing down, of curtailing our natural being, our reason, our will; it is a question of taking the indispensable means to exalt, to purify, to deify man himself as much as possible, without depriving him of remaining man, but by uniting him to the Man-God and, through Him, with Him, and in Him, to the intimate life, to the beatitude of divinity. To be sure what is often placed in the forefront, because it is the first condition to be fulfilled, and what is at first onerous, is penance to remedy a degradation that has to be healed before raising normal man to a higher state. But this purgative way, ever more or less necessary, prepares and already bears in it another still exacting phase even though it is no longer only a proof of divine love and a mode of transformative union.

Let us conclude then that the so-called intrusions of the Master—so readily accused of egoistic harshness as if he were intent only on making his susceptibilities, his jealousies, his sovereignty felt—turn out to be on the contrary for a purpose that is quite the opposite. How many times, because of faulty, ambiguous translation, the formula wherein Saint Augustine sums up all the élan of souls and all the divine provisions has been misunderstood: "You have made us for Yourself, O my God, and our heart is restless until it rests in You." But we must not translate this "for Yourself" as if it were *pro Te*, because of you, and for your benefit. The Latin text, untranslatable here, truly, means to say that this movement of the soul goes toward God for itself, according to the spontaneous élan of a being that with all its strength strives to deploy itself to attain its end and its felicity: *fecisti nos ad Te* [you made us unto Yourself].

But we must go more deeply into this doctrine of the two gifts and look for the common center where thought and will, according to the expression of Tauler, have to receive within them the divine generation. Let us not just play with words here without drawing from them a ray of light, if not a complete clarity, on this mysterious genesis of a new life and on the conditions of this new birth called for by the Gospel, *denuo nasci* [to be born anew]. It is easy to enunciate in words this renovation that confers on man something properly divine; but it is not as easy either to discern the difficulties of such a transformation, or to discover the means required to accomplishing it, or to define the reservations that remain metaphysically, morally, religiously necessary in order to avoid all danger of pantheism.

When we speak of our union with God, too often we interpret the words as if it were a matter of a liaison of friendship, and not of a real participation. And yet all the biblical and Christian literature evoke the strongest idea, the very one suggested by the Gospel when it speaks of two beings who are only one in their proper flesh, *duo in carne una* [two in one flesh]. Constantly, separation from God is characterized as adultery, and moreover spiritual union is presented as more intimate, more exigent than any other relation; whence the extreme purity of intention and desire required for this godly deiformity. Yet if we try to enter into this perspective of the perfect union between these two absolutely incommensurable beings, how are we to understand that one does not suppress the other or that the other should have something to offer, to sacrifice, when it has nothing of itself and finds itself entirely passive at bottom? This is where the highest sense of the two gifts comes to the fore: the first, which consists in the rational nature with its temptation to complacency and self-sufficiency, still has nothing yet that constitutes a truly autonomous life, since all it possesses is only a sort of loan, a means at the service of the Creator; but then the role of this rational nature is to make possible and meritorious the restoration, the submission of the faculties it has at its disposal to the only One who can be its total end as it is its principle.

Let us take one more step. We could not participate in God, who is pure act (*acte pur*), except by becoming also a pure taking action (*un pur agir*). Now, how is that conceivable? Let us use very simple metaphors here, but that will do better than subtle analyses in suggesting the master idea. God, in order to create free beings, has so to speak partially withdrawn from His sovereign domain, He has as it were gone into exile or committed suicide; and then it is for us to give Him back His empire, to make a place for Him within ourselves, and if we owe Him this power, He owes it to us to recover His own being within us. That is how far we have to go to grasp something of the divine inventions in the work of creation and deification; and from this point of view everything else seems unworthy of the divine intervention. Whence the saying: *nihil debuit, plus non potuit* [he did not have to do anything, he could not have done more]. God so loved his creatures that He subjected Himself to the possibility of deicide, which was however the condition for the theogony whose incomparable grandeur remains for us to glimpse.

Mystery of Truth and of Love

Closer and closer and through successive images, we are penetrating, it seems, into the literal sense of the divine plan, as only Revelation can make it known to us with a sufficient precision and a certitude without attenuation. All the metaphors we have used along the way are justified and contribute to opening the way, invigorating and orienting spirits, but they still remain insufficient and, even after tying their suggestions all together, they do not give us the central idea, the soul that animates Christian faith and piety. Without doubt the traditional word of "redemption" evokes the idea of buying something back; but this conception does not exclude in any way that of an elevation even independently of a separation and of an expiation. For its part, the idea of acquiring, of ascending is appropriate to mark the passage from a natural order to a supernatural life that we could not pay too much for; hence the evangelical paradox of the obligation we find ourselves under to sell all that we have in order to buy the precious pearl: a behavior that taken literally in the domain of temporal things would be folly, and that nevertheless is wisdom in the eyes of the Christian spirit. But here again the analogy is partially deceptive, because there is no proportion between the two terms of exchange, and what's more our goods are ours only in appearance: there is no partial sacrifice, no utilitarian calculation at stake here. We are thus brought little by little to understand that it is not for us to renounce some good already in our possession, even if we had to pay the heaviest price, but for us to renounce ourselves precisely in what is already most noble, most generous, most divine of ourselves, and to do so in order to restore to God what is, at bottom in ourselves, God's own proper and inalienable good—for even among the damned there remains a basic indelible being, an excellent reality, and it is this basic being precisely that prevents the destruction of the guilty as it causes its grief; for his chastisement does not come from without, it results from the sense he has of having misused the divine gift, the gift that remains without decline and without reproach.

Hence the metaphor itself of a deicide, as profound as it may be, does not exhaust all the sense of the mystery of creation and deification. To be sure it is already a lot to perceive that, to call us to existence and to beatitude, God placed Himself at our disposition, has lent Himself as a means for our ambition, has so to speak taken Himself out of the place that He destines for us in order that we would place Him back ourselves in it. And already thereby we estimate the horror of sin, the sin we ask the Holy Spirit to make us hate as much as God hates it Himself: for truly sin is intrinsically like a mutilation that takes away from God the kingdom about which the Our Father has us ask that it be on earth as it is in heaven the full accomplishment of the divine will. All that surely helps to penetrate somewhat into the providential plan and to glimpse the inventions of power, of wisdom, and of charity in this drama where, without there being anything necessary in it, there is nothing arbitrary either. But finally beyond the satisfactions that such attempts at explanation can provide us, there remains still something inaccessible; and the words of Saint Paul comes back to us, not as the admission of a discouraging obscurity, but as an apperception of inscrutable depths of which we know only that they are luminous and good: *O altitudines* [O the depths]! Eye has not seen, nor has ear heard what is contained, what promise this mystery of truth and of love holds. Such seems the sense that sums up the convergent unity of the sacred texts, of the commentaries, and of the experiences offered us by tradition: a perfect coherence, a response unhoped for in our highest aspirations, a surplus no one could have foreseen ahead of time and defined, but one that procures to the one who takes cognizance of it a plentitude of joy and a certitude of solidity, of security: those are some of the elements that make up, for those who live by it, the Christian spirit, that spirit the external observers of which are irritated by, are astonished by, or have to admit their envy of it.

Through the progressive analysis that has enabled us to spell out this testimony presented by the history of the Church, we have done nothing more than an inquiry as objective as possible. In order to render the result of this analytical inquiry a more decisive value in the eyes of intelligences who like precisely to take in the course we have followed in a synthetic view or even to grasp all at once its contemplative unity, we would like now to make an effort that is the reverse of the one we have just brought to its end. It is said with good reason that in taking one and the same route in both directions, we discover quite different aspects:

going to and from opens up new horizons. Let us confine ourselves then to reviewing in a reverse order what Gerbert called "the generative dogma" of Christian religion with all its consequences; and may we be forgiven, as Gerbert himself begged, for placing ourselves in a certain way inside God's secret council, in order to actualize this encouraging promise of the Holy Books when they place onto the lips of Wisdom this saying: *qui elucidant Me vitam aeternam habebunt* [they who elucidate Me will have eternal life]. Not that it would be possible to violate the mystery that was just expressed in the exclamation of the Apostle: O the depths! but at least, by using data from Revelation, which is well suited to illuminate us on the essential of our destiny, and also the data of reason as it raises the problem of the relations between beings and God, and the data finally of religious experience and sanctity, it does not seem illegitimate to hope for a confirmation and an increase of intellectual richness that makes up a precious part of the Christian patrimony.

There have been complaints recently concerning the lack of curiosity and the indigence of many contemporary minds with regard to knowledge of the Christian religion, and there has been a call for a rebirth of religious metaphysics. Perhaps this expression itself calls for some reservations and criticism; for the issue is not to speculate on our dogmas to extract from them some philosophical truths; such attempts have often led to a semi-naturalism that denatures the original and properly supernatural sense of Christian Revelation. But at the least it can be hoped that, from a frankly and integrally Christian point of view, as Saint Augustine had foreseen, by placing ourselves, if we can so say, at the intersection of the historical order and the rational order, in such wise that, proceeding from the transnatural state that is ours, we might see unfold this struggle of the two Cities that, within each one of us as in humanity and in the entire universe, must come to one and the same judgment. The role of philosophical speculation must tend to anticipate on that judgment; for it is only by looking ahead to the final ends that order can be constituted in thoughts as in actions. Bossuet had studied successively the sequence of empires and "the sequence of religion." What we have to describe is also a "sequence," in the sense he understood it; and all our effort now will be to lay out the congruence of all the parts that form the ensemble of the Christian dogmatic and practice under the aspect that philosophical analysis can legitimately look into.

CHAPTER 9

Synthetic Exploration and Progressive Elaboration Starting from the Generative Idea of Christian Religion

Vos dii eritis [you shall be gods]: this phrase from Genesis can serve as the inscription for one or the other of the two cities. It is the divine promise. It is the satanic temptation. To understand the opposition of these two slogans and to grasp their significance is the highest service human intelligence can render in the light of Christian revelation. The danger is to feel the pull of pride that moves man to the pretense of deifying himself. Its fault is not having a sublime aspiration; it is not imposing on oneself the necessary means and not entering into the dispositions that one could already judge by oneself to be just and salutary, but that Christian religion teaches one and gives one the means of practicing with a clear-sightedness and a force of which we are naturally incapable.

What does God ask of us? and what prospect does Christian religion indicate as being the unique and supreme goal of creation and in particular of humanity? Saint Thomas sums it up in a proposition of extreme forcefulness: the entire movement of nature, the entire progress of knowledge has as its reason for being and as its ultimate end to multiply spirits in view of eternal life. And elsewhere he adds that God, in willing to elevate man supernaturally all the way to participating in his life and his beatitude, had treated man as if man were the God of God himself, *tamquam si homo fieret Deus Dei ipsius* [as if man were to become

God of God himself]. Behold strange assertions indeed. One does not imagine any that are more astonishing. The purpose here is to explore their content.

God then has willed (and this project is the very reason for his creative intervention) to make alongside Himself, who is nevertheless fully sufficient and leaves nothing to be fulfilled, other beings, and so to speak other gods. Freely, without any need on his part, without susceptibility or any trace of egoism, if we may speak in these terms, He insisted on communicating His own beatitude, on producing other himselves [*d'autres lui-même*], to love, to bring forth spirits that are themselves free and capable of resisting Him, because their docility and their love could not be meritorious, truly real, truly divine, except under this condition and at this risk. But, if we reflect on it in the least, does not this project seem like a dream, something chimerical, an impossibility? Are there not absolute obstacles, an irremediable incommensurability between the Being that is all being and what has nothing of itself and by itself? Yes, that is true, it will be eternally true, and all fear of confusion is forever to be set aside as nonsense. And yet the divine invention has consisted in "communicating the incommunicable itself," through an admirable stratagem we have to discover, in order to render God the tribute of recognition and to help man fulfill his role in the economy of the providential plan.

But is it not to play on words to speak thus in contempt of the principle of non-contradiction? How are we to communicate what, speaking absolutely remains according to the very words of the Scriptures, the privilege of the One "who gives his glory to no other," of the One who, according to theology, can only love Himself in us and only crowns his own gifts, according to the famous expression of Saint Augustine? And is this not exactly the supreme objection that has often been opposed to this thesis, deemed necessary from the standpoint of reason as from the Christian standpoint, to the effect that, having nothing lovable in ourselves and by ourselves, we cannot be the object of divine complacency except on the condition of putting on the form of the Word, and of consenting to the presence and to the vivification of the Holy Spirit; so much so that what God loves in effect is not the human, but still and ever the divine that is infused in us?—It is against this objection that we must react, so as not to leave Christian religion under the impression of discomfort, of defiance, even of hostility that repels so many spirits from it convinced that they have a higher ideal of goodness and that the theological conception is nothing more than the leftover of a bygone age where injustices and the harshness of political and social life accustomed men to bow before the yoke and the caprices of an absolute master. How then are we to pull ourselves out of this embarrassment where, from the start, the affirmation of our deiformity has placed us? How especially are we to render conceivable a communication of what, by definition, remains jealously reserved for God alone?

The illusion to be dissipated here is this. Too often those who have spoken most intrepidly of the supernatural elevation conferring on man a *consortium divinae naturae* [consorting with the divine nature] have kept the feeling that we receive a kind of gracious implantation by which we become, next to God, analogously divine beings. A sort of still spatial or conceptual image persists in our thought, that allows us to believe in a sort of redoubling, of expansion, or of infusion of the divine life in beings naturally outside of, foreign to, and inconvertible with it. And so it is not surprising that we run into insurmountable difficulties: for we cannot understand how finite beings can, on their own ground, see divinity itself rise up; and it is clear, in a perspective such as this, that the expression of our deification is a simple analogy. It is also the case that the truth saints live by, and in which all Christians participate by grace, is quite other than the usual analogy whose usual formulation we have just explored. Let us try then to react against a deformation that, for being very frequent and quite tenacious in many spirits, constitutes nonetheless a mutilation of the divine message.

What must be seen first as clearly as possible is that the *consortium naturae divinae* [consorting in the divine nature] does not make of man a God somehow juxtaposed to God. We were saying earlier that the entire aim of the Creator is to multiply beings enjoying beatitude and united to God's own life. But this is in no way to say that this beatitude, this divine life would be other than the one that resides exclusively in God. Let it be well understood then, even as we speak in our blunt human language, that the problem consists entirely in obtaining that God be in man without man ceasing to be himself and without the disappearance of our own limits under the pressure of the flow of divine life and of felicity that invades and dilates our personal life. Thus God remains quite the incommunicable in itself and yet He communicates something of this very incommunicable: there is no other God than God; there is no other beatitude, Saint Thomas said, than divine beatitude; that is indeed what is given to us, but remains God's very own even as it is, through grace, our own fruition, according to the technical expression of the theologians. Have we then succeeded in grasping the new problem that we now have to resolve? God has found the means, not only of giving us other goods than Himself, but of giving Himself, while leaving us ownership as it were, or the creation as it were of this divine being residing in us, since it is well and good a matter of the inhabitation of the Trinity in the justified and supernaturalized soul. Now this it seems is the only way such a wonder can be realized. Let us attend carefully to this decisive point that holds the key to Christian dogmatics as well as practice.

In order for Being in itself to call creatures to partake of His own felicity, as One who is pure act and infinite Charity, He could not be content with creatures that would have been pure passivity. For them to be in his image and likeness, they too would have to produce and even to produce themselves in a way, so that they would become, like their author, *causa sui* [cause of oneself]. But what of the means of such a creation? Starting from what we are at bottom we could form only caricatures of being, and all our divine aspirations of themselves, when they pretend to self-sufficiency, lead only to idolatry. The only thing that can free us in absolute detachment from our egoism, is the substitution within us of the divine will for our own sense of ourselves, is the renunciation of our properly human aspirations in order to truly make room for the divine operation. Earlier we were saying that, for God to make us be, God had withdrawn Himself as it were, *Se ipsum exinanivit* [He emptied Himself] (*Philippians*, II, 7), Saint Paul says: it is then for us to restore to Him the sovereignty over us of which he had let go in order to allow us to restore it to Him also freely and out of love; hence it is a radical mortification of our natural and human being that makes way for the advent of the supernatural and divine Being. Truly then must we say, literally, that we beget God: for, without our fiat God would not be in this inviolable dungeon of our freedom that it depends on us to open up to Him or to close off from Him forever. God owes it to us then to shine anew; and his external glory is indeed to obtain the full generosity of souls that willingly undergo all the passive purifications. The measure of the supernatural being in man and of his future beatitude is the very degree of his courage in the testing that substitutes for his own will the exigencies, apparently cruel, but in reality tenderly paternal, of the One who can only view all from the standpoint of eternal truth and perfect joy.

So is it understood now how God loves Himself in us, how He wills infinitely to find Himself there, how it is for us even more than for Himself, that he has accepted all the deicidal humiliations and sufferings in order to render to man the possibility of his divine generation or of his regeneration? Is the sense of the provisional harshnesses understood as well that have led some to accuse the Christian religion of being the religion of sorrow and humiliation, when it is the religion of felicity and of glorious exaltation? Is it understood how the links of all this plan where the strangest paradoxes are resolved in a coherence of light and of goodness?

Indeed from this standpoint are explained the series of dogmas as well as the connection between the ascetical life and the Catholic discipline. It used to be said, concerning the expression "devout humanism," that these two terms howl for being coupled with one another: yes and no; for there is a false and even destructive, and there is a beautiful and salutary way of understanding them. If we wanted to signal with these words that man has only to remain himself with all the charms of science and art, save for conferring on this civilization the sumptuous mantel of a glowing devotion, then we would have to declare that this optimism is contrary to what Bossuet called "the incomprehensible seriousness of Christian life"; and we would run the risk of misunderstanding what we referred to as the intrusion, the insertion, the crucifying exigencies, all that pulls man away from even his most noble and most elegant satisfaction: the reality of the facts, the truth of the dogmas give the lie to this conception of a Christianity at a discount. But if, with humanism, we mean to protest against the theories of a divine egoism that would bring everything back to itself; if we keep in mind the expression of the apostle speaking of "God's philanthropy," Who has done everything for us, for the love of us and our salvation, then it is well and true to insist on the mystery of charity that in itself alone contains and brings forth all the others.

The question has been raised at times about what would have been, without the original fall, the condition of humanity and how it is that a trial could have preceded the entrance of innocent humanity into glory, and also how this single trial could condition the entire course of history. The foregoing considerations will help us elucidate this difficulty that has stumped certain minds, as if the providential plan had never been anything but a succession of adjustments or of "jolts," according to the expression of a recent critic. Yet there is nothing more coherent than the biblical account if, amid the data that can be termed historical, without even being obliged to take the detail of the narrative literally, we look into the intimate significance of the facts under their literal covering. What we are taught is that, in the primitive state there was an interdiction limiting the expansion of human curiosity and ambition. In what did this sacred prohibition consist, such that it could be imposed on a being in a state of nature and of naïveté so to say. Adapted to this infancy of the sensible and avid being that the "human composite" is, the trial seems to have been brought to bear on a renunciation prescribed by God in order to obtain a sacrifice of the natural aspirations on the part of the flesh as well as on the part of intelligence. The fruit of "the tree of the knowledge of good and evil" was the spontaneous and so to say normal covetousness corresponding to the primitive gift of the rational nature. That is what one had to forbid oneself to remain in the divine order of things; and such a renunciation, which seemed to mutilate the most noble élan of the spirit, could not but appear onerous and provoke a temptation of rebellious pride and of redoubled covetousness: *non serviam* [I will not serve].

Thereby is explained somewhat the possibility of a fall that has often been judged to be unlikely; for, as it has been said many times, prior to the ignorance and the concupiscence that are only the consequences of the original rebellion, how could a temptation resonate in the reason and in the heart of a naturally upright man, healthy and illuminated by a divine light? Well, for Adam, as for the Angels also, according to tradition, all having had to undergo the necessity of a decisive option, the trial to be passed through is of such a nature that an intellectual evidence, a natural rectitude is not enough to triumph over it: it requires a generosity that comes from what is most intimate in one's being, as it passes through an obscurity and a sort of immolation and of death. Yes, in all cases, access to the supernatural life requires the sacrifice of the most profound, the most legitimate of natural goods, even before seeing or tasting the compensation for such a holocaust. We have already noted, and now we discern better still the conditions of supernatural genesis, of the theogony that we have shown to be the highest reason for the whole of Creation.

But, it will be objected, was it not unworthy of God, unworthy also of man, to lend Himself to this *capitis diminutio* [head shrinking], to this abdication of all virility, in such wise that a state of perpetual childishness would have kept the Edenic humanity in a trivial interplay consisting in cultivating the garden without any need for doing so, without any usefulness, *ut operaretur terram* [so that the earth would be worked over], a superfluous task since everything was supposed to be offered abundantly to the desires of man? And, it is added, is not the corollary of such a conception what is admired in our present humanity, the frequently heroic effort of labor, the noble joys of science, the moral drama, the masterpiece of social life and all this struggle for the City of the good that makes for our greatness, all that would then be a simple consequence and as it were a backlash of the initial sin?—To this there are two appropriate answers that are added to one another. Yes, in a sense, the Fall, allowed by God, became the occasion for a greater good from the standpoint either of the supernatural itself, or of the natural elevation of civilized humanity: *felix culpa* [happy fault]; it nonetheless remains that these advantages are compensated for by increased risks, by individual or collective failures, by a transposition of being put to the test: for if the science of good and evil, far from being forbidden, is [now] prescribed, it entails precautions, renunciations, rectifications of intention that are onerous and that expose each person in isolation to pitfalls that the primitive trial, if it had turned out more favorable, would have dispensed with for all the human generations that came after.

What we can bring to better light than ever with the help of the Augustinian teaching, to answer difficulties that have arisen in modern consciousness, is the idea of a test antecedent to all eventualities at stake in the use of human freedom. Within the perspective both one and flexible of the Creator's plan, whatever was to be the case of fidelity or of rebellion by man, there was one primordial condition imposed absolutely for the being called to a supernatural vocation to be elevated in effect to this dignity of the *consortium divinum* [divine sharing]. What varies are the modalities of this elevation, modalities logically contained in the previsions of the Creator, so that His plan, albeit entirely gratuitous and imperious, came to be modified in fact according to what use man would do of his own willing. Thereby falls the objection so often repeated against the harsh and arbitrary character of the consequences of the Fall. How often, before or since Voltaire and Victor Hugo, people have inveighed against the apparent absurdity of these dogmas that seem to offer us this illogical stance: man was guilty; to save him he had to become more guilty still by crucifying Christ! Purely superficial and totally incomprehensible reasoning, which subordinates to the law of time and of abstract deduction the eternal order and the sequence of spiritual realities. What makes the incomparable beauty of the divine inventions is precisely this acceptance of charity that confers on the creature the power, either to restore God by man's filial submission, however onerous that may be for him, or to become properly deicidal by preventing God from being reborn, so to speak, in this being to whom he had granted the possession of a power to opt; so that the sacrifice of Calvary had to take on a double significance. First, the sacrifice was manifesting the required consequence of the divine condescendence regarding man free and rebellious; whence the idea that recurs constantly about the exigencies of the heavenly Father and of his implacable justice condemning his celestial Son to the punishment [of death] that results from the guilty will: things were so preordained that already the creation of supernaturalizable man implied, so to speak, a mortal danger for God. But at the same time what is implacable consequence, obedience imposed on Christ, historically ineluctable necessity in the hypothesis of rebellion, has to take on a character of voluntary immolation, of reparation generously consented to, of loving pardon: yes, Christ dies by necessary submission, *factus obediens usque ad mortem* [made obedient even unto death]; but, yes also, Christ offers Himself and dies because he did will it; and the reparation of pure justice would not have been redemptive mercy, if Christ, in undergoing the logical consequence of the rigorous plan, had not added to this expiation the pardon that erases the crime committed against him by an act of charity infinitely surpassing the very rigors of justice.

Thanks to these two aspects of the redemptive mystery, everything becomes explainable, the exigencies of reparation as well as the mercies of grace, without any proportion with the merits of man, whatever may be the efforts of repentance and penance. How far we have come from this indigent moralism that reasons about our destiny as if it were only a matter of some fault to be compensated in the finite order by some rectifying of our own will, without even having to take into account the so often irreparable consequences of a bad act that proliferates unto infinity! If truth be told, the sense of sin, of its divine nuisance, of its humanly incurable consequences, has disappeared too much from Christian consciousness for it not to be urgent to insist on the extent and the gravity of the drama playing itself out within us between the soul and God.

CHAPTER 10

Unity of the Work of Creation for the External Glory of God through Supernatural Elevation

If we envisage from a central point of view the train of Christian dogma in all its radiating directions, we cannot but be struck by its cohesion that renders it as satisfying for the logical mind as it is solid for our sense of the real. At the same time what dominates the whole is the impression of a charity that uses the most extreme, the most paradoxical means to communicate to the creature the maximum of elevation and beatitude. How is it then that most often in our day Catholicism is reproached with being as unreasonable and incoherent as it is contrary to justice, to the dignity, to the goodness people supposedly imagine to be appreciably higher, but that in reality is diminished and idolatrous?

The great need for the apostolate is to make manifest the unity of this Christian spirit, which is quite the contrary of a synthesis, notwithstanding the allegations common among historians who consider it to be as it were a syncretism made up of oriental and Hellenic factors. Let us try then to present briefly, we dare not say its directive idea, for it is a question of something else than only an idea, but of the soul, and this word is not yet forceful enough, or of the divine thought, better still of the charity that spreads its rays into the entire ensemble that constitutes Catholicism and that the masters of sacred science name "the external glory of God." Strange expression and difficult to comment on, this word *glory* that recurs so often in the Sacred Scriptures and in the liturgical prayer. Glory, that is metaphorically like the shining forth that manifests the intimate splendor; and it is first of all, in God Himself, this plenitude that is concentrated on itself, with nothing that can exhaust it or add to it, nor translate it exteriorly. But there is also the external glory or, as the theologians say, the "accidental" glory of God; and this is where we have to beware of false analogies or of explanations that fall short. Too often it is thought that glorifying God means representing Him as a master avid for adulation and servility; and the rigorous exigencies of precepts, of tribulations, of mortifying transformations are interpreted in this sense. The truth seems to be much broader and much more beautiful. We must dare to use the most brutal, the most childish terms, in saying that the external glory of God is, surely not to spread His divinity outside of itself like a sphere that would explode to let go of its overflow of heat and of force, but rather to produce other beings, other true beings, beings that as such have a value of their own, beings capable of knowing, of loving, of possessing something of God Himself by participating in His beatitude; so that, without going out of Himself, without creating other gods, God still lives in others Himself: they are themselves, and therefore they remain eternally distinct from their author, and still they are Him by participating in His divine life. What could be more glorious than this expansion that enriches unto infinity the universe resounding with the hymn of joy and recognition? This glory is, in one sense, quite exterior to God; and yet it is still and ever the same divine light, the same charity, the same beatitude that shines in this celestial city. That is the vision offered by Christian metaphysics; and no less admirable than this glorious plan is the manner in which it is realized, as we shall show from this center of perspective.

Before giving Himself to His creature and to enable it to become, according to the Thomist expression, *capax Dei* [capable of God], God asks it to renounce the independence He had bestowed on it, but in order to confer to it the power to make the only act that could proceed from a secondary cause without ceasing to be truly taking action [*agir*]: to renounce what has been received, when one could close oneself up in one's egoism and admire oneself in the gifts of nature. In that there is an initiative that supposes the entire created order, because it implies that beyond the received qualities and the natural capacities one affirms, one wills the infinite as the negation of one's own limits; this indirect way, as Denis the Areopagite remarked, is the most positive way of all as denying negations and as excluding limitations. Whence this conclusion, which is not only that of the mystics, but that of the common law of Christian life: one acquires the infinite only by accepting beforehand the voluntary renunciation of all that is finite insofar as it is finite. Not that Christian asceticism should be pessimistic, hostile to nature, with a tendency toward Buddhism or Manicheanism; far from it: nature, in spite of the risks and abuses for which it is the useful occasion, is doubly good, first, because it constitutes a first patrimony to be put into effect and an original gift destined precisely to serve as the price of entrance; second because, once the spirit of abnegation has deadened the natural élan, all the purified affections participate in the new life of grace, so that perfect detachment and holy indifference attach us purely to everything and encompass all beings with a solicitude that slights none of them.

We should take care to reflect at the same time on the metaphysical conditions that are necessary for the realization of a truly personal being, of an activity of which we can say that it is original, *causa sui* [cause of itself], of a felicity whose sense could not come except from a merit attained; and then we will be brought to recognize that the law of tribulation, as fundamentally mortifying as it would be, is the only conceivable way to lead a creature to the *summum* [the highest], the *optimum* [the best], in short to a truly supernaturalizable reality able to enter into communion with the divine life. The question has been posed in familiar fashion: "If I were king, what would I do for the well-being of my creatures?" The question may also be asked, at times more seriously than Jaro of the fabulist: "If I were God, what wouldn't I do to facilitate and promote the multiplication and the felicity of my creatures!" Well, it is at justifying the true response and the austerity of the means necessary for this elevation of the created order that we are aiming here with all the force at our disposal. The humanitarian conceptions, the facile deism, the pretensions of the Overman, all these conceptions that give the impression of surpassing the Christian ideal, are in the sight of a piercing critique no more than impossibilities, worse still, deflations and depreciations of an aspiration that remains congenitally a desire to know, to possess, even to be God, in accordance with the tempting word: *dii eritis* [you will be gods].

It may be objected that in linking the Christian order to the metaphysical élan of human thought and will, we lend ourselves to a confusion that would compromise the gratuity of the supernatural, as if, from the foundation of the reasonable nature, a seed were given that, as it would develop, would of itself open up finally in what seems to be the domain reserved to grace. Such an objection has to be set aside at all costs; for, if it were grounded, it would be the ruin of Christian dogma, discipline, morality, and practice in what is most specific and most essential about them. No, the supernatural is not the prolongation, the blossoming, the conquest of our humanity unfolding its primordial gifts. No, the law of tribulation and the role of the Redemption are not restricted to reestablishing us in the state prior to sin. No, Christian dogmas do not require that they be interpreted as parables serving to illustrate a drama that is simply moral where man and God would enter into an alliance, as if the advent of charity resulted from a simply intelligent generosity. If the objection we are protesting against has an appearance of speciousness, it is only when the supernatural is reduced to being a knowledge disclosing truths that escape the natural grasp of spirit and to being a submission to precepts imposed by an authority. For in that case we could not claim, without betraying the exigencies of such a supernatural characterized by the fact that it is entirely extrinsic to our thought and our will, that the Christian order finds a foothold [*pierre d'attente*] or, better still, a spring [*ressort*] in some innate desire. The case is taken quite otherwise once we understand that access to the supernatural is conditioned by the renunciation described earlier, by the humble, dependent, confident disposition it supposes on our part. Far then from presenting it as a prolongation, as a conquest, and, according to the words of Father Rousselot, as a "captation" that would allow our intelligence to take hold of God if He did not establish protective barriers for the supernatural, we have to put on a spirit that is quite the opposite, to agree interiorly that nothing coming from us can procure for us what we have to receive from God by offering Him the entire renunciation of all that pertains properly to ourselves.

But, it will be further objected, if it is true that there is indeed a radical opposition between the natural attitude and the supernatural attitude of the soul, don't we fall again into inevitable difficulties and errors under the weight of this dilemma: either it is still from ourselves that we take this metaphysical view and this religious disposition according to which we acknowledge the salutary necessity of this "total and sweet renunciation," according to the word of Pascal; of this transfer of will resembling a wager of which we are told that in the end we understand that we have on the whole given nothing, paid nothing, but gained everything; and then what we have is still only a double phase in one and the same purely human development;—or else we have to admit that, to renounce ourselves, we need the divine aid, to the point that without grace we would remain invincibly in egoism and naturalism: a consequence that aggravates the Jansenist error itself, which condemns nature to being fundamentally impotent or even evil, and which renders inexplicable or chimerical the conception of a "soul of the Church" in which people of good will can enter into communion; and in this case, as was then maintained, the supernatural city, born of a grace not given to all, remains apart; and, alongside this restricted supernaturalism, is found brutally juxtaposed the human world, following its way of enjoyment, of science, of ambition, of humanitarian civilization, without the possibility of building bridges between these two cities.

But these two interpretations are both false; they both proceed from a partial misconception of the modes of intervention by grace. In the first case, if it is true that we make an effort ourselves to get out of egoism, that is not to say that this labor of the soul is not stimulated and sustained by a prevenient and supporting grace. As [Juan Martínez de] Ripalda says in his *De ente supernaturali* [*On Supernatural Being*], the supernatural concurrence of grace knows how to insinuate itself into acts that appear most natural to cooperate with our decisions, to confer a value upon our freedom worth more than it would have by itself, in a word to resolve under the guise of human appearances the divine problem in which salvation or damnation depends. What is at issue is no longer merely a moral question to be resolved, what is at issue, be it anonymously, is an option in which our divine destiny is at stake. Thereby is explained the possibility, for grace issuing from the Incarnation and Redemption, to attain, to vivify, to save even those who are unaware of the precise teachings of Revelation. Hence let it not be said any more that in trying to orient souls toward the problem we call that of the generation of God in us, we run the risk of falling into naturalism, Modernism, or immanentism: the truth is exactly the contrary of this, since the spiritual attitude we are calling for theoretically and practically is entirely opposed to that of these doctrines, in serving as an antidote to them. Indeed, upon the slightest reflection, we become aware that it would be absurd on our part to pretend deifying ourselves or finally to substitute ourselves for God by denying all that surpasses the Overman, whereas in fact we are insisting as hard as we can on the restoration of God, of the one true God, of the incommensurable God absolutely surpassing every created and creatable nature; a restoration that surpasses a first gift from God to reasonable beings and this second gift of which Saint John tells us that God, having come unto his own, leaving them masters to refuse Him or to receive Him, gave to those who welcomed Him the power of becoming His sons, His adopted children,—the Gospel even says, more forcefully, His own progenitors.

In the second case, the presence of supernatural action in even the most indifferent, perhaps the most hostile world to the Christian beliefs and to the very idea of the supernatural, is no less misconceived. To pretend that the Church goes its way, that modern civilization goes its own, is to restrict illegitimately the outpouring of charity and the duty of the apostolate. We even have to say that one of the most dear hopes in souls desiring the extension of the kingdom of God, as the *Pater* [*Noster*] calls for, is the convergence of efforts that are unaware of one another or that sometimes militate against one another, but that secretly proceed from a Christian inspiration. Undoubtedly our contemporary world appears to be distancing itself from its Catholic origins; and yet the positive sciences, the material advances, the social institutions proceed in part from the stirring given to the human consciousness by the Christian ideal. Provisionally many are unaware of this or then believe the opposite; but we must aim at bringing the prodigal sons, who remain sons, to the paternal house, while hoping that the brother who had stayed at home will finally show himself more welcoming, more understanding than the one in the parable.

Thus in both cases we avoid the reproach of compromising the pure transcendence of the supernatural, while showing that it can descend to the lowest, to the most obscure, to the least noted of souls and of peoples. Its superhuman character in no way depends on the fact that it is promulgated from outside; for it acts within without ceasing forasmuch to be higher and exterior to what is most interior to man.—From the fact that the supernatural is not just some metaphysical secret to be defended as if by a taboo or to be unveiled before our intelligence prevented from the outset by some divine ukase from going to the peak of its capacity to capture being, as if being were only an intelligible object, we come to the result that in the order of grace, the issue is more essentially one of life and of a loving will than one of seeing, or rather of an obscure adherence that depends on an ulterior vision, deferred as a matter of order and precaution. We should add that, if in fact there is in the supernatural, a promise of vision, this sight will be all that it has to be only as the effect of an infused life and of a charity capable of assimilating the divine secret to us as an intimate and lived trust, and not merely as a presentation that is exterior and speculative,—no matter how real the reciprocal causality and stimulation, the alternating priority and superiority of the assimilative knowledge and adherence may be.—And from the fact that it is not of a totally speculative secret that we are provisionally deprived of, but of a union of life and of charity that it is for us to receive and to accept as an absolutely gratuitous gift that is naturally, metaphysically incommunicable and unpredictable, it follows that the supernatural is not a barrier of separation, but that it consists in a wondrous invention of generosity to make into *one* what was, what remains, what will ever be inconfusable. Whence it is that, without any fear of transgression, the plan of Revelation and elevation, *a parte Dei* [on the part of God], and the effect of penetration and assimilation, *a parte hominis* [on the part of man], imply as their principal aim less the affirmation and the maintaining of differences to prevent any risk of confusion (since this risk does not exist in this perspective of thought and of life) than a desire and an élan of maximum conjoining, *miris et occultis modis* [in wondrous and secret ways]. And then it is in fact quite the contrary of ὕβρις [insolence]. Now we are at the point where we have a new objection to discuss: how is the suture possible, and how is human dignity respected?

CHAPTER 11

The Conditions for Realizing the Divine Plan for Surmounting the Difficulty of Uniting Two Incommensurables, the Creator and the Creature

On the One Hand, the Invention of Divine Charity to Cross the Abyss through the "Verbum Caro Factum" [the Word Made Flesh] and the Hypostatic Union, on the Other Hand, the Testing Imposed on Man by the Transformative Union

We have arrived at the main idea that tends to take precedence concerning the supernatural. All the recent controversies seem to converge finally toward an interpretation at once more precise, broader, more vital, of the notion of the Christian supernatural. Even from the side where for a very long time there was a jealous insistence in saving its totally extrinsic character, there is more and more agreement about recognizing that there is a preparation and, as the encyclical *Paschendi [dominici gregis]* [1907] says, a fittingness [*convenance*] that, in nature itself, gives rise to a desire to know and to possess God, as a foothold for the supernatural vocation. And from the other side, among those who had at first exaggerated the inclination we have toward God, as if through it we could develop and perfect our destiny without another revelation than that of moral conscience, people have become more and more conscious of the impossibility of equaling the Christian ideal with a natural religion and with an immanentist doctrine. But to bring these two movements closer together from their prolonged divergence, it seems indispensable to give of the supernatural an idea that has never been made completely explicit, even though it visibly inspires all of the patristic, theological, and mystical tradition. That idea is the following: the supernatural does not consist only in the sharing of a metaphysical secret, nor in the sudden promotion of anything that we would have a taste for because it would have no connection with our innate aspirations; it consists in a transformation of our faculties, of our hopes, of our natural possibilities; and it confers on the relations between man and God an intimacy that reason could never have foreseen, desired, or procured.

Hence, it is not in the order of ontological truths, as if it were a question of a new creation *ex nihilo*, it is in the order of attitudes, of wills, of affections, of actions, that the relation between Creator and His creature finds itself modified. The charter for the Christian life is undoubtedly founded on the promulgation of truths not known and inaccessible; but these truths themselves are useful to know and have "knowability," so to speak, only because they are Good News tied to the advent of the Kingdom of God in souls and to the outpouring of a vivifying and transforming grace. Undoubtedly, the enunciation of the truth precedes, prepares, commands the new life; but, more profoundly still, it is the vital finality and the intimate assimilating of a divine reality that allows these truths to be illuminative and active within us, even as they remain obscure under the veil of faith. The term that sums up the Christian spirit is therefore not the key to an intellectual enigma; it is this gospel saying: *jam non dicam vos servos, sed dixi amicos et filios* [I will no longer call you servants, but I have called (you) friends and sons].

Therein lies what it is important to meditate on with all its consequences.—To begin with, from the fact that the supernatural is not principally the manifestation of a metaphysical thesis, or of a secret that would be jealously kept from the curiosity of an intelligence that is congenitally capable of grasping Being, it results that the fears of theologians regarding the danger of transgressing by rational inquiry are found to be conjured away: it is not of course that we should not have to prevent absolutely any intrusion, any presumption of philosophy regarding the Christian order; but rather such intrusion is rendered impossible the moment that we show that in fact Revelation proclaims something totally other than mysteries to be considered speculatively, and that such truths, too profound to be penetrable by purely human thought, are related to our vocation and our participation in the very life of the Trinity.—Whence comes this other complementary and still more important consequence: for, from the fact that the supernatural, even after it is revealed, appears as absolutely gratuitous and requires an inversion of our properly natural dispositions in order for us to substitute what Saint Thomas calls the "divine mores" for our natural virtues, it results that the problem to be resolved is not to make people understand and respect the separation by forestalling all confusion (for confusion is entirely impossible), but on the contrary to show how the union becomes possible and more and more intimate between the God of charity and man, be it innocent man, or especially guilty and fallen man.

In the perspective we were criticizing earlier, it seemed that the supernatural could not subsist except by considering it as an extrinsic furnishing, protected by sacred prohibitions, by a taboo; and all the more so if we conceded to the spirit the faculty of knowing and willing God and his beatitude: whence the further necessity of fortifying the barricades and of insisting on a metaphysical fast provisionally imposed on the *intellectus impeditus* [impeded intellect], while waiting for this intellect to resume being itself, in some way, *intellectus ut sic* [intellect as such], that is to say as capable of attaining its only and true object, which is Being, which is God.—In the perspective where we have been brought to establish ourselves, the question is quite on the contrary to come to see that the divine plan has in view, not the separation nor even the distinction of the two orders as its first and principal aim, but on the contrary their convergence, their intimate cooperation, the transformative union that, without suppressing anything of human nature, makes it participate in a more than human life.

It would be impossible to exaggerate the speculative or practical, the intellectual or the social repercussions of the choice to be made between these two conceptions of the supernatural. The second, laid out in all its fittingness, seems to include all that is positive and truly traditional in the first. But conversely the first seems at times to have misconceived certain truths that remain indispensable for the economy of Catholic dogma. That is why, if it is good to give their due to the salutary precautions that come from the first of these conceptions, it will be to prevent the second itself from failing, by reacting against too narrow theses, into contrary exaggerations by an excess of breadth. That was what we had in mind when we were insisting on the radical mortification, on the gift of fear that is the beginning of all wisdom, on the infinite disproportion of the Creator relative to its creature, however elevated the creature may be. We would not want, nevertheless, even to safeguard these austere and necessary truths, to give the impression that there subsists a fund of divine egoism in all these rigors of what the mystics have called "passive purifications," for in the last analysis all that is but the proof [*preuve*] and the test [*épreuve*] of love, according to an expression of Saint Francis de Sales. It is to raise man higher and to unite him more intimately to Himself that God submits him to a more profound destruction of the obstacles that nature opposes to the fusion without confusion of the two wills, the two loves to be joined together spanning the abysses that separate them.

But, it will be said, is not all that, which may seem verified in the heroism of sanctity, inaccessible or even foreign to the common existence and to banal piety? To this objection we have to respond without hesitation, as the masters of the spiritual life do more and more clearly, that the least degree of faith and of grace already bears within it the seeds of the most elevated states, and that there is only a difference of measure or of development, but not of essence or quality between the humble beginnings and the highest forms that tend toward the future union. And it should be added, as a psychological and moral truth that helps us to ground our Christian synthesis on universally verifiable data, that even implicitly accepting the common tribulations and death, without rebellion and without despair, is already itself a more than virtual adherence, one that is already real, like a mustard seed that is enough to prepare the growth of the great tree of divine and immortalized life.

Clearly then we see that neither in theory, nor in practice, is there any danger of naturalism in the idea of the supernatural we are trying to present, because speculatively and effectively this supernatural implies the avowal of a gift impossible to naturalize and implies as well the consented sacrifice, even unto death inclusively, of our natural being. But then we encounter an objection that is quite the opposite, that of sinning through an immoderate supernaturalism, by an exclusive "transcendentism," as Luigi Stefanini once indicated in the *Convivium*, or as already in 1894, the *Revue de Métaphysique* had expressly reproached regarding the book *L'Action*. The question now then is to respond to this serious and delicate difficulty: have we not so exalted the supernatural, so shown its transformative mission and power, so called for the disappearance of the old man to the benefit of the new man, that we risk suppressing one of the two terms, as we face the supreme term of our ascension or rather (since this word still suggests the idea of a personal effort) of our assumption? or, if it is still granted that, at least in intention, we maintain man's role as the matter of the holocaust or even as the wild stem to which is grafted the branch that alone is fruitful, is there not still some worry about what is left of our nature itself, about the suture that allows the circulation of the sap in two lives that seem hardly compatible with one another? This is what we shall now study, for the question has become so important for the most cultivated consciences that it is worthy of being examined in depth.

CHAPTER 12

The Doctrine of the Supernatural Considered under Its Triple Metaphysical, Ascetic, and Mystical Aspect

This term *supernatural*, too often used in a manner that is imprecise and even false, needs to be defined in a technical sense, so that it can be used without equivocation in Christian philosophy.

First we must not be content with its etymological meaning: what lies above a given nature could be called, in some vague, but hence confused and uninteresting sense, a supernature; this is how the living being has been spoken of as supernatural with regard to inorganic matter, or the thinking being with regard to organic life. Some have even tried to approach the Christian supernatural at times by claiming that in the ladder of beings there is a hierarchy that ends with one highest rung. Such an image is more dangerous than useful: it conveys an easily falsified idea of the true supernatural.—Some have also often abused this term to designate what is extraordinary, unexplained, mysterious: people are struck by sensible facts apt to arouse the imagination and to satisfy the need for credulity and of occultism that stirs so many spirits detached from religious beliefs. Such use of the word "supernatural" must be condemned absolutely.

In a way that is already more precise, some facts have been dubbed supernatural for which only the epithet of "preternatural," classical in theology, would be appropriate. What difference is there between the realities designated by these two terms? As Cardinal Dechamps used to note, the states themselves that proceed from the divine power and exceed the natural strengths of the creature should not be called indiscriminately supernatural: anything pertaining to the physical order, to the psychological order, even to the metaphysical order could not justify the use of any other appellation than that of preternatural, no matter how great the miracles of the divine power and charity, whether in bodies, or in vital phenomena,—be it the resurrection of someone dead,—or in the graces of mystical illumination and vision. Only that is supernatural, says Dechamps, which goes toward union through charity and in a manner that escapes all grasps of human consciousness and intelligence.

Let us try to be more precise still concerning the notion of the "absolute supernatural." To be sure the expression "supernatural" has often been applied to what is only preternatural with reference to the distinction of what is simply supernatural with regard to ourselves, *quoad nos*, or to what is such with regard to its mode of realization, *quoad modum*; but this extension of the term, although habitual, presents so many more distortions than advantages that it is better, it would seem, to abandon it as much as possible.

Having set aside the abuses, the false senses, the useless extensions, let us try to see the exact idea that we should make of the Christian supernatural, in the strong and absolute sense of the term.

1. It has often been said that it is God, taken in Himself, who is the supernatural itself.

God, it is said, is above every nature; according to the strictness of the terms, He does not have a nature, He is his own essence: hence He constitutes that absolute supernatural that Christian religion reveals to us.—But such an explanation does not dispel the difficulties it pretends to eliminate: like it or not, the word "supernatural" implies a relation between what is the natural and what is surpassing; it is therefore a word with anthropomorphic overtones; and the disadvantage there is in projecting it, so to speak, into God Himself can be dissimulated only at the cost of consequences that we can call, for want of a better term, denaturing. If God alone were supernatural, what could supernatural life be in us? We would have to reduce it to a simple extrinsic knowledge of the divine transcendence; we would have to limit the promised union to a simple vision that would risk absorbing the creature into the divine life or else that would allow only a representation by interposed intermediaries. The result would again be that Revelation would have a bearing only for what subsists for all eternity and with all necessity in God alone, without constituting a new order, a gift of grace, an invention of pure charity.

Then the supernatural so conceived would oscillate between two shoals: either it would seem attached, imposed, as if a happy accident depending on a divine decree as an incomprehensible intrusion of God in his creatures; or else it would risk reducing the supernatural to the object of intelligence itself, as if every spirit were tending congenitally to capture God and as if the normal end of this intelligence were provisionally taken away from man through a sort of taboo. In either case the supernatural remains equivocal, whether we consider it from the human point of view, or we try to place ourselves in the divine outlook.

2. To rectify and complete this doctrine of the supernatural, theology has proposed more and more clearly a more balanced conception. In what does it consist precisely?

The supernatural, as the word itself suggests, presupposes to begin with a given nature, a human order; and it is that nature that is, not the starting point of a new creation, but the leveraging point and the giving of an elevation that confers upon the creature a participation in the divine life. Let us note first that grace implies a first gift, an already subsisting nature; and it is these faculties that have to be elevated, fortified, sublimated in the transformative union. Let us note then that there is in this a new relation between God and man. The supernatural, then, is not God Himself; nor is it a created thing that would be attached and added to man: it is a sort of hymen between the soul and God. Consequently, we must not think of a simple accident, an arbitrary enhancement, a form extrinsic to man or a truth intrinsic to God: it is, in the consecrated phrase, an adoption, an assimilation, an incorporation, a consortium, a transformation that at once assures both union and distinction of the two incommensurables through the bond of charity.

Such a conception of the supernatural liberates us from the danger we were indicating earlier in describing the oscillation between two equally fearsome shoals, the shoal of a merely tacked on supernatural and the shoal of a supernatural that would be no more than the highest flourishing of an intelligence attaining and capturing its object. There is nothing of the sort here, since the issue is not one of grasping God in Himself, be it without Him and in spite of Him, but of accepting a friendship that, freely offered, asks to be freely accepted. Is not the formula for the supernatural in the Gospel: "I will no longer call you my servants, but my friends and my brothers"? Hence the supernatural appears as a bond of love rather than as a metaphysical rapprochement; and it is through charity that knowledge itself is perfected rather than by a speculation that would leave the two beings as if external to one another. This is not to say that vision does not precede and does not accompany the union of charity: some knowledge is always required and included to allow for the certitude of possession at the same time as the sense of distinction between the Creator and His creatures. But while this distance maintains the humility and the personality of each spirit, the assimilation of human life to the divine insinuates into the created intelligence an accrued energy, to the point that the Sacred Scriptures speak of an intimate face-to-face, going as far as affirming that it is in the divine light and by that light that we know God *sicuti est* [as He is] and that we know ourselves in our true relation with Him.

How is such an intussusception possible and realizable? and by what purifying testing does the prior gift of nature serve as the cost for gaining the precious pearl that is the grace of the divine union?—That is the object of the study, entitled *On Assimilation*, following this one.[1]

---

1. Compare also the more technical study of the supernatural found in the first volume of *La Philosophie et l'Esprit Chrétien*, Part III. The new edition of this work has gone to press.

CHAPTER 13

How the Order of Grace Completes the Natural Order and Forms with It in Us a Life and a Personality That Is Truly One

In the conflicts that put at odds with one another the defenders and the adversaries of Christian religion, even in those that have arisen among the representatives of the Christian spirit, the principal difficulty could be expressed as follows: the distinction of the two orders, natural and supernatural, is such that either we cannot explain the passage from one to the other without compromising either the validity proper to reason or the transcendence of grace; or else what is maintained is a simple juxtaposition of the two orders by affirming, without rendering it intelligible, the celebrated formula: *gratia non tollit naturam sed perficit* [grace does not take away nature but perfects].

It is important then to enter more deeply into the question of the supernatural's adherence to human nature, this indwelling of the new life in a nature that does not cease being itself even as it is transformed. *Theandric* is the name given to this mysterious state that by definition brings into communion two beings, two lives, through a grace of the *Verbum caro factum* [Word made flesh]; but if such an assertion is clearly promulgated, it remains, from the standpoint of rational thought, to discover a mode of possibility that will keep it from remaining in the state of a brute and opaque enunciation. Now, that is not an easy task; but forasmuch as we can succeed in introducing some rays of light here, the benefit will be very great for those who want to practice the *rationabile obsequium* [rational service] and set themselves, according to the Apostle, in a position to render reason for their faith. Quite often Christians who have been in relation with incredulous people able to reason their own incredulity have encountered this objection, the shock of which is felt even by simple folk: it is nice to speak of divine life in man; but are those not just words, unthinkable words, words discredited perpetually by the very impoverished realities of these devotees who, according to the words of Montesquieu, make their piety consist in believing themselves better than others, when in fact they are lacking in the most delicate and sometimes the most essential natural virtues? Theoretically and practically, then, the objection is quite real, quite telling, quite urgently to be refuted.

If we were to remain exclusively at the standpoint of notional knowledge, we surely could not surmount the difficulties of a response to such an embarrassment. To define on one side a supposed nature, a state of pure nature, and facing that an absolute supernatural that no faculty of man could suspect, desire, define, or procure, is to be fatally exposed either to the rejection of the supernature as of an added factor or as an unjustifiable intrusion, or to be exposed to a servile absorption of human dignity, to what has been called a slave morality, to a vilification of courtesans held in tutelage as perpetual minors. To allow the debate to remain at this level where incredulity has every interest to keep it, is to render the teaching of Catholic dogma and morality easy to despise; and the apologists who have heroically taken on this task of exposing and even of imposing this conception, that has been given the name of "extrinsicism," have in spite of their intention turned toward the contrary error of immanentism many minds who could not resign themselves to a solution as unintelligible to critical thought as it is revolting to a will enamored of a generous sense of human dignity as well as of divine goodness. There is then another attitude to be taken than the one that consists in abstractly opposing nature and supernature, as has too often been done under the guise of preventing any confusion and of avoiding the dangers, otherwise quite real, of semi-rationalism, of the new Pelagianism of liberalism or of immanentist idealism. Let us declare once and for all that we as much as anyone else abhor and reject these doctrines, and even that it is to take away from them any occasion for seducing minds that we take our stand in another perspective than that of extrinsicism.

To understand at least partially how supernature, while remaining entirely transcendent, completes and reshapes nature itself from its foundation up in order to form with it one single whole, it is indispensable to dispel an equivocation and to bring to light a truth seldom adverted to.—The equivocation is this: it is imagined spatially that, for the supernatural to remain transcendent, it must necessarily be imported from outside, under an explicit form, as addressed through sensible signs and formal notions to a reflective knowledge. However, these vehicles, as legitimate and as indispensable as they are to reveal to us the factual existence of the supernatural order, do not constitute the supernatural itself: this true supernatural takes place interiorly; it is to be sure not from us, *ex nobis, ex natura* [from us, from nature]; but is in us, *in nobis* [in us]; and it is under this interior form that the supernaturalization takes place. Hence, those *interna auxilia* [internal helps] that the [First] Vatican Council indicates as "necessary" for the genesis and the efficaciousness of faith have, so to speak, their transcendence in an immanent form, their superiority in interiority rather than in the exteriority to which it has been prejudicially subjected. Hence the problem is no longer to make some material import coming from the outside cohabit in our innermost thought, like a thorn that would penetrate our flesh,—which is still not to say enough, for it is more difficult to introduce a brute object into the flow of intellectual life than to have a foreign body tolerated in organic tissues. The question becomes this: how can an influence of a spiritual and supernatural order act at the core of our intellectual and moral personality, without compromising that personality's existence, by helping it to develop, but without ceasing to be distinct? What was an intelligible and deadly intrusion for the intimate life of the spirit therefore appears as nothing else than a cooperation that we must now define by showing how, according to Sacred Scriptures, the spirit of man by adhering to God forms, without any confusion whatsoever, but one spirit with Him.

Through this first regression the problem is therefore reduced to terms that are no longer at odds with one another as if it were an issue of transforming into a spiritual truth a totally material letter. It is the letter itself that contains, conveys, and reveals a spirit more truly spiritual than our own thought. Consequently, those who accuse Catholicism of materializing the Gospel, of transposing the religion of spirit and truth into a religion of authority, understand nothing of the exact meaning of our dogmas, of our discipline, of our Christian life. What they claim to wish for, they do not obtain; and contrary to their pretense of adoring a God who is pure spirit, they subject their religion to a philosophical conception and to an ideal that remains a simply human ideal. It is in this sense that Revelation must, as has frequently been repeated, prevent natural religion from weakening, indeed from denaturing the religious spirit: this spirit withers away to the extent that deism invades it by confiscating for its own profit what has been called free Christianity or neo-Christianity: an illusion that has brought about many victims and that keeps outside the Church many souls who are nevertheless generous and clear-sighted, but who go only half way, let us not say in the supernatural order, which is not given by half, but in what natural reason itself admits and demands.

Having dispelled a fearsome equivocation, we have still to bring to light a truth that has been little noted because it has remained masked by the misunderstandings from which we have just taken our distance. This truth is that of the appropriateness [*convenance*] there is between the spontaneous, albeit inefficacious, aspirations of nature and the unforeseen responses, the unhoped-for satisfaction that the supernatural order brings to the imprecise, but positive, wish of our spiritual nature. This point, of capital importance, is beginning to be studied methodically from many sides at once: it is important to take advantage of these converging efforts that will help us to understand how in effect supernature, far from breaking up and crushing nature, perfects it.

Earlier we were showing that it is less from outside than from inside that the supernatural, as superior as it is, enters and dwells in us; and already thereby we were dispelling the oft-repeated reproach against the alleged heteronomy and against the materialistic tendency of Catholicism, the religion of authority and of literal observance. Now we have to establish a yet more intimate truth, and that may seem more paradoxical; the issue is to show that the supernatural does not and cannot come into effect except by way of interiority, whatever may be apart from this the material vehicles and the literal practices that it uses normally to reveal itself and communicate itself. If this thesis is understood and admitted, we will have radically excluded the charge of heteronomy and the objection that consists in declaring incomprehensible and even impossible the union of the rational nature and of the supernatural gift. With the same stroke we will forestall the contrary exaggeration and the danger of confusing the two orders, because it will be in the orders themselves, through this adherence to one another and their inherence in us, that their distinction in the very unity of their cooperation will appear.

If it is true that the grace of filial adoption, which constitutes the new state to which the Christian is called, entails much more than one sort of knowledge, if this elevation of man, without creating other faculties than those he possesses naturally, has for its object association with divine life at the cost of sacrificing his purely human nature, it is not therefore like something transmitted from the outside or like some exotic truth to be received, it is as an intimate renovation that the supernatural order presents itself and has to be received: whence it follows that a personal disposition, an internal conversion, even if it be obscure and implicit, is really necessary for grace to insert itself in a soul and bring about in it this second birth of which the Sacred Scriptures constantly speak. To be sure, with the child, with the uneducated, even with the most educated, the superaddition of grace is normally tied to a sensible sign, to a sacramental rite, to an external act; but this vehicle, which serves as a mark of the introduction of a gift and of the submission of the one who receives it, does not impede the truth about the entirely intimate, the entirely spiritual, from being what is principal and what is essential; and hence we have to say that the birth of man to grace implies, not a pure passivity, as a magical incantation would be, but a conformity of the active being that we are with a vocation that for its part calls for an adherence, a cooperation, a union from the inside and not simply in the domain materially subject to constraint and passivity.

In this way, the strongest and the most subtle obstacle of reason collapses against the imperative exigencies of Catholicism: it is neither a materialization, an exteriorization, a suggestion, nor do the truths it infuses in us enter without a moral act, without a meritorious acceptance, without some at least tacit and virtual consent. It is therefore wrong to have willed to oppose this religion of authority to the religion of spirit and truth; for Catholicism has this unique trait of uniting those two aspects and even of showing that they are possible and stable only as both together and the one by the other. That is what remains for us to understand better. For without a doubt indeed there is a cloud that enters here into many minds. We see quite well indeed, it will be said, that supernatural life presupposes some moral support, some human preparation; but does it not tend to absorb, to annihilate the work of nature for the sake of such a superhuman state that often appears inhuman? Or else, if we insist on what has been called devout humanism, do we not run the risk finally of attenuating the divine exigencies, of dulling Christian heroism and of ending up with a confusion propitious to the illusion of semi-rationalism or of theoretical and practical liberalism?

To this difficulty, which we have already encountered in less radical forms, we have now to oppose a no less radical explanation. The entire movement of nature leads to two conclusions at once opposed and solidary: on the one hand, human aspirations and the effort of civilization orients us toward an ideal that has to approach ever closer to the Christian ideal; but at the same time, the law of renunciation is imposed as the condition *sine qua non* of access to the truly Christian life: so that in order for us to attain what we have to affirm and will, we have to go through a state contrary to our natural élan. This is the interior drama that is clear to upright and generous souls, but that remains obscure and as it were scandalous or insoluble to spirits full of themselves or backing off from onerous effort. But, for being contrary to one another, these two tendencies are no less both profoundly in conformity with reason, if it goes to the very end of its own exigencies. Moreover it cannot be said that the law of submission, of sacrifice, of humility, of mortification is contrary to the dignity and to the human aspirations of reason and the will. Here again, here especially, grace, while appearing to contradict and deaden nature, does nothing else than fortify it, enlighten it, perfect it. But on the other hand the conflict between our two wills always remains such that we cannot, without the help of grace, effectively triumph over the law of our members and our congenital egoism: that is what has been strongly noted by Saint Paul, Saint Augustine, and so many others who have experienced and described the struggle in which grace, without violating nature, frees it from a yoke that of itself it would be too weak to shake off.

From these analyses we have to draw these conclusions: it is by insinuating itself into the most profound depth of our nature; through a sort of subterranean channel, that grace, as supernatural and as higher as it is, acts in man; but man is not thereby chased out of himself, nor a prisoner in himself, nor reduced to an entirely passive and subalternate role, nor condemned to self-annihilation: often through the most mortifying purifications, it is always toward the elevation, the exaltation, the full utilization of our human powers for deification that the supernatural action aims at and accomplishes. We have to say then that the graft is very deep, well into the very root of our personal life: there is such a close suture that, even under the scar, the unity of life assimilates man to God, to constitute this wonder called "theandric being," that is to say, this duality that seems to enrich God with an external glory, that of being Himself in another and making of this new being another Himself. Can one conceive a more wondrous invention of charity, an achievement of union without confusion and as it were an increase of the uncreated richness itself?

Let no one say again then that we have to choose between extrinsicism and immanentism: the Emmanuel [God with us] can be entirely within us without thereby ceasing to be above us: but if, by hypostatic union, the eternal Word personally united Himself to human nature down to its material form, we can, we too, profit by this incarnation and be incorporated, through the Mediator, into this life of the *Verbum caro factum* [Word made flesh]. To be sure, the mystery subsists; but the dogma is not entirely obscure, and a very fruitful light reveals to us dispositions that are enough to set objections and doubts to one side.

Doubts, for it is not allowed to have any, and there is, here again, a difficulty to be overcome. One might imagine that a conditional faith is enough; and it has seemed more meritorious to some to perform, without certitude, as if it were certain. Did not Pascal propose the argument of the wager? Now this argument (astonishing as it is that its Christian incorrectness has not been denounced) is not acceptable in any way: to the extent that it puts forward interests, where it establishes probabilities and where it lets some incertitude subsist, as faint as it may be. Such a method of demonstration, which has been criticized from a logical and mathematical point of view, is to be condemned from the Catholic point of view, as specious as it may seem from the psychological and moral point of view. We are not authorized to think and to act as if faith did not give us a certitude higher than any other, absolutely and divinely founded. How then can the part of the will in the act of faith be preserved, when the assurance of the truths to be believed has to be full and total? The fact is in effect that we not only have to affirm more or less obscure truths, to adhere to the data of a Revelation that brings strange news to our world; we have to have a docile and loving confidence in the Revealer Himself who makes Himself known only to give, only to make us live and to make Himself loved; now does one doubt about love without offending the one who should be loved?

The very idea of the true supernatural we have proposed excludes all doubt from faith, which either is or is not, but which could not be hypothetical without destroying itself. Thus is explained this ominous exigency, albeit logical and beneficial: there is no half-faith, no conditional faith, no faith out of interest or calculation, no faith out of prudence or with the benefit of an inventory. For better or for worse we have to commit our whole selves in our response to the call of our destiny. In this we can explain also that, even in acts that are at times childish, the problem of the option that fixes our eternal responsibility can be resolved. There was once proposed a theory according to which most men, not being conscious of the revealed dogmas, of the imposed precepts, of the gravity of the stakes, were to remain between heaven and hell as simple folk not having reached the adult state of reason. This invention, which has no roots in the traditional teaching, misconceives, it seems, the weight of decisions having to do with alternatives that do not need to be notionally tagged to bring into play the secrets of hearts and of wills. Here again we have to say, with Saint Bernard, that, under the humblest of species, grace and nature cooperate without confusion between them, to form together an indivisible act that can hold for eternity or bring to bear on the culpable soul an indelible sanction.

To sum up, the very paradoxical association of grace and nature, in spite of the internal revolutions it provokes or imposes, does not cease to be a work of peace, of concord, of profound calm. The greatest mystics have expressly noted this. After the hours or years of spiritual combat, of tragic sufferings, of extraordinary states, there comes finally an appeasement, and, in this higher serenity, all the forces of nature, henceforth sublimated and transformed, deploy their quiet activity in a higher joy and under the guidance of the divine Spirit. Proof that in fact, in spite of the concupiscences that never quite die down entirely in this world, nature and supernature can prelude the supreme accord of a happy life in which even the glorified bodies will participate. We see then that Catholicism, far from being a religion against nature, against reason, against freedom, is essentially the path of the triumph of man and of humanity. In order to bring out better this beautiful continuity that the conflicts of this world too often mask, it will not be without benefit to examine the applications of the doctrines that have just been set out. We shall see to what profound realism studies bearing on the relations between grace and nature lead us in the sensible, the moral, and the social order. There will be in that a sort of counter-proof at the same time as an extension of our Catholic synthesis.

CHAPTER 14

The Union of Nature and Supernature in the Practical Order Itself

We have just gotten a glimpse of how philosophical speculation surmounts the difficulty of uniting, at least theoretically, two beings, two lives that seem incommensurable. But if this union can appear realizable in the outlook of the metaphysician who accepts as possible the data of faith, is such a union practically realized? and how does this mysterious alliance that could not remain without efficacy manifest itself?—Thus, then, we find ourselves before a new domain to explore, that of the implementations, of the failures, or of the fruits of this theandric life whose permanent character we have glimpsed.

Let us begin by examining the effects visible to observation and that nevertheless can be explained only by the influence of a supernatural power: those are, according to the consecrated expression, the "notes" or the psychological and moral proofs of the Church, which, by its unity, its sanctity, its universality, its perenniality, provides for all eyes some reflection of its invisible glow.

Judging from the history of the people of Israel or of Christian religion through a display of details, one might be tempted to look mainly on the human miseries, the incessant failures, the apparent or real indigence of results. It has been said that the Bible, as studied by a critical thought that places the Jewish people back among the others in the general flow of history, presents itself as a very poor reality, "a long fastidious story of battles," as a great mind once told me, with continuous disappointments for centuries of a deceived expectation and with the insignificance of a small state seen as a lowly figure in the ensemble of great empires and brilliant civilizations. And yet it is from this that what has been called the Jewish miracle breaks forth best: the more our sacred history is reduced to its humanly minimal proportions, the more this way of restoring the truth of history brings out the paradox of the influence spiritually exercised by this small nation, charged with maintaining a monotheist tradition that had everywhere withered, and with safeguarding the alliance, the immense hope of a universally proffered salvation. This apologetic, which has been termed glacial, stripped as it is of all factitious ornamentation and warmth, is also the most decisive for spirits capable of understanding and admiring the miraculously preserved purity of a teaching upheld amid the passions and all the revolutions that make of the history of biblical times a chaos of religious errors and political ruinations.

Is it not the same, and more so, for the Church, surviving after Christ almost before having been founded otherwise than on words and examples? As we look upon its origins, its gropings, its internal crises, its struggles with Oriental cults, with Hellenic thought, with an imperial domination, we become astonished with the spirit that persists, thanks to a pliable adaptation to the most diverse, at times the most hostile realities. That is how a spiritual assimilation came to transform the temples, the rites, the institutions, the customs, the souls little by little; so that from the Pantheon itself a church came to be, and into the pagan superstitions, as into the forms of ancient art, a new civilization was infused inspired by the all-new unity poured into thought and into society through the Christian leaven. It may be objected that such heterogeneous elements have at times been ill digested, corruptive, ruinous for the early institution of the Good News: upon closer examination, it is the assimilative power of Christian religion that finally triumphed over the difficulties resulting often from its very success with peoples with whom the Church seemed to be adapting in order better to redress and to divinize all that could be converted and purified in the most diverse traditions. Hence here again we see (and the most independent historical critique has restored the truth of this active and triumphant assimilation by Christian ferment) that the provisional condescensions of Christian religion have achieved a synthesis in which the most refractory human elements have sooner or later been as it were transubstantiated by a principle of permanent life and unity.

But it is in the intimate order of personal life that this power of absorption is manifested. Words fail in trying to name adequately the continuity that is established in thoughts and in the acts, penetrated at once of human aspiration and of supernatural life. We were speaking of transubstantiation and of absorption: those are inexact metaphors: for, unlike in the hypostatic union that makes of the Man-God one single person multiplied by the Eucharist, the beings supernaturalized by grace do not cease being merely human persons; and we could not insist too much on the inviolable distinction that forestalls any fear of false mysticism and of pantheistic absorption. The term "consubstantiation" has been proposed to indicate the cohabitation of the two elements in us; as if two substantial beings resided in the Christian in the state of grace, as one might tend to believe from that vision that had shown in Saint Catherine of Siena the Christ appearing in the saint's own face: but this expression is still inexact, too strong or too weak, because there are not two lives developing in parallels and substantially in the supernaturalized being. There is one and the same life, but that is not an essential unity; there is union because whoever says union, says at once difference of being and intimate relation of voluntary, meritorious, and savored adherence; it is triumphant symbiosis.

We find here once again the truth we had earlier looked at in its speculative aspect, but whose application in detail it is good for us to consider. The supernatural consolidates nature itself: if, from the standpoint of metaphysics, there is inconfusability between the Creator and the creature, this incurable disproportion, which maintains a sort of material barrier against any suppression of the human personality, is, from another standpoint, a will of love and a condition of spiritual value, of personal beatitude for the created being itself. The two faces, rational and charitable, of the providential plan appear here to complete and to perfect one another. But, as can be seen, the distance remains, and the God of majesty ever subsists in the God of charity; so that the apparent multiplicity of divine perfections is resolved, even with regard to us, into the absolute simplicity that makes one and the same truth of all these attributes distinguished in our discursive anthropomorphic thought. This is the illusion we must always beware of, when objections are raised against the rigor of divine judgments, against the exigencies of justice or of charity itself: not only must we reconcile these attributes, but we have to show that they compenetrate one another, even for us, if we can arrive at the point where nature and supernature help us to surpass the notional viewpoint and to realize the union of the two orders that are not limited, in us, to a mere juxtaposition.

Let us take some examples that will help to concretize these explanations. If it is true that the Christian, according to Saint Paul's expression, is buried with Christ through a sort of mortification of all natural appetites, the Christian is nevertheless at the same time virtually risen with Him. Whence the twofold attitude noted in the Christian marking the most legitimate feelings, aspirations, and loves; and that is what the world does not understand, because the world does not know the secret of this twofold attitude that strikes it as paradox, contradiction, insincerity, even hypocrisy, when it is the matter of a disposition that is profoundly beautiful, justifiable, and meritorious. Let us consider a few more samples of these contrasting attitudes, that it would be wrong to see as isolated or as opposed to one another, although they are not always combined even among the saints.

Take for example the love of nature, the blossoming of the aesthetic sense, the natural chant of the soul in the presence of great spectacles and of human heroisms. On another side, all that can and should be reduced to a sense of infinite smallness, of a passing vanity, of a supreme detachment, or of a meritorious sacrifice in view of practicing a holy indifference that annihilates everything in the presence of the one thing necessary and the divine infinitude: Saint John of the Cross wrote the canticle of the nothing in the face of the All.—But Saint John of the Cross also wrote the canticle of universal love and, like Saint Francis of Assisi, he found everywhere the visible traces of the invisible beauty. So that his perfect detachment very softly and very joyously attaches Him to the entire order of creatures, loved and admired, not just in their author, but in themselves, at once for God and for the ones who are going toward Him and who should incline us toward Him.

Let us analyze likewise the desire for glory and for influence, a natural passion of noble and generous spirits. To be in the esteem of a soul, Pascal says, is the most beautiful place and the most worthy to be sought. Such a vivid sentiment must at first be subdued in the Christian who is looking for humble abjection, who loves "to be ignored and counted as nought," who puts others ahead of himself for whatever honor and who gives, according to Newman's remark, the impression of belonging to those wretched people, to those "poor of spirit," to those little ones where, in fact, Christian religion has so often found its recruits: to the extent that one of the tests to be gone through by many converts is to fall in with this flock at times justly decried. But let us look at the other aspect and, after or along with this profound mortification of an appetite for glory and for action, see what Christian religion draws from this mortified and transfigured inclination. *Duc in altum!* [Lead on to the height!] This precept of the Gospel applies to every intellectual challenge, to every search for truth, to every initiative in the apostolate and in action, to every salutary enterprise. Much more, if we are asked to renounce the false glory of renown, which has to do only with a show of brilliance and an illusion of resounding words in the present order of phenomena, on the other hand nothing is lost of the secret influences, of the unknown devotedness, of the hidden alms, of the truth sewn in souls, that will be known only later or never in this world; and glory, true glory, alone substantial and eternal will rise from the Christian who has acted for God and for his brothers amid obscurity: *occulta omnia revelabuntur* [all hidden things will be revealed]. Thus the natural inclination that, left to its own resources, would have found only vanity and deception, receives therefore, through Christian humility and the fecundity of grace, a full satisfaction. On one side, the fearful word for the proud: *receperunt mercedem suam* [they have received their reward] . . . , *vani vanam* [vain for one who is vain]; on the other side, the promise: *merces vestra erit magna nimis* [your reward will be great indeed].

It has been claimed at times that the Christian religion has done no more than appropriate for itself, as if they were supernatural, profound tendencies of our nature capable of leading man to heroism and even to pathological excesses; such as the attraction to suffering, the strange pleasure of privation, the need to be devoted and to sacrifice, the exaggeration of penance and expiation. But if these tendencies are in fact spontaneous among certain people, they find in Christian religion, not just their complete explanation, but also and especially their regulation, their moderation, even their correction, where ascetical rigor exceeds reasonable austerities, as in false mysticism and in what has been called the sadistic search for suffering. That is one of the points where we find revealed best the reasonable character, the intelligible sense, and the marvelous equilibrium of nature and grace in their most paradoxical union. For, unlike Buddhism, fakirisms, Stoicism, and all doctrines or sects that have exalted the cult of suffering and of mortification or that have depreciated enjoyments accessible to man, Christian religion remains a stranger to any pessimist conception, even where it encourages detachment, including voluntary suffering. Far from causing a sort of proud and scornful insensibility, Christian asceticism increases gentleness, mildness, compassion, humility, profound and soothing tenderness, interior joy, fortifying hope, lively and heartfelt charity. Here again then, the contrary aspects are united in this life where grace and nature complement one another and mutually enrich one another, even where at first sight one might have expected a conflict such as has appeared among those who have been called, with Frances de Sales, the "holy folks," who are not holy at all.—But we shall presently have to examine the objection that is often drawn from accidental imperfections and for which Christian religion is not in any way responsible.

To better understand, from a standpoint that is not only moral, but also fully realist, the unity wherein the relation between nature and grace is consummated, let us examine for a moment the problem of the reversibility of merits and that of pardoning prescribed by the *Pater* [*Noster*] as the rule for the will to follow in judging ourselves. It has often been found incomprehensible and hardly just that innocents should take the place of the guilty and that there be this obligation at times to sacrifice justice to mercy. Now there is in this one of the greatest commandments of the new Law; and it is important to bring out what there is that is grounded, intelligible, good in such a prescription. The mystery of the redemption is the full and efficacious expression of such a law; and the law of pardoning imposed on us is an extension of the redemptive task itself. How is that possible and justifiable? And what light can come from a meditation on this rather disconcerting point?

As we have seen, moral relations and religious obligations are grounded on the natural order itself. Saint Thomas says: what is in conformity with nature is good; evil is a fundamental disorder rooted, not just in ideal intensions, but in the real relations of beings. Thus there is in evil a consistency that can be termed realistic and ontological, even though evil by itself is not a being and results only from falsified relations among beings. That is why an ideal change, a regret, a conversion of desires and of intentions is not enough to heal and expiate the wounds caused by fault and even more so by sin. Fault, in the natural and human order, is the betrayal of values and the preference given to lower goods. Sin is the betrayal of the divine order establishing the universal hierarchy of goods and the obligation to obey the divine law. On either side, disorder has brought about a positive and durable state whose consequences are virtually unlimited and irreparable: for we cannot keep what has been from having been, nor from having its consequences stretch to the infinite. Hence, fault and sin have something indelible about them; and repentance is not enough to rub out the evil perpetrated that no reparation could compensate for absolutely.

Whence comes the call for a pardon that renounces justice in the name of a merciful goodness. That is the sense of the texts from Scripture declaring that no offering or sacrifice could have disarmed justice, that the heavenly Father had required the fulfillment of deicide as the expression of a strict equity, that the Christ had obeyed this inexorable sentence implied in the intrinsic force of the sinful will; but then, in order for this necessity, as rigorous as a logical consequence, to have its saving and expiatory effect, it was required in addition that the victim transform this necessity of justice into a free and loving offering, whence the words Scripture attributes to the incarnate Word immolating Himself: *tunc dixi: ecce venio . . . oblatus sum quia ipse volui* [then I said: behold I come . . . I have been offered because I willed it myself].

In this justice and mercy truly embrace one another; and the way is thereby open for us equally, in the commandment imposed by the law of pardon: we have to grasp all the realist reason and all the charitable beauty of this. For if, according to a word from the sacred books of India, if vengeance and hate respond to hate and to evil, how will hatred ever end? To remedy the damages committed by a human freedom and woven into the reality of a past and a future that escapes our grasp, there is in spite of partial compensations, only one means: it is by the reciprocal condoning of the harms and damages experienced. If we demanded what is due us down to the last farthing and if we ask God to avenge us, we then remain chained and we enchain others and Christ Himself in an inexplicable responsibility. On the contrary, in renouncing the requirement that remains impossible to fully restore, we lighten, so to speak, the burden that weighed on the shoulders of the Crucified and we grant our culpable brothers a remission that, as it profits them, profits us also, by serving as the measure for ourselves of the mercy accorded to the other we have thereby discharged of the burden of justice that weighted on him in vain.

Do we not understand then the very coherent, very really grounded and extensive significance of this redemption and of this law of pardon, of which some have said at times that it is a denial of justice, an aggravation of faults, a contradiction of the moral order, an unacceptable humiliation and degradation? Do we not see especially, here again, how perfect the connection is between natural reality and the mysterious laws of supernatural charity? There is no confusion possible between what is free and what is necessary, between the rigor of positive facts and the generosity that turns the severity of an inexorable justice into an occasion for goodness and into an invention of charity. So much so that, considered in its entire articulation, the plan where nature and supernature come to be united does not expose us to any confusion, not any more than to any dissociation. The plentitude of Christian life does not then create, as some have maintained at times, a *homo duplex* [twofold man], a sort of interior schism that would turn into a monster perpetually oscillating or divided in its affections and in its thoughts. A new proof of what we had called the profound realism of the Christian order. And therein in effect, for those who know how to see it, is also found a confirmation of the truth that Christian religion is to be taken as alive, that it adapts itself to all needs, that, as something solid, it presents indefinitely varied aspects, all of them in concord with one another; all the more so when, instead of looking at its many facets from outside, we enter into it in order to discover the spirit that animates and unites all functions of this theandric life.

It has often been said that compared to Christian religion pantheism is the most captivating doctrine for souls enamored of spiritual life, of absolute, of harmonious diversity. Perhaps it should be objected that on the contrary the pantheistic synthesis, rather than being harmony, richness, absolute, caricatures the solutions offered by the Catholic unity; for the absolute of pantheism is only the relative perpetually oscillating between the contraries; its richness is no more than a privation of infinite transcendence for the sake of an ever-mutable and indigent immanence in its indefinite extensions. Catholicism offers at once God in all and God in itself, and, without compromising perfect transcendence, it incarnates the divine Word into the depths of the flesh and into each one of the singular beings capable of personal life and free will: nowhere else is diversity as completely assured, and yet nowhere else is unity as completely attained.

The fact is, indeed, that there are two kinds of unity, quite different and even opposed to one another: that of monism and that where Christian religion leads us. The first mixes in together, in an identity of nature that goes to the point of joining contraries, all the diversity of things, all the patent distinctions of beings, in order to arrive at an absorption of everything into a single and impersonal being, into a substance that contains all of becoming, all the relative, all the imperfections, but that altogether excludes thereby the perfect, the absolute, pure thought, existence in itself and for itself. Understood in this way, unity and identity are more mixture and confusion. The Christian conception answers the supreme wish of the spirit in quite another way. It does not confuse the whole with a sum of juxtaposed and successive parts, through a kind of materializing image that, even in the idealist Spinoza, makes of the body a divine attribute. True unity consists in the presence in all and in everything of one and the same real mediation, of a concrete universal that, without being mixed in with the imperfection of creatures and with their finite mode of existence, is nevertheless Himself everywhere and in its entirety, God of power who makes all things subsist, God of light who enlightens every intelligence by making it participate in the light of the Word and in the life of the Spirit, God of charity who conveys to the faithful souls the union whereby He gives Himself entirely to all those who consent to receive Him. This is the sense of that spiritual unity that is not limited to relations of nature, but that presupposes the intervention of thought and of will, in order to maintain the distinction of persons, along with the merit and the joy of intimacy freely consented to.

We were inquiring into how nature and supernature can be united, and how the first of the notes of the Church can be realized and verified, both in its members and in the entire organism we salute with the words: *credo in Ecclesiam unam* [I believe in the one Church]. This unity, as we have just glimpsed it, is, notwithstanding the paradox of the coming together of two incommensurable orders, a lived reality to begin with in the intimacy of Christian souls, each one in its one-on-one with the interior Master, Friend, Bridegroom. It is realized and lived in the diverse human societies: family, nation, Christendom, humanity, catholicity, with reservations we shall presently have to indicate, not to cut short, but to deepen this essential truth. And this unity is realized again and lived through the generations that come after one another in this world, in the continuity of Tradition, in the City that includes the suffering or the triumphant Church as well as the militant Church. Unity of dogma, unity of practice, unity of discipline, all that comes from one and the same spirit about which we cannot lose sight of one aspect without losing thereby the life He alone infuses and to all.

The ancient moralists had the sense of an analogous truth, albeit in a subalternate way, when they said: *bonum fit ex integra causa; malum, ex quolibet defectu* [good comes to be from an integral cause; evil, from whatever defect]. The good, however particular it may seem, always supposes for it to be good an intention that is right and complete, which is to say that we must attend less to this or that particular good than to what represents or contains, in a given occasion, the Good itself in its integrality. It is in this sense that Socrates said that virtue is one, even in the most diverse forms. But what is true of the dispositions of our will struggling with the difficulties of moral action, how much more is it true still when what comes into play is the unity that all the metaphysical foundations of nature, all the development of our thought, all the aspirations of the heart and of the will, all the order of grace and the divine provisions for our supernatural vocation and election. Donoso Cortés used to say: only the Catholic is a living unity, being a supernatural being, because he possesses God within himself. Such an assertion comes to light and is justified by showing how the unity of the Christian, the unity of the Church, the unity of the providential plan form only one and the same truth, even though it is seen in different frameworks and, provisionally at least, in a sort of shorthand that eternal life will develop without ever exhausting it.

Is this to say that this unity ends up in a uniformity that is only a false identity? By no means; for the infinite resourcefulness of the divine power, wisdom, and love does not proceed by those general ways to which our discursive reason is subject. The more perfection is rich, the more it diversifies itself in original implementations that manifest the very variety of its gifts. Absolute simplicity can be imitated only at the cost of an immense multiplicity. That is why there is not, in the world of nature, of thought, of grace, two facts that are entirely superimposable, two indiscernible beings, two totally identical vocations: it is beauty and charity all at once; for love, which attaches itself to what is unique and living, always needs this variety that, according to the words of Bossuet, is the entire secret of pleasing, by allowing to love uniquely and incomparably each one of the beings expressing some perfection and some design from the One-on-High. Let us not then understand unity as contrary to what is its highest condition and its inexhaustible charm.

CHAPTER 15

The Philosophical Problem of Sanctity

Are we not however painting the Christian spirit too rosily, not only by describing what it is in the ideal order where speculative philosophy tries to contemplate it in its doctrinal scope, but also by canonizing so to speak from the onset those who are inspired by it, who should live by it, who sometimes claim to incarnate it, while falling so far short of the perfect harmony it requires? Among the marks of the Church, after that of unity, it is sanctity that is proposed to the attention of the world, as if this privileged fact reserved as an exclusive possession of its own defied criticism and imposed admiration or adherence. Do we not have to discuss, from a rational viewpoint, these pretensions, to examine the many objections evoked by the weakness, the failures, the deficiencies of Christians, by the social or political inferiorities of Catholic persons or societies, and even by the strangeness, to say nothing more, of many lives proposed to the public cult of the faithful?

To begin with, are there saints outside the visible Church? The question cannot be resolved without a prior distinction. We shall examine it further on. But for the moment we have to say that the formula "outside the Church there is no salvation and no sanctity" contains an ambiguity we have to free ourselves from without delay: the invisible Church, the one called the soul of the Church, goes beyond official cadres, but does not forasmuch cease to participate in redemptive grace; and there is nothing to prevent us from admitting that some day the visible Church will honor, in some way that it will be for it to determine, a saint who will not have known or recognized it, as was recently proposed regarding a Muslim mystic and martyr, Al-Hallaj ([1]).

This being said, let us examine precisely, not the objection arising from the perfection of non-Catholics, since that can be an extension of the grace of Christ, but the difficulty arising from the imperfections, often quite serious, quite disconcerting, of many of the faithful who make up the common flock and even of the leaders who direct it, the figures who are supposed to illustrate the faith by their works. We shall not insist on the most obvious argument, the one more commonly advanced: the fragility, the consequences of human nature, which are in fact without assignable limit. But, it may be added, it is not a question of simple failures that even the wisest, who "sin seven times a day," do not avoid; it is a question of those devout types, whose devotion, as Montesquieu suggests, consists in thinking that they are holier than others, when they are often lacking in the virtues that are the most delicately and the most nobly human, only to remain satisfied with practices and formulas compatible with an offensive mediocrity or even an unconscionable morality.

Without coming to the defense of these insufficiencies or these deformations, it has been maintained, not without some truth, that such imperfections, at times allowed by God, would be either to foster humility in those who take note of them and secretly suffer from them, or to mask the more profound virtues that escape notice, but are not legitimate grounds for a severe judgment against Catholicism and its efficacy. Of course it is desirable, as we have already said, in keeping with the wish of the [First] Vatican Council, that the spiritual sparkle of the Christian people would catch the eye and serve as irrefutable, indubitable proof of the divine truth that shines in the Church at each moment of its history, so that it should be enough to see it living before us to conclude legitimately and necessarily to its founder and to its mission. Nevertheless the problem of sanctity is of another order still; and if it is true that we need a faithful flock as numerous and as fervent as possible in order to justify before all spirits of good faith the supernatural character of Catholicism,

---

1. A sizable thesis for the Doctorat ès Lettres by the well-known erudite Louis Massignon studies, with the support of documentation, the extraordinary life of this Muslim mystic.

it has been repeated more often still that we especially need saints in the full force of the term, in order to bring warmth to a world that is getting cool, as we read in the office of Saint Francis of Assisi, *frigescente mundo*. Why so? What then is a saint? whence comes the importance that surrounds canonizations? and how on the other hand are we to explain this contemptuous or irritated hostility of the world, recently attested to a candidate to the baccalaureate naïvely declaring that "the state of sanctity is an immoral state"?

There is a sort of challenge to the world in the habitual and otherwise always new and original allures of saints. They seem, like Christ, a sign of contradiction, an occasion for scandal, giving the lie to the fearful prudence and the seeming virtues inspired by the worldly spirit. Whence the problem saints pose for the conscience of those who witness their initiatives, their austerity, their "folly," according to an expression often applied to them as it once was applied to their divine model. Of course we have had to insist more than once on the profoundly human and fully rational character of the Christian life, and John of the Cross declared that the mystic is the most sensible of men. But finally another aspect is even more striking: supernatural wisdom on the whole contradicts the common precepts, the counsels of philosophers and of moralists, the moderation of which Aristotle said is a just midpoint between contrary excesses. To this prescription of pagan thought comes the reply of the Evangelical teaching that, in imitation of the excess of divine charity, calls man to an excess of the same kind: the only measure for loving God, Saint Bernard says, is to love without measure as if in a contagious folly. We should not think then that the Christian ideal is one of bourgeois virtue and of equilibrium in repose. Though there have been great saints who have realized this unalterable peace of the "little virtues" whose continuity and perfection are enough to cause one to attain the highest degree of spiritual union, still it seems more ordinary to see incarnate in the heroes of sanctity certain particular traits, certain paradoxical initiatives that provoke surprise, disturbing interpretations, even persecutions. Saints then, in the divine plan, seem intended to awaken souls from their torpor even when it is virtuous, to keep the Christian ideal from becoming banal, from humanizing itself, from degenerating into a sort of idealist philosophy, in the manner of the [Stoic] sages of the Portico or of the heroes of metaphysical ascetics. Destined to make the presence of the supernatural explode into the very world that is bent on denying it or on relegating it to the past of history or of legend, sanctity justifies the perpetual declaration of war of Christ on the world and consequently of the world on Christ.

Hence it is not astonishing that the Church keeps the privilege of this methodically perturbing state and that forces the secret of hearts to reveal itself in keeping with the judgments souls will bring to bear on the fruits of the apostles of the Gospel and the imitators of Christ, who did not shy away from harsh words, from the fearful warnings against pharisaical wisdom, from humiliating acts and from obedience going all the way to the suffering of slaves. Slave morality, has it been said of the Christian law, which prescribes humility, gentleness, forgetting injuries, love of enemies, everything that seems to contradict natural pride and magnanimity of character. And nonetheless if we reflect on the ways that alone lead to the transforming union without allowing us to stop at our human level, we have to agree that the so-called natural virtues, when they are too confident in themselves and turn into self-admiration, deserve the name of *splendida vitia* [splendid vices]. Let us consider the words of the *Magnificat*, of which some have dared to say that they are full of venom that the Church has had to expurgate with its sacred music: they express, quite to the contrary, the fundamental truth that illumines a soul full of God, a Truth that does not apply to the political realities of this world, but that contains the most mysterious depths of grace at work in human baseness to elevate it all the way to divine union. Those who esteem themselves powerful, rich, satisfied, and sage are the ones who remain hollow, starved, bereft, downcast. Sanctity is also held in contempt by spirits closed to the summons of grace, because the latter, according to the words of Scripture, pours only into empty vases, empty of self-love, empty of all complacency in personal accomplishments.

Taking this into account, there is no longer any reason for contesting that true sanctity is found only where there is the spirit of God, that is, the invisible Church of which the visible Church is only the organ. And it is understood also that the irritation of people against the importunate witness of this spirit is in its own way one more proof in favor of the unique character, impossible to contradict, always unexpected and disconcerting, of the Catholic truth. From this standpoint, we are armed to answer the repeated objections against private or public infirmities, against the particular failures or collective deficiencies of Catholic people or nations. Providence has no need of what we may call ostentation and glorious proofs. Truth in the order of religion is revealed humbly, in the intimacy of souls, much more by discreet proofs than by showy manifestations. The latter, it is true, have had this useful role to play in history, but not without some admixture and some compensation often more onerous than these triumphs have seemed advantageous followed by regrettable aftermaths. In truth, the mixture of obscurity and clarity is, as Pascal noted, the rule of the game in the divine governance of the world; and Pascal did add, in admitting the error of his outrageous logic, his own desire for either a total charity or a total obscurity regarding the certitude and the merit of faith; but no, he concluded, it is the mélange of obscurity and light that best allows a revelation of the secret dispositions and of the mysterious commerce between God and souls.

Besides the ever recurring millenarist illusion is the one we must be most wary of: we are always inclined to cut short the kingdom of God on earth for tomorrow; that is the carnal illusion to be avoided at all costs, because it is loaded with impatience or with violence, with disillusionment or with discouragement, not to say with abdication and with betrayal. Nothing then can nor should keep us from recognizing for the Church the authentic, specific, permanent, inalienable, irreplaceable, conclusive mark of sanctity: a character so original that no fake intimation of it has been given that was lasting, general, or plausible. Is that not a proof of this theandric realization, God in man, man in God, which seemed at first to be a chimerical and absurd dream, when Aristotle was declaring that love between God and man would be indecent, out of place, irrational, impossible, so marked is the disproportion from one to the other?

CHAPTER 16

The Proof of Christian Religion through the Idea and the Very Word—Catholicism

Among the most subtle and perhaps the most influential objections for highly cultivated minds, we find one that must also be turned into a proof and an enlightening confirmation. Many generous souls have the idea that any religion with established dogmas, with rigorous precepts, with an authoritarian discipline is a leftover from the past, and that, if we have to stay with the idea of a Church, it is to see in it an assembly of free believers, an organ of human solidarity, a means for communing with the common Father of all beings, with the divine light that enlightens spirits, warms, and guides wills: that, it is said, is the only true Catholicism, the one that justifies its name by remaining faithful to the etymology that makes it signify universality. Have we not said ourselves that there is an invisible soul of the Church? And is that not where we must place the center of equilibrium and of propagation for all religious life, for all cult of God in spirit and in truth? Thoughts such as this inspire many congresses for the union of Churches and for that parliament of religions where some have been astonished to find historical Catholicism failing to answer the call as though it were betraying its name and its function. It is important to study attentively this specious difficulty.

Saint Augustine said that the name alone of Catholic is enough to keep him in the bosom of the Church, because this Church alone gives itself this name, manages and will always manage to have everyone give it this name that is its proper and irremovable trait: did he speak and see

Christian Religion through the Idea and the Word—Catholicism

rightly? And what precisely does this pretense mean that history has upheld up to now? For no one takes it amiss when we sing in the Creed of *Unam, sanctam, et catholicam Ecclesiam* [One, holy, and Catholic Church]. Through this word we simultaneously designate many sorts of universalities; but we exclude that promiscuity of religion that has been compared to a tower of Babel. Let us try then to indicate these diverse ways of taking the term and the entire extension of the word "catholic"; for, in understanding it well, we shall see at the same time how it is the trenchant sword that separates what must be disconnected, without confusion, without any possible diminution, of the truth besieged on all sides by multiple errors and weaknesses.

The most obvious sense applies to the extension in time and in space of a Church that comprises men of all races, all ages, without distinction of borders nor any limitation foreign to the pure spiritual order. Officially, catholicity is defined by adherence to the highest magisterium and to the hierarchy that is the channel of authority, of infallible teaching, and of sacramental life. But this historical, geographical, juridical, and canonical way of determining and justifying the etymology and the application of the word "catholic" still does not render its complete idea, however precise the indications previously given may otherwise be. Let us try to show how Catholicism, without losing any of its precise contours, has yet another breadth than the one people generally limit their sight to, attentive more to the visible realities than to the invisible aspects.

The catholic spirit extends not only in time and space, nor to the group of the faithful who explicitly bear its name and its livery. It makes us participate in immensity, in eternity, in universality: it justifies thereby the plenitude of the meaning attendant on the Greek term signifying more than ecumenical, more than perpetual; for this term applies to what is totality, not just in the human and terrestrial order, but in the metaphysical, the spiritual, even the divine [order]. The Catholic then is not only part of a large human community, be it through ages and generations past, present or future, as in the cult of Humanity that positivism takes pride in by supposing that it is the largest object possible and the highest end of a realist religion. Catholic realism includes, along with the cosmic order and the human order, the universality of beings; and that is still nothing, since communion with the latter is effective only by their common relation with one and the same Creator and by a final destiny that will realize the providential plan in unity. Hence, the Catholic is indeed the one human being who, united to all others because he is united to God to begin with, leaves nothing outside of Himself that would be foreign to Him. The poet spoke of the bond that associates him to all that is human: Catholic life is infinitely more inclusive: everything incorporated and intelligible to it, to the extent that the will of God is done on earth as in heaven.

Judging from appearances, Catholics seem a minority, a *pusillus grex* (little flock), usurping a presumptuous title; and already the author of the Letter to Diognetus took note of the contrast between the grandeur of the name and of the role and the tiny minority of those who fulfill the mission of being "the light of the world," "the salt of the earth": we seem to be in a dungeon, he said, prisoners and despicable; and it is nevertheless we who contain the world and have within us its salvation. Thus, from the apostolic age on, the double sense of the word "catholic" comes to light vigorously, one restrictive, the other immense and letting nothing fall from its hold.

But, it will be said, isn't that falling back into the confusion previously denounced and proscribed? Must we not have to lower the barriers of orthodoxy and of discipline and confer on all souls of good will a sort of implicit baptism or, with Origen, an ultimate return to salvation? To put down this objection or rather this misunderstanding, it will be enough to say that it is not only the saved or the elect who give homage to truth and to the universal action of Catholicism: it is an error to imagine that those who separate themselves from it and who shut themselves off from it are outside of it. It could be so perhaps under the hypothesis where the possibility of salvation would not be offered to all and where grace would not have a universal bearing. But it is of faith that Christ is the universal Mediator and that no one perishes except for having refused to profit by the vocation secretly proposed under forms perhaps impossible to define, but that we must believe to be really accessible. Hence the reprobate themselves are not outside the order; they express an aspect of divine justice, the aspect consequential to the appeals of infinite charity: from the side of God, the essential has not been lacking, and damnation itself is but a personal consequence of the bad use of liberty and of grace, both munificences of the sovereign goodness.

Thus, even in what appears most contrary to it, the Catholic order remains at the same time perfectly coherent, intelligible, and good. Nothing therefore escapes it; and even the complaints that we hear from the Holy Books never have the accent of blasphemy. It is an arbitrary and even a false interpretation for authors whose poorly enlightened zeal depicts the place of chastisement as a tumult of menacing gestures, of sacrilegious violence, or of crimes of divine *lèse-majesté*. Better inspired were those ancient painters who represented the damned as bending before the revelation of misconstrued graces, accusing themselves or accusing one another, and all the more painfully for having before their eyes the wounds of the Redeemer, having died to offer them salvation, without their having been willing to make use of the mercies and the infinite love.

We see thus how far Catholicism extends, which, according to the liturgical expression, embraces heaven, earth, and even hell and which encompasses, along with the Church militant, suffering, or triumphant, still more than the entire history of humanity; for this humanity itself is only a part of a plan whose grandeur still escapes us, even though Revelation raises some part of the veil that surrounds the angelic world and perhaps other histories of which ours is not totally independent. The future Jerusalem will undoubtedly include many other marvels: *multae mansiones in domo patris* [many mansions in the house of the Father].

CHAPTER 17

The Character of Apostolicity in Catholicism

Through its universality, the Christian spirit seems to surpass every limit and to be identified with the total spirit and all of history, because no understanding, no fact escapes its jurisdiction. Nevertheless, one restriction does appear as restricting Catholicism under the law of a narrow condition: only that deserves the name of catholic which bears the mark of apostolicity. With this blow, would we be going from extreme openness to extreme rigor? How is that possible? And what meaning can we give to this "mark," which reverses, it seems, our foregoing conclusions, on the immense harmony comprising all centuries and all races? We shall see nevertheless that, to be catholic, the Church has to be no less apostolic than one and universal; and contrary to appearances, it could not be one and universal without satisfying this precise condition of apostolicity.

But first of all what exactly does this fourth mark of our sweeping Creed mean: *Unam, sanctam, catholicam et apostolicam Ecclesiam* [One, holy, catholic, and apostolic Church]? According to the common and quite clear interpretation that etymology justifies, it is from the apostles, sent by Christ, as He Himself is sent from the heavenly Father, that the Church was born; and by an uninterrupted transmission of doctrine and of authority, the apostolic succession continues through the centuries, in such a way that, according to the expression of the councils, the sacred deposit of dogma, of faith, of powers, of rites, in a word of all that constitutes the most positive, the most historical, the most regulated religion one can conceive has been preserved from hand to hand: from the least curate of a rural parish to Saint Peter, to Christ, to the heavenly Father, an unbroken chain of continuity binds the whole hierarchy, and it is from this source that the teaching of the Magisterium as well as the efficacious administration of the sacraments proceeds.

If that is the way it is, how are we to understand the persistence of a soul of the Church broader than this visible body? Here we must remember the distinction made earlier between the explicit knowledge of Revelation and the effective participation of the soul, even unknowingly, in the Redemption and in grace, even if it be anonymous. The capital truth that the mark of apostolicity has to underline is therefore of the real order much more than of the temporal order of our explicit knowledge. From this first point of view, the idea to maintain at all costs is that dogma and grace come supernaturally to us by a mission from on high without human thought, even stimulated by invisible supports, being able to discover and procure anything of what Revelation alone can make us expressly know of. The profound meaning of the mark of apostolicity then is essentially this: Christian religion is not an invention of man, not an initiative of his consciousness even mutely worked over by God. There has to be, at the origin a formal mission, a Revealer who alone called Himself Master, the inner Witness of the inviolable secrets of the Trinity, a Mediator who, by the hypostatic union of the two natures, human and divine, in Him, makes the supernatural sap circulate in each one of the members who constitute the Christian humanity. Thus is radically demolished the heresy, ever recurring, according to which Christian society would be merely an organ of religious solidarity for souls aspiring to a moral perfection and seeking in Christ only a model, an exemplar more perfect than another, but without there being any need for a direct action, for an inner cooperation, for a superhuman aid, for an agnition[1] of the supernatural character as implied in the idea of apostolic transmission.

---

1. Translator's footnote: A term coined by Blondel here to characterize learning from a tradition flowing from apostolicity going back to the first envoys of the Redeemer to the ends of the universe and of time. It is not cognition properly so-called, but something that comes with it regarding the supernatural in practice. Nor is it simply faith regarding any truth, natural or supernatural. It is a kind of recognition of authenticity in a tradition going back to its origin.

From a second point of view, the apostolicity of the true Church implies, no longer just for a real participation, but for a formal adherence and an effective docility toward Catholic authority, consequences and exigencies no less precise than rigorous. If it is true that invincible ignorance does not prevent a soul of good faith and of good will from adhering to the soul of the Church by participating in the effusion of grace, still, from the moment when a more complete knowledge of truth dawns in a spirit alert to it, a duty of probity can render inquiry absolutely obligatory; and above all recognition of the truth entails a serious and urgent duty to join into the visible body, under pain of no longer belonging to the invisible soul of the Church. Cardinal Dechamps tells of an Anglican woman, with a long experience of security in her fervent Christian religion, who was brought to the study of Catholicism, and who was troubled and then soon became convinced, but was still hesitating to convert, saying that her religion, which had been sincere and fruitful, could surely still remain just that, while it was repugnant to her to deny her first fervor and to abjure a Christian religion that had been authentic,—as if she was regretting a surge of new light disconcerting for her inner equilibrium. "It is too late for you," the Cardinal replied to her; "after what you have seen, you would no longer be in good faith; you would no longer be Christian if you did not become Catholic, whatever hardship of the soul or of family a complete conversion would require for you."

Thus, on two counts, apostolicity is the necessary condition for the properly supernatural truth of Catholicism. It has often been denied that this fact, contingent like historical realities always are in some way, constituted an accidental element more embarrassing than profitable for the much desired reunion of Churches. But that is a shortsighted view. Within this contingent fact of an uninterrupted transmission, there lies the necessary truth of the divine origin, without which the transcendental character or the supernatural base of authentic Christian religion disappears. What seems to constrict the extension of Catholicism is therefore precisely what assures its integrity and also its integrality, two words close to one another, but with quite different, albeit complementary, meanings. Integrity is what maintains the pure idea of Christian religion without losing an iota of its letter and its law, consequently what constitutes, as logicians say, its comprehension, its essential definition.

Integrality is its extension, its total applicability, its universal judicial standing. Now if Catholicism has in fact, as we saw in examining the mark of catholicity, an infinite hold on souls, on societies, on all of history in time and in eternity, it is precisely by reason of this supernatural character of which the mark of apostolicity underscores and safeguards the necessary and unalienable transcendence. On this point, no dealing is possible: in hoping for concessions, one would only prove that one does not understand the economy of Christian religion and that one has no idea of the imprescriptible reasons of an intransigence that is at once probity and charity.

The good we hope for in a return to the Christian sense is possible only if it is inspired by the veritable and complete Christian spirit. Also here the role of the papacy shows itself to be capital. The attitude of minds with regard to the rock on which the Church is built brings out the contradictory dispositions agitating in the depths of souls. To rise up against the "powers of the keys," against infallible authority within the limits in which it is exercised, is to misunderstand the divine institution to which one might otherwise imagine being able to adhere all the more by leaving aside this painful and as it were scandalous point for many consciences. But have we not seen that, according to the words of Saint Augustine, it is through humility and sacrifice that one enters into charity and into truth? Not that we should exaggerate what has been said or exceed the constraints prescribed to docility: the Magisterium itself does not go without the concurrence of those it has to instruct and confirm in their faith. The role of the faithful is not one of mute passivity that on the other hand does not always avoid joining criticisms and insubordinations to its protestations and adulations. Authority is assisted in settling controversies relative to faith and morals within the universal Church: it is not there to suppress them and to prevent the movement of spirit at the very heart of the spiritual life. Assisted, we say, but not inspired (for inspiration ceased at the death of the last of the Apostles), this holy authority itself needs to consult, to seek enlightenment, to add to prayer the study of works that have penetrated pending questions and on which precise decisions become and seem opportune to it. It is not in opposition to science and reason, but with their concurrence that the power of interpretation and of direction vested in apostolic authority is exercised. It never innovates, it preserves a living deposit; it is the organ of Tradition: and this word, better yet than the word "transmission," expresses that mix of fidelity and intrepid initiative wherein is manifested in time an eternal truth that never any discursive expression will exhaust.

Such are the ideas implied in the mark of apostolicity and that were already strongly emphasized by the name favored in the Middle Ages for the Sovereign Pontiff, *Dominus apostolicus* [apostolic Lord], the one also suggested by the more habitual appellation nowadays, Vicar of Christ. The one who sees the pope sees Peter, and the one who listens to Peter hears the Christ, and the one who hears the Christ hears the One who sent Him: the word "apostolate" has, in the Greek language, this meaning of sending.

It results also from this that the Church is apostolic, because it is essentially missionary: it is never resigned to living in itself and on itself, to confining itself, as has been suggested, in a dungeon, in a sacristy, in a quarantine; it goes everywhere, sends people everywhere to preach the word of God, and when words cannot yet be taken in, heard, and understood, it sends both for spirits to see people of God, who, by their attention to physical miseries, by their silence, their prayer, and their immolation, become a living proclamation. It has often been reproached for this indiscretion; it has been forbidden public manifestations. It remains nonetheless ever-present, active, importunate when it has to be, and taking advantage of its visible and vulnerable body to intervene amid facts that impose themselves, amid beings that suffer blows, like the old man saying to the enemy who was mistreating him unjustly: hit, but listen. Therefore it thus has and always will have its apostles and its martyrs; and its apostolicity, which has never failed, encounters, seemingly, so many obstacles only to bring out the supernatural merit, generosity, heroism of missionaries of the Gospel, as well as the coalition of sentiments that Bossuet dubbed "the hatred of truth," the fear of God, the horror of the supernatural. So that everything converges toward a justification and an illustration of the Christian spirit: those who really incarnate it as well as those who resist it and sometimes fight furiously against it.

Nevertheless let us not oversimplify the conflicts of this world. It has been said without paradox that Christ is at work in souls and in human societies in two ways, through those who love Him and make others love Him, but also through those who oppose Him by taking

Him for what He is not. Among initiatives coming from outside Christian religion or even at times apparently against it, there is some good done, some good prepared. The Gospel itself speaks of a trait often too little noted. The Apostles once asked Christ to stop a healer in whom they saw perhaps a kind of emulator or competitor; and the Master prescribed them to let him go on: there are indeed many sheep who do not yet seem to be of the fold of the Good Pastor, but who may enter later on. Amid the transformations that stir up the world let us not rush too much to judge or to condemn: just as there are consciences where the invisible Church lives, there are initiatives, institutions, where a Christian spirit, at first not adverted to as such, can come to light and some day return to the principle whence they drew what is already generous in them.

Conclusion

How many judge and condemn the Christian spirit because they do not know it or do not understand it! If, in the presence of Christian religion, philosophy has a first role to fulfill, it is precisely to put in practice the precept of Spinoza: *haud admirari, haud indignari, sed intelligere* (hardly to be in awe, hardly to be indignant, but to understand); but this understanding is itself difficult, even for the most learned, because it presupposes less a systematization of intellectual points of view than an intimate disposition of the entire spiritual being. Nevertheless let us not belittle the value of the speculative proofs or the truly intelligible character of a teaching that alone gives the complete word of the enigma of the world, of man, and of destiny. The aim of this study is especially to bring into view this total cohesion, to the point of not leaving out of the catholic unity any hold against it, anything that escapes it, anything that turns into opposition, but to discover a convergence of objections for the benefit of the very truth that they seemed to be menacing or to be destroying. Catholic truth has therefore also justified the criterion invoked by Spinoza, when he said: *verum est index sui* [the true is the indication of itself], the true has no need for justification extrinsic to its own consistency: it makes itself manifest by its solidity. And this is the testimony that Christians render whose conviction is expressed thus: my certitude is made of all of myself and of the perfect conformity of my faith with all of my experiences, all my aspirations, all my knowledge, and all my hopes.

Undoubtedly many objections come up at times; but far from finding in them reasons for doubting in the end or causes for weakening, the Christian spirit turns them into confirmations and reinforcements; for, in a way that is more realistic than what pantheism has done, Catholicism has always known how to reconcile contraries and to draw from obstacles an additional force. *Oportet haereses esse* [there have to heresies]: these tests of faith, which become for some occasions of falling, are for the Church as a whole a principle of advancement. From the great intellectual difficulties that have arisen in recent times Christian religion must draw and can hope for an increase of vitality, as much for the intelligence of dogma as for the purity and the generosity of practice.

I.

How the objection against Christian religion drawn from the inadequacy between the ideal it proposes and the realities history tells us of the customs and the ideas of those inspired by it and who swear by it can be overcome by discovering in this persistent fact of the earthly life of the Church a providential aim of the divine pedagogy.

An objection against Christian religion has always been drawn from the deficiencies that it has shown in every age by the disparity between the ideal that it teaches and the realities that the history of the customs, of the ideas inspired by it and depending on it. This inadequacy has been at times contested on the basis of biblical and liturgical texts presenting the Church, as spouse of Christ, without wrinkles, without a stain, without any weakness. But such an optimism, found in orators and souls more ardent than judicious, is nevertheless hardly in harmony with the official teaching and common evidences. How are we to understand and appreciate this disproportion that, in fact, afflicts, disconcerts many souls and that keeps many spirits far from the Church or closes the way of returning for so many, who are easy to scandalize when there is a question of avoiding the onerous effort that a conversion would require.

Many attempts have been tried to explain such a fact in order to console, encourage some, or to prevent others from finding a pretext for evasion. Recently Karl Adam devoted an eleventh and final chapter of his book, translated under the title *Le Vrai visage du Catholicisme* [*The True Face of Catholicism*], to the examination of this point that he recognized as very important, very delicate, very full of consequences. It does not seem, however, that he pulled together the more decisive justifications for this discordance one would love so much to disappear: he pleads in fact the attenuating circumstances of the creature or even, if one may say, those of the Creator, rather than finding in this permanent fact in the earthly life of the Church a providential purpose; whereas it is only this aspect that would offer a profound and appeasing solution.

(1) Would we have to say as some do, among whom Malebranche, that Christ, because he is man, suffers from the limitations of the flesh, finds thereby his knowledge restrained and his redemptive action limited to a number of the faithful and the elect that could not be indefinite? Does not Karl Adam invoke for his part a character that turns out to be deficient for all that is incarnate, singularized, known by concepts, exposed to the imperfection of science and to the failures of the will? But such an explanation leaves one with a discomfort, not to say more, when it is an issue no longer of only the members, but of Christ Himself, unique soul and divine chief of the Church, absolutely perfect, omniscient, in his hypostatic union with the eternal Word.

Another series of arguments is invoked, as if God were playing hide and seek with us, allowing scandals to conceal the beauty of his work, in order to lend more merit to faith and in this way to put to the test the ingeniousness of our interpretations with an artificial pedagogy. That in fact the deficiencies whose afflicting spectacle should be allowed to develop the heroic generosity of believers who have to be at the same time suffering, that is a truth generally admitted and besides justly encouraged; but that is only a palliative, it is an accidental means of making virtue of necessity and of admitting as a fatality of nature this defectiveness about which we persist in thinking that it would be better for things to be otherwise than they are. Now this is the disposition that does not seem to be fully in conformity with the plenitude of faith: in his work, God accepts as permanent and characteristic only what corresponds to a freely chosen purpose for a higher good, and it is this good that has to be unveiled if we want to truly enter into the divine perspectives.

(2) What gives us courage in following this way is that Christ Himself wanted to disconcert human wisdom, to give the lie to messianic expectation, to become an object of scandal, according to his own expression: yet will we say that he Himself participates in this psychological, metaphysical, moral imperfection from which an argument was made earlier? No, that would be impious and certainly false. But, one may add, is not Christ, impeccable in Himself, participant in the errors in his members, the faults that he assumed in Himself, so that, against his will, the facts often betray the ideal he teaches and that he is Himself?— Undoubtedly we have to take into account what we could call the immense disappointment of the Savior with respect to what the way of the cross shows us as the worst suffering, the uselessness of the effusion of divine blood for so many impenitent rebels. But what is at issue nevertheless here is something else; what is at issue are the living members, those who prolong the Incarnation, and in whom the blood, the sap of Christ, circulates: how are we to explain the misery that goes with this infinite richness? That seems to be the true problem; and what must be understood is how it is that so much holiness in the source, which runs always in all purity, takes on so much bitterness in the course of this life that circulates by pouring out the divine water itself.

Here, let us make a remark whose importance Saint Augustine and many others, including Fénelon in particular, have noted: underlying the infinite and the perfect, the differences between the degrees that appear to us as the lowest and the highest count for little, since between the creature, as beautiful as it may be, and the Creator, the distance remains always incommensurable. The first point of this divine pedagogy, of which we spoke earlier, is to prevent infatuation with all that is of created origin and to recall the beautiful verse Corneille offers us: "God does not bow before souls that are too high." His glory, His privilege, the liturgy tells us, is to be condescending and to pardon: *cujus proprium est miserere et parcere* [what is proper to Him is ever to have pity and to forgive]. But there is more: in following this orientation of thought, we come to see that this deification with which God wants to glorify us in ourselves, is not possible except through the most mortifying experience and that the beauty of the heavenly Jerusalem is acquired at the price of the intimate humiliations, the apparent shortcomings, the failures that we can call normal and providential in the Church here below. It is perfect in its Christ and in its eternal hymen, but it is constantly mortified, even in its provisional triumphs that are often in this world the occasion for spiritual depressions.

Thereby the mystery of the Church is explained by a disposition that, while seeming paradoxical at first, is fundamentally justified in accordance with all that we have explained concerning passive purifications, and the mortification that leads to the transformative union and the glorious life. In the meantime, there is the laborious existence, doleful, and that we must not try to exalt too much in its present form with earthly victories, in order to remain in conformity with the truth of the facts, with the secret testimony of consciences, with the justified judgment of impartial witnesses, and, to sum it all up, with the authentic purpose Christ is pursuing who, according to the word of Pascal, is in agony in his suffering members until the end of the world.

II.

How, through an accommodation that is the highest proof of Catholicism, a complete intelligibility matches in it an integral solution of the problems in the moral and religious order, that reaches into the depth of man, takes and claims the whole of man, and that is sufficiently clear and justified to engage his responsibility, as it maintains, under the tutelary veil of the present life, an enclosed form that allows for the merit of an option in righteousness and in generosity.

It is to make evident some of the aspects made more clear, more useful, of the Christian Sense that we would like to have contributed in this philosophical study. The idea that inspires this study is summed up in this theme: Saint Bonaventure said, after Saint Augustine, that our philosophy was the Christian religion; and Saint Thomas replied: philosophy has a proper domain of its own, a rational method, a relative autonomy; to reconcile these diversely true viewpoints seems worth making the effort. There is in fact an independent, truly critical, way to approach the study of philosophy, by raising the problems that only positive religion can resolve. But these problems, which a separated philosophy has the fault of setting aside or of claiming to resolve by itself, have repercussions on the ensemble of methods and conclusions that constitute the proper domain of rational speculation. Besides, it has always been noted that doctrine worthy of the name is formed out of two elements: on one side, a dialectical element that is necessary to define, to tie together, and to order a grounded and coherent system; on the other side, a final intention that orients toward a moral and religious term the entire effort of the intellectual dialectic; but these two elements are not always in accord with one another, and often the partiality of the intentions tries to justify itself by the apparent rigor of the logical arguments and of the rational connections. Now, what may be given as the mark of Christian religion is that, in it these two elements each for itself entails an entire development, and that both are adapted to one another in a complete concordance; so much so that we can say that in it is found an integral solution of the problems in the moral and religious order. Such an accommodation, for spirits able to grasp it and to whom we can succeed in demonstrating it, is the highest proof, one in which nothing human is lacking and that justifies a certitude stronger than all convictions about details.

Pascal said: "Contradiction is a bad mark of truth." He did not mean to say that opposed theses denounced the error of the one or the other; but quite on the contrary, he signified thereby that the divine truths, more vast and more diverse than our personal views, can appear to us as in conflict, whereas in reality they are complementary and solidary with one another. That is why, in gathering together all the reproaches, all the objections in which Christian religion has been assailed, we see them not so much as destroying one another but rather as concerted in a harmony that reveals the very transcendence of its principle. The Gospel, it has often been noted, prescribes contrasting attitudes, peace and war, gentleness and energy, mercy and rigor. Similarly the spirit that runs through the Sermon on the Mount knows how to bring together the most diverse prescriptions and promises without ceasing to be one and the same spirit.

To be sure the external witnesses could not comprehend as much as the faithful the unity of these contrasts, which must be experienced internally to see and taste their harmony surpassing any expression. But it is in conformity with the doctrine itself that there be such a disproportion between a purely erudite, speculative, or extrinsic knowledge and an experienced science that conveys to truth a life, a warmth penetrating to the very sources of intelligence and will. Hence it is a confirmation and not an objection that this hardening of the heart or this clouding of thought of which the Scriptures speak so often as an effect of justice itself, that is, as a normal consequence that derives from a disposition of man and not from an insufficiency of truth and of the Revelation conveyed to us interiorly or exteriorly.

But, it may still be said, does there not subsist any obscurity, even among those most advanced in the ways of speculation, ascetics, or mysticism? And is it not of faith that faith remains under the veil? But let us be careful in understanding the kind of obscurity that persists, as long as we are, according to the word of the [First] Vatican Council, on the way of the present life, *in via:* at issue is not some sort of divine dissimulation, of enigmas proposed as a means of preventing indiscrete curiosities, of an invention meant to mask truths that could have been more clearly proposed. Such an idea, too often admitted, seems to falsify the entire economy of the Christian Revelation: the obscurity is not brought in or maintained casually; and the merit of faith does not depend on running a risk as if we had to get beyond normal uncertainties. There is really nothing obscure for the soul that follows the interior light; and the truths essential to our decisions are known sufficiently so that the certainty about the route to follow for souls in good faith and in good will escapes any risk of a painful wager. The actual necessity of the test is salutary; whence the shrouded form that allows righteousness and generosity the merit of an option. But nothing more than this tutelary veil; and, in the night where certain souls are led, the issue is never one of speculative curiosity, it is an issue of an effective response; consequently the obscurity is brought to bear less on adhering to the very object of faith than on the effort of docility and on the practical orientation of the will.

In this sense we can say that the Christian spirit can be philosophically justified to the point of producing a truly philosophical conviction; but this view, as complete, as decisive as we suppose it to be, does not constitute thereby the adherence required for faith. Without having to go into the supernatural order, even on one point, where faith alone can come to life by grace, we must still, as philosophers, and from this side of the dividing line, note that, to surpass the inevitable obscurities, salutary and ever persisting, there is necessarily an act of the will, a rectification of intention, a resolution, and a submission to be produced within ourselves. Concerning other philosophical doctrines, nothing of the sort is required, but that is precisely because they do not go to the depth of man, they do not seize and do not lay claim on the whole, and they do not touch the highest point of man's insertion into God or of his desertion from God; our study of this Christian spirit would therefore be incomplete if we did not indicate this singularity, and, we must say, this exclusive and unique superiority.

It has been said that, to remedy the religious ills of which philosophy has become the principle, a profound philosophical renovation was necessary, an effort of high metaphysics in order to renew the higher sources of human thought; and, it has been added, it is a long time since it has snowed on the summits of doctrine to sustain the glaciers and the fecundity of the plains. Without doubt it is very desirable to manifest all the intellectual complementarities, all the rootedness of Christian religion, all its doctrinal sublimities. But after all philosophy is always reduced to doing little by itself; the furthest it can get in its greatest ambition is to anticipate in some way the final revelation that will come for all of us and to dissipate the concocted difficulties we take pleasure in by incriminating the supposed obscurities of the Church, which nevertheless the [First] Vatican Council presents to us as the source of light and as the standard of salvation raised for all nations to see. Yet let us not belittle the task to be accomplished for the benefit of intelligences; for such an effort is not in vain by itself, and it goes with the one, more pressing still, that consists in supporting and redirecting wills against the objection recalled by the poet complaining to God: "You want them too pure, those you make happy." Let us look for more from those who, in the face of the true Christian spirit, will answer on the contrary: no, never too pure, happiness is and can never be but at that price; and that is why the Christian spirit holds, along with the words of eternal life, the promises even of the terrestrial future.

2

ON ASSIMILATION AS FULFILLMENT AND TRANSPOSITION OF THE THEORY OF ANALOGY

FOREWORD

This study, dictated nearly twenty years ago, was supposed to constitute chapter XII of *The Christian Sense*. By reason of the amplitude taken up by the development on supernaturalization, I thought I should deal with this problem separately. It sets out, without getting technical, a view underlying my philosophical effort in a more profound research into the conditions implied in the Thomist assertion: *Omnia intendunt assimilari Deo* [all things intend to be assimilated to God].

Indeed, among the notions regarding which misunderstandings remain frequent, one of the most equivocal, but also one of the most important, is that of *assimilation*. Many conflicts arise between theologians and philosophers from the ambiguous fashion this same word is used, without noticing at times that it is used according to quite different meanings.

A scrupulous examination of the notion of *assimilation* will dissipate confusions, highlight distinctions, and open the way for true reconciliation. It will further shed light on the conditions for realizing the authentic destiny of man. We shall see then why this destiny cannot be integral if we restrict it to the simple development of reason and of our natural powers—even if this development were normal, indefinitely progressive, and humanly perfect. Thus, man will appear frustrated, and even culpable, if he refuses his real destiny, which is supernatural. But this is on the condition of not talking only of an analogical imitation of God by man. For at issue is rather an incorporation of the divine life in man, and a presence in man of a supernaturalizing action; at issue, moreover, is a cooperation wherein God and man each bring their contribution to a true symbiosis, which the sacred texts compare to a hymen. So that to refuse this union is to commit a sort of adultery. So true is this that the call to the supernatural is for man a fact at once imposed and consented to, which takes away any possibility of avoiding it reasonably. All of Christian morality and mysticism are conditioned thereby and are intelligible and viable only from this fully comprehensive standpoint.

To this present study, the reader will find joined a "reconsideration and comprehensive view," adding complementary precisions both on this capital question of assimilation and on multiple connected problems on which our philosophical effort has been brought to bear.

Allow me also to reproduce, as an appendix, despite their length, the contents of two letters addressed to a correspondent a few years ago and quite appropriate, it seems, for shedding light on the method we are using or even on certain essential aspects of doctrine.

CHAPTER 1

Twofold Traditional Sense of the Word "Assimilation"

In *Summa against the Gentiles*, Saint Thomas sums up the movement of nature in its entirety and, more still, that of spiritual beings in this emphatic formula: *Omnia intendunt assimilari Deo* [all things intend to be assimilated to God]. Is this term given the same meaning that it has from Saint Augustine or Saint Bonaventure, who, for their part, speak of our interior illumination and of our spiritual assimilation? In the first instance, the issue is rather one of resemblance, of imitation, of an essential nature that tends normally to be more or less of a reflection of the divine perfection to which each being bears a similitude, but without by this reduplication or by this mimesis tying into the divine life and into the vital union that would make these beings resembling God members of one and the same whole, organs diversely adapted to one common function. According to this conception then, *assimilatio*, far from uniting beings substantially to God, constitutes them in themselves and leaves them outside of the divine model, like imperfect copies alongside the true original. Thereby we come to a solution we can only call speculative, only a vision that yields only an extrinsic reproduction, only a double, however exact it may be, of God considered ever as object of cognition, rather than as term of a real love and union. Clearly, what dominates in this thesis, whatever connection or complement may be added to it, is the idea that *assimilatio* means resemblance, *similis*, but not assimilation in the biological sense of the word, that is, an intaking that transforms the lower being into a life, into functions, into a perfection of being of a higher order.

From that, we are led by contrast to conceive of another sense of the traditional formula, a sense itself traditional and grounded in the most repeated teachings, in the most expressive parables of the Gospel, in the most profound of the patristic texts. According to this interpretation, assimilation, which is the ultimate aim of the entire created order and especially that of spirits, is more than a semblance limited to producing multifarious copies of a divine object, it is the authentic and vivifying incorporation of beings into the divine Subject who inserts them into itself like a shoot into the stem of a vine and who tends to make of this scattered multiplicity a real unity, in keeping with the wish that ends the elevating discourse of Christ after the Last Supper as recorded in the Johannine Gospel. According to this conception, the world is not just a mirror, ever imperfect, of the divine perfections; and the beatitude promised to the spirits faithful to their destiny is not merely a frigid contemplation in the immobility of an ecstasy without any élan of possession: it is an unceasing penetration, an ever-accrued participation, an ever-warmer effusion and one drawing ever closer to the very source of charity. It results from this that the union could only be freely given by grace, since it is an issue of acceding to the very intimacy of the *Deus absconditus* [the hidden God] and, according to the expression of Tauler, of being invited to the secret banquet and to the eternal generation of the Trinity itself.

In the first conception, the danger remains always great of compromising the transcendence of the supernatural, since spiritual beings tend normally to knowing and seeing God, seeking through the fundamental desire of their intelligence to contemplate God as he is, but reasonably, as if from outside and without the suspicion of anything more than an extrinsic vision. Also, from this point of view, to avoid naturalizing the knowledge of God or totally losing personal consciousness in a totally static absorption, one looks for ways of raising barriers and of insisting on the impossibility of attaining naturally what nevertheless appears to be the inescapable object of the *desiderium naturae rationalis* [desire of rational nature].

In the second conception, on the contrary, such a danger is radically eliminated. For if it is true, according to the word of the Apostle, that each consciousness bears its own inscrutable secret and that only the spirit of man knows what there is in man, it is all the more rational that the divine secret could not be known except by gracious revelation; moreover, the divine life, the adoption by the heavenly Father could not be realized except by a charity that is totally free, truly paradoxical, and above all inventions, all pretentions, all capacities of the rational nature.

We find in all this the cause of many conflicts about which it is of no use to discuss and that we cannot bring to rest in the light of day without first approaching the ambiguous problem of assimilation, in order to know on which side we have to look for the precise sense of tradition, the dogma generative of our entire destiny.

To be sure, it has been said that the two interpretations, whose contrasting aspects we have just indicated, reunite with one another or at least are juxtaposed in the history of Christian speculation. With M. Saudreau, we can even add that there have always been more or less opposite spiritual temperaments, as exemplified in the angelic choirs, some more struck by light, more desirous of seeing, more contemplative, and those are the souls he calls cherubic; others, in contrast, more ardent with charity, more capable of union than of vision, and, in the hierarchy, they are more perfect, the seraphic souls. But such an opposition, however partially grounded it may be, should not delude us about the common and indispensable obligation of seeing and loving, of contemplation and of transforming union, which are never separated, although proportions may vary in one sense or the other. Hence what we must retain from this examination is that we must not limit ourselves to either one of the two exclusive interpretations of the word "assimilation."

Now, once [we see that] the second conception could not be legitimately excluded or passed over in silence, we must conclude that the first cannot without fault limit, as has often been claimed, the horizon of the Christian synthesis. We should note that there is not an equality of parts between the two forms of assimilation. The second has never pretended going without the first or discredited it, since in order to arrive at love and at union, a knowledge, an analogy, an initial and progressive resemblance are manifestly prerequisites; hence, in the more there is the less, and the vital assimilation through grace and charity implies a congenital similitude, an acquired resemblance and a more or less infused contemplation. But in the less there is not the more, and many of the sufficiencies of our religious vitality, as also of our philosophical and theological speculation, come from narrowing excessively the doctrine of assimilation by trying—without success (and that is felicitous)—to reduce it to a pure problem of intellectual conformity. The question of the supernatural, so much in dispute in recent years, makes this all too uniquely specular theory explode. Yet to complete this salutary refinement, it seems very useful to entertain directly and in depth the other thesis, which, it seems, has not in truth been the object of any systematic work. That is one of those vital points on which it would be urgent for philosophy of religion to come to bear; and we shall see now what problems come up in a more critical and more penetrating examination of this problem.

CHAPTER 2

Getting beyond the Metaphors That Risk Masking the True Problem

The question of assimilation brings us to a more profound and yet even less explored problem. How are we to understand the difficulty that goes unnoticed to begin with, if not under the form wherein the mystics have felt all its grandeur?

To resemble God, what does that mean? Or what is to be done to understand and to realize this program? Too often we are content to interpret these words according to images suggested by our common experience, as if it were the question of a human model to be reproduced by another human or to be copied by an artist. Even metaphysicians, like Leibniz, have been satisfied with simple metaphors, when they have spoken of creatures as of a mirror of the Creator or as reproductions that imitate the perfections of the sovereign Being. With such formulas, it is thought that satisfaction has been given, but only for the imagination; and in fact the true religious problem is masked, which begins to present itself only if one has a sense of the divine incommensurability; for it is truly the vivid idea of the mystery surrounding the majesty of God that has prostrated pious souls before the secret wherein resides the mystery of the Absolute.

Let us try to scrutinize more closely the difficulty where the analysis of the two senses of assimilation we have attempted brings us; and, taking up the words of Plato declaring that the end we are aiming at is resemblance with God, let us try to understand what such a claim, the very claim indicated more emphatically still by our sacred Books, the one that was also the principle of the original temptation: *eritis sicut dii* [you shall be as gods]. How does such an ambition arise? And how is it realizable?

It would seem natural, for as little as one might reflect on the fundamental dissemblance between man and God, to conclude, with Aristotle, that it is out of place and even absurd to maintain a bond of similitude and of attachment between two beings as disproportionate to one another. And nevertheless the normal knowledge that, according to reason and according to the most formal dogmatic definitions, we should have of God proves that disproportion does not prevent analogy, nor does it prevent the congenital aspiration of human intelligence and will toward God conceived as first Cause, as highest Truth, as perfect and beatifying End. Hence, we cannot keep ourselves from tending to know as much as possible and to possess this infinite good toward which our fundamental inclination draws us. Now, if intelligence shows us the truth of this perfect and only fulfilling good, the will, moved by this knowledge, is borne not to an incomplete or veiled possession, but to one as full as possible, because it has a presentiment that this possession of the Good is its own good. There is in fact, Saint Thomas says, only one beatitude, that of God Himself; and that is the one man aspires to, even when he is unable to name it or to define it.

It is by following this analysis that we have been able to demonstrate the place of the supernatural in philosophy itself, at least if philosophy goes as far as it can go and has to go forward. There lies then, at the most profound level of the human being, a problem of fact that calls for not just an abstract analysis, but for a concrete solution: if we take ourselves such as we are, within the actual plan of Providence, how is it that our destiny does not remain in suspense? And how does the divine design become intelligible and realizable, in spite of the abysses that seem to separate the creature, as elevated as it might seem, from the altitude of God without common measure with any being, created or creatable? This is where we encounter the supernatural in what is gratuitous, inalienable, inconfusable about it with any natural gift. Let us be attentive to this point, which we must now clearly elucidate with all the lights that reason and Revelation combined can make converge on it.

CHAPTER 3

Is the Issue One of a Simple Ideal Participation or Do We Have to Conceive of a Truly Vital Participation?

If grace consists in uniting man to the divine life by an assimilation that incorporates him in the intimacy of Christ and of the Trinity itself, would it be enough, in order to obtain this sublime elevation, to have a theoretical knowledge, a representational image of this participation that, according to this hypothesis, would remain purely ideal and would be only a given to be undergone as in a passive viewing? But this idea of a purely specular passivity, of a lazy contemplation, is the very error that was condemned in quietism and in many false mysticisms. Supernatural elevation, according to authoritative teaching, is neither a creation *ex nihilo* nor a totally inert receptivity: it is, as the name "elevation" indicates, the promotion of already existing energies, entailing a response of the assumed being to the God who elevates it, but not without the consent and the cooperation of man. That is why we must consider as fundamentally insufficient the first conception of assimilation that we considered: the issue is not, for God, only to produce images, copies, that are bound to be imperfect; the issue is to have us participate in His own life and in His own beatitude: *ut vitam aeternam habeant homines et abundantius habeant* [so that men should have eternal life and have it more abundantly]. It is in this sense that we must take the Evangelical saying according to which a second birth, a new gift is indispensable to accede to the kingdom of God. And that is now for us to understand better in order to grasp, in the very unity of the divine plan, the distinction of stages, the role of mortification, and to resolve also the terrible difficulty that the problem of evil as a whole represents.

CHAPTER 4

Irreplaceable Role of a Laborious Trial of Parturition for the "New Birth"

It has been asked at times why the divine charity did not have, from the start, its full effusion: would it not have been a better God who, instead of exposing us to trial and to the risk of damnation, would have given heaven at once and associated to his blessed eternity others like Himself? Whence is it that we have to have successive gifts and that there have to be adjustments, as it were, for there to be, after the generation, the vocation, and the purification, a labor of sanctification, when it would have seemed so easy to furnish the elect with a gift that is at once initial, total, and final? To speak thus would be to prove that we do not really understand the exigencies of Goodness itself. It is not only because man, in what is noble and generous about him, would not want a happiness for which he would not have made himself worthy; for at issue is a difficulty more profound than this otherwise legitimate susceptibility: the possibility of becoming a being for good, of acquiring personal consciousness, of tasting a true joy, and, even better still, of participating in the pure Act and of uniting oneself to the divine willing, is conceivable only on the condition of going through, according to the words of Saint Paul, the trial of a parturition.

The main idea to be brought completely to light here is therefore this: for man to be really elevated to the properly supernatural and divine life, he must, through an ensemble of steps (whose intelligible significance and spiritual value we shall see), undergo the trial of an alternative where he has to opt between two destinies, without having anything to take the place of this act of opting that fixes once and for all his personally and freely chosen fate. This is what the first gift of our rational nature, of our moral freedom, of our supernatural vocation serves: it is all of this that we have to hand over before a new gift, one that cannot be received unless we restore to God the egoistic use of the first gift received. It seems that in conferring upon us our human nature, God has left us masters of excluding Him from it, that he has as it were withdrawn himself from a part of being and that, notwithstanding his omnipresence and omnipotence, he has consented to annihilate himself to give us a place of sovereignty; but then it is for us to reestablish Him in us, to give Him a "new birth" and to thus obtain that this divinity, restored by our loving acceptance, should become all ours. Do we not understand therefore the radical impossibility of replacing this sublime history, the inappropriateness of obtaining at a discount this genesis that somehow creates God in us and that reestablishes us in God, as if we were somehow the free authors of this new creature wherein are found, amalgamated, and united two lives and two loves in an exchange of perfect detachment and of complete possession of themselves?

CHAPTER 5

Paradox of the Tribulations of the Just and Scandal of the Sufferings Judged According to Our Human Views

There is still more to be taken from this study of assimilation, wherein is effected, through passive purifications, what mystics have called the transformative union, which, under more humble forms, takes place in every soul in the state of grace. Notwithstanding all the explanations by which we can try to justify the onerous ways by which charity leads and elevates man toward an "indeclinable" destiny, according to the quite forceful expression of the [First] Vatican Council, there still remain aspects that have been called scandalous or even revolting. Let us not fear to face these difficulties head-on, all the more so because, in order to resolve them, we will undoubtedly be led to understand better, that is, to love all the more, not the limitations, but on the contrary the extent and the depth of the divine work and of the providential ways.

One scandal to begin with that certain very generous spirits have difficulty accommodating themselves to, like the good Frederick von Hügel, is the frequent occurrence of physical and spiritual tortures inflicted on the better people, on the more saintly, and that often seem all the more humanly inexplicable by the fact that such trials sometimes fall on other beings and that they even seem to cause a prejudice in the spiritual order for those who find themselves in what has been called the terrible proximity to saintly souls being tested. There is in this without doubt a very harsh paradox for reason and for the heart; but in this we must not reason by arguing from the unknown to the known: Baron von Hügel seemed to think that the undeserved hardships, apt to embitter and not to enlighten, would lead to belief in a sort of cruelty on the part of God, who, as if to elevate some according to arbitrary preferences, would not hesitate to submerge others deeper into revolt and perdition. That is an abusive interpretation and one that is surely false. Without going as far as saying, with Herman Schell, that suffering, even undergone without acceptance, is like a sacrament that works *ex opere operato* [from the work as worked] (which is excessive and has been censured), it is possible to grant that submission, though blind, *ex passione patientis* [from the endurance of the one enduring], has an expiatory and already purifying power; we must never conclude from the insufficiencies of resignation to the uselessness of trial, to an accrued indebtedness of the poor patient.

But, it might be said, is that not to make of Christian religion a religion of pain, on the path of the pessimism of certain oriental sects where is practiced an asceticism that goes all the way to frenzy? Not at all; since, for the Christian, the worst trials are the condition of an infinitely higher felicity. To the Evangelical text, *oportet pati et ita intrare in gloriam* [it is incumbent to suffer and so enter into glory], Saint Paul adds this somewhat mathematical affirmation: between the sufferings here below, *passiones hujus temporis* [the sufferings of this time] and the celestial joys, there is an infinite disproportion, *non sunt condignae* [they are not of equal value]; and God, he concludes, does not let Himself be surpassed in generosity. Hence, let us not be scandalized by crucifying exigencies; let us not even see in them mere expiations and penance; it is not uniquely to compensate for faults, for evil pleasures, or for excessive pride that there is in the depths of human life an incurable pain, a torturous yearning; it is to prepare for the advent and the exaltation of the supernaturalized human being that profound humiliations, internal ruptures, mortifying destructions are the direct and the only possible ways for a love that has its place, not in our terrestrial viewpoint of perishable beings, but in the perspective, alone real, alone definitive, of a blessed eternity.

Evidently, the scandal of the sufferings of the just and even the scandal of sufferings poorly understood, poorly used in keeping with our human judgments, this scandal, which has troubled and darkened so many souls, must cease in the more intimate light projected by a deeper understanding of the doctrine of assimilation. When we imagine that we have only to lead a middling life to enter into a heaven tailored according to our human ambitions, yes, then we can rightly be troubled by what the Germans call *Weltschmerz*, the pain of the world. It is no longer the same if the descent into the abyss appears as the road to justice and to glory, beyond any proportion with the conceptions of a mediocre wisdom and of an inferior generosity. We should not fear even to bring out the sharpness of the evils that weigh on humanity, because that is also the way of bringing out the immensity of the drama at play and the transcendence of the destiny from which we cannot escape, and for which the evils of this world are meant to remind us imperiously, to prepare us, and to make us attain. Nothing is more dangerous than a semi-optimism that misconstrues the double reality of evils and goods, and that conceives a kind of paternal God who will not punish too much and who will reward only in a childish way.

In this way the examination of the first scandal that struck us turns into a higher idea of the supernaturalizing destiny that keeps man from being complacent at his human level and from misunderstanding a destination that he cannot debase all the way down to his finite nature. We could not insist enough on the inappropriateness there is in reducing our relations with God and also, indirectly, with the world to the level of a simple moral or metaphysical conception. To be sure the relations of man with lower beings or with the rewarding and vengeful God that deism speaks of have to be acknowledged, defined, and observed: but, what a superficial view of things, if, like Aristotle, we represent the world to ourselves in the image of a hierarchy of scaled essences where each degree has its own validity, its own fixed role, its definitive stability! How much more living, more stimulating, more exalting is this conception that Saint Paul sums up when he tells us that the world is in a labor of parturition where every creature groans as it aspires to this new heaven, this new land, where precisely the body will become spiritual and where, through this transformation prepared in suffering, will arrive the perfect fulfillment, *initium aliquod creaturae quod ipse perficiet Deus* [a certain beginning of the creature that God Himself will perfect]! Let us not then restrict our views to a simple moral anthropomorphism that would reduce the providential plan to a sort of humanism or of indigent pragmatism.

But, it will be insisted, how are we to answer this persistent objection: how are we to understand what the sacred Books call the peace of sinners, the tribulations of the just, before which conscience remains hesitant and troubled? Is it then possible that God takes pleasure in the suffering of his friends, or that, if trial is a grace, God refuses it to those that it might bring back to Him? More generally, whence is the apparent cruelty of the passive purifications and of certain mystical states? Do we then have to admit the judgment arrived at by a historian of religions to the effect that Christian religion is, not a doctrine of beatitude and of charity, but the religion of suffering and harshness?

Put in this way, the problem is wrongly misformulated, misconceived; because one is trying to approach it from the viewpoint of sensibility, of duration, of human appearances. But as Plato was already showing in the *Philebus*, that is to start from a false perspective that ends up in pessimism and even in nihilism. In a decisive analysis, Plato has shown that our sensible states have validity through memory and foresight, through the ideas that fix them and interpret them, through the metaphysical and religious conceptions that give them meaning. In other words, it is only from the standpoint of God, of eternity, that a truthful explanation and justificatory judgment can and must be brought to bear. Now, from this perspective, the scandals presented as objections turn into edification; and how can this be so?

If it were only a case of leaving man in his natural condition, it would seem that in fact God can let Him follow a more gentle path; but is it conceivable that a spiritual being, able through its reason to know other joys than those of sensibility and of the terrestrial life, should find its integral satisfaction in ephemeral delights? Is there any true happiness for him apart from beatitude, which, according to Saint Thomas, is not truly beatitude unless it is that of God known and somehow possessed? Consequently, man could not perfect his destiny as a spiritual being without facing the problem of his union, his more or less complete assimilation to a beatified life for which he does not find within himself the conditions and the possibility.

But then, it will be said, why would God not accord purely by grace this felicity that he offers at such a price, and how is his infinite charity compatible with so many rigorous exigencies? This is where we have to come to terms with the difficulty of our elevation all the way to God, and where we shall see, in the apparent cruelties, the height of justice and of merciful charity.

To insert as completely as possible his own life and his own beatitude into a creature, the Creator could not make of it a passive thing, a thing without moral value, a thing that would resemble Him so little who is all act, all generosity, while it would remain on the contrary total inertia and total subjection. But then how can the initial passivity of the created being transfigure itself into a divinely creative activity? There is only one way conceivable and realizable of effecting such a prodigy that consists, according to a theological expression, in "communicating the incommunicable"; which is to say that, in order to merit union with God, the creature must empty itself of itself, voluntarily and through a veritable cooperation accept the substitution within itself of the divine will for the egoism proper to its own nature (*fiat voluntas tua* [thy will be done]). Whence this provisional and as it were annihilating destruction of the natural joys, of the apparent goods, of the activities that seem the most legitimate and the most elevated in the order of the gifts of nature, and of all these strippings, these disappropriations, to obtain a vivification, the birth of that "new man" who is henceforth configured with Christ, better still, who is the very life of Christ in a creature delivered from its congenital limitations and infirmities and superelevated to a theandric life. From such a point of view, everything that offends common sense or the susceptibilities of a purely human conscience lights up, is justified, solicits admiration and love. But such a disposition presupposes, under grace, a correspondence of free will; and that is why, for those who resist or turn away, callousness is possible, even to the point of producing in them a certain peace, a certain indifference, a certain serenity, even a certain hostility, that surprise so many superficial observers, as if the grace of religious yearning could have been constantly refused to some human beings.

CHAPTER 6

Supreme Objection

The Problem of Evil in Its Most Universal Form

In spite of all this, there is still a lurking thought at work in many spirits haunted by the problem of evil in its most universal form. How many times I have received this complaint, this anguish, almost this accusation: but could God not have produced, from the beginning, this world that Scriptures call *perfectum* [perfect]? could He not have created heaven with its elect from the beginning, without exposing some unfortunates to the risk of suffering, of unworthiness, and of becoming lost forever? could He not have spared Himself, not just the sufferings of the Redemption, but also the spectacle of the Fall, the hateful cries of the impious, the eternal evil of damnation? Does not creation, in all its phases and all the way to its final state, manifest powerlessness, a semi-failure, a failure of goodness, or at least a partial triumph of evil? In this way there subsists in many minds a base of Manicheanism: it is as if God could have done better if He had not come up against resistances, and that the partial failure of His plan is because of a limitation of the good by an unavoidable evil. Therein lies a supreme objection that it is important to set aside and that must constitute the ultimate objective of theodicy, that is, in keeping with etymology, the justification of God.

Let us try to make this wound bleed to its depth that risks poisoning so many consciences, even among the most generous, and let us tell these consciences first of all that it is not surprising that the supposed justifications of God, such as those of Leibniz in his disappointing *Theodicy*, leaves them less than satisfied. For, is it acceptable that the happiness of some should come from the unhappiness of others, that the ransom for the good should be an evil, and that we should console ourselves by crowning this very evil with a misleading name, by calling it a lesser evil? Is it even enough to distinguish, with many classical philosophers, three kinds of evil, as if to crumble the difficulty into bits and pieces, in order to resolve it more easily and to make it vanish in a way so as not to be crushed by what is massive about it? And this "metaphysical evil" (as the principle and the condition of physical evil and of moral evil is called), is it enough to present it as inherent to every creature to escape the sadness of thinking that in many cases it would be better not to be, when so many beings seem destined to pain or to deprivation? Besides, is it not said that, for the traitor Judas, it would have been better if he had not been called into existence? We thus encounter here a more radical problem still than what our preceding analyses enabled us to suspect, the one formulated in the doctrines of predestination and of pessimism, the problem also that dualism was subject to in advocating the part of divine powerlessness in the face of an irreducible principle and of a kind of positive resistance to the action of the sovereign Goodness.

It is this tenacious dualism, this latent Manicheanism that we must finally come to terms with. Let us first understand how it is engendered in the mind of so many men, of so many philosophers, even in those who believe themselves to be indemnified from it and who reason nevertheless as if God had not been able to do better than he has done, as if his work were partially and inevitably deficient, as if evil, the reality of which is incontestable, remained indirectly imputable to the Creator and to Providence, to the limited character of the divine action. As in the case of Malebranche invoking always the esthetic preoccupations of divine governance, sacrificing to the beauty of the simplest of ways the interests of the greater number and even attributing to the ever-finite bearing of the person of Christ the restriction of his graces and the failure of a lack of total expansion of the Redemption.

Such a way of reasoning proceeds from our habit of abstracting, of naming our abstractions, of substantifying and considering these entities as being truly subsisting and acting. Thus it is that, in spite of God's gifts, we imagine, in the face of this totally free and totally good bestowal, a contrary aspect, an antagonistic concept, at some point a positive reality that normally enters into conflict with the divine charity to push it back and to contradict it in its applications as well as in its essential depth.

Let us free ourselves from these idols, and we shall see how we quite naturally rise above these last temptations, these last traces of dualism. But, to succeed in doing so, we shall have to embrace as completely as possible the formidable problem of the creature facing up to creative generosity.

To make creation worth the effort, was it enough to fabricate a sort of architecture for the sake of proving the power and the wisdom of the supreme artist? No, this external glory adds nothing; it would only copy or even caricature the very intimate splendor of the Trinity. Will it be enough, in order to justify what the theologians call the exodus, God's operation *ad extra* [to the outside], to declare that it is good, in order to attest to his sovereign majesty, that there be adorers to send him back some reflection of his light, courtesans to celebrate his favors in contrast to the wretches who will serve as eternal witnesses to his justice? Again no: such thoughts do no more than dishonor God, to the extent that we would think of Him as of an autocrat in need of flatterers and of victims.

If there is one sufficient reason for creation, it cannot be, according to the most profound traditional teaching, anything else than charity, a charity that, while being sufficient uniquely and perfectly unto itself, willed, nevertheless, in total liberty, to multiply itself, and to give meaning to the apparently crazy wish expressed in a Hindu book relative to the thought of divine solitude: "if only I were many!" God is not solitary: he is altruism itself in the Trinitarian mystery of his internal life; but love is *par excellence* that which spreads itself out, that which makes be, that which elevates by giving as much as possible of itself; and the creative design consists precisely in realizing not just creatures that would remain exterior and infinitely inferior, but as well participants in the divine nature itself, *divinae consortes naturae* [in consort with the divine nature].

And inasmuch as Revelation gives us in fact this incomparable light on the authentic sense of a creation that without it would remain incomprehensible, it remains for us to show how this design, entirely of goodness, can be realized, without any limitation from an evil that, from the divine viewpoint, is entirely outside the perspectives of creation, in spite of the paradoxical character of such an undertaking: to bring into the divine life, without absorbing them into it, new beings that, by nature, could only be at an incommensurable distance from this union and from this prodigious assimilation.

CHAPTER 7

The Only Appeasing Solution of an Assimilative Theogony by Way of Renunciation and Even Death

Given that, according to revealed teaching (which lets us know what it would have been impossible to discern or even to conceive and to desire by reason, in spite of the fundamental aspiration at work in our spiritual nature), we are destined to the life of beatitude, how is this divine genesis possible, how is it realizable?

We have seen that this destiny could not be plastered on like something passively imposed and undergone. Salvation would not be salvation if it were put in us without us. What then is this part that we have to bring into the elevation, into the assumption, into the deification to which we are called? It is here that will appear the exigencies of a goodness that, from our infirm point of view, we risk taking as arbitrary exigencies of a susceptibility, of a majesty, even a harshness that are at first disconcerting: in order to serve as a foundation, as a support, better still, as a ransom and as a holocaust for the supernatural order and for the kingdom of God that must establish itself in us or rather that must become our very selves, there is no other means, no other conceivable and valid toll than this one: the first gift, the reasonable nature, the spiritual being that we receive from our first birth as properly our own,—so that we are, in some way, at home with ourselves and so that, according to the expression from the book of Wisdom, we belong to ourselves, truly masters and given over into the hands of our own counsel,—this is what we must resign from, sacrifice, destroy in some way, so that the wondrous transformation will take effect that makes of a creature, undoubtedly already intelligent, free and able to know God, but as if from the outside and as an ever-mysterious object, one intimately associated with what is reserved, secret, apparently incommunicable in the divine life itself. Hence, it is the first solidity of our moral being that serves as fulcrum and as the price for this raising, for this deific assimilation; and we understand, thereby, how we have at the same time to affirm the original value of our nature, but also to recognize that starting from it our elevation takes place as an apparent expression, as a vivification through a provisional mortification, as a supernaturalization into the divine form through a consensual annihilation, so that nothing can dispense the created being from going through these generative phases, these trials that, as painful as they may seem, are the only means, the proof, and the supreme grace of an infinite charity.

No one sees God without dying: what is that to say, in the spiritual and esoteric sense of this initially literal truth? It is that in fact, to see God, to enter into Him and to possess something of His intimacy, we have to renounce ourselves, to restore to Him in ourselves His total peace, to undergo the purifying and transformative trial that mortifies the natural appetite for being, for making ourselves the center, for self-sufficiency, for deifying ourselves by ourselves. Whether it be an issue of corporeal death or of total abnegation, in the land of sin or in Eden, a reversal of perspective, a renunciation of egoism, a sacrifice, a death, are and cannot not be the condition *sine qua non* of the illuminating and transforming union. We see God only by participating in his light, in his incommensurability, by admitting our nothingness and by the loving gift of what would allow us to close ourselves off from the call of charity.

We must go all the way to this apparent destruction, to this annihilation of egocentrism, all the way to total abnegation, to understand what it is to love God and to love oneself *ad majorem Dei gloriam et ad majorem sui amorem et beatitudinem* [for the greater glory of God and for the greater love of self and of beatitude]. To love God is to renounce everything for Him, except Him and what He is and wills in all and for all and for each one and from each one. Not to admit, neither in spirit nor from the heart and from the will, this deifying mortification is to radically misunderstand the Christian way, the grandeur of the divine gift, the sense of charity, the supernaturally integral plan: truly generative charity in God and in us, creative and parturient of God in us; otherwise, *morte morieris* [you shall die the death]; and the first death is but the recalling of the infidelity, the symbol of the renovating option, the toll of the Resurrection, but also the image of the second death; also, in a sense, death is the synthetic act that resolves the alternative and that we must undergo actively both in the *quotidie morior* [each day I die] and in the *semel mori* [dying once and for all] in the unique and total summation.

It is strange that no one has integrated death, the *act* of dying as man, any more than has been done, into philosophy and metaphysics: supreme "mortification" that we must render intelligible and voluntary, "vivification" also, from which we must draw the divine part both for expiation and for the purification and for the deifying preparation. Even in the trial preceding sin, there had to be an abnegation, a passing away, a repression perhaps of the curiosities and the virtualities congenital to the spirit, a renunciation regarding the conquering ambition of nature and of "civilization" as understood in the modern way. It remains always that, for us, dying has to be an act, an adherence, a consented abandonment, an integral humiliation by the destruction of our own belonging and dignity.

Death, understood and accepted in the fullness of its providential, penitential, and transformative sense, can and must therefore become the act par excellence, the act that, delivering us from egoism and sin, conforms us to the divine will, to the universal order, to the totally disindividualizing, but personalizing, singularizing, and consuming expansion *in unum* [into one]. Death remains the highest vehicle of the common trial, to which is adapted the means grace uses for salvation, possible for all. And if it is true that knowledge of the highest goal and of the integral conditions for the transformative union, at the cost of mortifying purifications, is infinitely beneficial, stimulating. and perfective, still we can say also, in response to the beautiful variety of the providential leads, that there is, even in the ignorance and the obscure acceptance of the crosses, the sufferings, the agony, and of death, a grandeur of sacrifice all the more meritorious for the aridity of a submission that is more painful.

This is not simply a "return to God," it is at once arriving at the Principle and participating in the divine fecundity, which is not limited to a *status quo* like those we imagine in duration or that make us conceive, so wrongly, the beatific vision as an immobile sleep: hebetude and not beatitude. There is newness in God who is Spirit of life and of nearness, active act, pure acting, and not purely native and naturist act; there is newness for man, and even by man, in God who in his immovable eternity encompasses all the riches of a perpetually generative Love both of God and of gods.

From this viewpoint, the objections, the scandals that trouble spirits more generous than perspicacious and docile to the suggestions of love, are dissipated; and here again what seemed revolting is transformed, for whoever can understand and love, into a new reason for admiration and for giving thanks [*action de grace*]. How desirable it is, to dispel preventions and acrimonies, to broadcast this apology for the ways of God and to lead souls into letting themselves melt before the unveiled sun, as Plato reports in the explanation of the myth of Boreas: the pilgrim, against the effort of the icy wind that would strip him of the cloak of rationalizations and recriminations he wraps himself with amid the tempests of this world, sheds of his own self all the falsely protective wrappings as soon as the warm ray of the sun and of love has penetrated through his incomprehensions.

CHAPTER 8

Exigencies of Divine Charity

One final rebellion nevertheless stirs reason up against this partly unveiled mystery that it persists in finding too burdensome and ultimately cruel for those who resist the call of charity. Why is it, one asks, that, instead of chastisement, God does not impose annihilation on the wretched ones who have failed in the test and in whom the terrible genesis of their transformation aborts in a second birth more disruptive than the first? Well, this dream, which was that of Origen and of many others, this supposed "end of Satan" celebrated by the poet, is but one more misunderstanding of the goodness of God and of the grandeur of man. The being we receive is not just a game, a make-believe, a pure mimicry: it has an indestructible consistency, and the moment we have, through reason, entered into the order of transcendent and imperishable realities, we participate in eternity; whence comes what Bossuet called the incomprehensible seriousness of this life that is forever, of our acts that remain indestructibly, of our option that confers upon us a sort of power to create, since, in the choice that depends on us, we decide about our total and definitive attitude: with God and in God in the eternal order, or against God in egoism and in an irreparable disorder. "It is not just for fun that I loved you," Angela of Foligno heard it said to her: this warning is addressed to all; it only expresses the logic of a goodness that never fails and evokes a power that is either deifying or deicidal conferred upon man and to which God submits Himself.

In our diverse modern societies, even among those that are Catholic, the sense of *sin* is getting lost, or if some esthetes boast of possessing it, is it not to spice up their sensualism? In our prayer, we must ask to know the horror of sin and to "hate it as much as God hates it Himself." What then is that to say? and what makes it so profoundly contrary, repugnant, mortal to God and to man? We could not come to any idea of it in the least exact otherwise than by thinking of the deifying intention, of the provisional *exinanition* of God who is soliciting from man His full restitution; so that to sin is to become deicidal, it is as it were depriving God of a part of Himself, and it is depriving man of his divine birth; it is therefore going against the most profound *instinct of conservation*, if we dare say, that attaches God to God, and that is in man the most fundamental élan: to persevere in his being and to increase his being to the infinite. It is not a question of only a fault easily corrected and compensated for, of a stain on a garment easily brushed or washed off: *sin* attacks what is most intimate, what is most essential; and what is the being it smashes and annihilates somehow? It is God in His own subsistence, in His creative and beatifying intent, and it is man, in his total destiny.

Let us not think that the chastisement is the expression of a revenge, of a vindictive anger: it is quite the contrary, for it is only the clear manifestation of an unrecognized Goodness that has itself suffered, even to the point of dying, from the human revolt that has become intrinsically deicidal through the force of sin. A beautiful image makes us feel the truth of this perspective, by showing us also the deviations so often allowed by the insufficiency of a moral and Christian sense: Let us compare, in effect, two famous frescoes that represent the final judgment, the one of Michelangelo, the other more ancient one of painters who had meditated, not as artists or as humanists only, but as men of faith and of piety, the mystery of the divine sanctions. In the Sistine Chapel, the painting, undoubtedly touching, represents in Christ a powerful and terrifying athlete, who, conqueror of the world and of the devil, overpowers by his gesture of crushing malediction the rebels, who, under this thunderbolt of justice and anger, can only sink into the abyss of eternal sufferings: this is the triumph of strength, of irresistible constraint, of implacable justice; but is that the God of truth and of goodness, is that the Christian solution to the remorse aroused by the problem of evil, of suffering, and of sin? Let us consider, on the opposite side, a certain painting of an ancient anonymous painter of the fourteenth century, or a certain tableau of Fra Angelico: it is almost the same gesture that Christ makes and we could almost believe that Michelangelo had only to be inspired by his predecessors; and yet what an abyss separates him from them! If the Christ raises his arm, it is not to strike, not to crush, it is to show the wounds of His passion; if He holds and shows in his other hand a book, it is so that we can read there the Beatitudes and the appeals of his heart to humanity; and it is the saving love that the true pain of the culpable, the pain that comes forth from their own conscience, the pain that is in some way that of the very passion of Christ, suffering more from the sentiment of the uselessness of His redemption and of the loss of souls than of his own tortures.

Thereby we also understand that the sense of chastisement arises from the intimate conscience of the guilty one and does not in the least resemble a purely external torture that, unable to bring about any amendment, would appear as a useless and brutal vengeance, like something bad added to something else bad. The complaint that Scripture places on the lips of the damned is not a cry of defiance, nor a malediction against the one doing justice, and even less the boast of one revolting glorifying himself for remaining impenetrable to God Himself: the admission that is the very principle of the suffering is this exclamation that sums everything up: *ergo erravimus* [therefore we erred]. It is against themselves that those being punished rise up; and therein lies a more acute source of regret, more torturous than would be the pains inflicted from outside to a being that nothing could have dulled: it is this division at what is most intimate in the criminal consciousness against itself that gets translated in the image of the devouring flame, rising and maintained in the very interior by the clear light that makes manifest the unacknowledged warnings and the rejected graces. We even have to say, with Julian of Norwich, that, even in the extreme suffering of the soul, man keeps this primitive base of attachment to the existence that had been given to him by goodness and for the good: this is what renders indestructible the being now dead spiritually, and it is this conflict between the initial goodness and the final mistake that constitutes the very sanction, without anything in all this story taking anything away from the charity of the Creator and the Redeemer; quite the contrary, from the abyss of evils, which derive entirely from the human fault, arises still an indissolubly united testimony celebrating the grandeurs of justice identified with mercy that lets this loving plaint be heard: *quid debui facere et non feci* [what should I have done that I did not do]?

No doubt, to adapt itself to popular language and to the most efficacious feelings, the divine pedagogy, which makes itself all things to all, uses metaphors that take hold like sharp warnings, like those of a father who menaces his children with all the more severe solicitude that he loves them in order to spare them dangers by alerting their imagination against risks of which they do not always discern the true nature. No doubt also, it would remain for us to explain what is taught us about contagious rage, which we observe ourselves about the proselytism eager to bring other souls down. But, besides having described earlier only one anticipated consciousness and the fundamental reason for the imperishable despair, it is appropriate to add that in fact the spirit of rebellion, the hateful fear, the desire for perverse pleasures, the ambitions of a dominating pride suppose at the same time accomplices, the support of the greater number and the ardor for obtaining the necessary concurrence for our powers of enjoyment and of destruction; hence there is nothing surprising if, in the drama of this world that Saint Augustine traces in showing the two Cities constantly at odds, one founded on the love of self to the contempt of God, the other on the detachment and the annihilation of self up to the triumph of the divine love. The two armies are recruited, intermix, and constantly seek to get dedicated recruits to the supreme sacrifice. This very spectacle is well drawn to make manifest, through confusing appearances where so many spirits lose the sense of the drama in which they are the actors, the immense stakes and the secret organization that will finally line up distinctly on one side or the other the belligerents in the war of this world.

But, one may say also, how is it possible that such great issues are decided almost unbeknownst to all men? is this description of a sort of divine genesis or bottomless and endless fall not a chimerical dream? is it conceivable that, in the banality of common existences and preoccupation, the work of an eternal discrimination is being prepared and determined with a sufficient clarity so that a sufficient justice will follow?

For this difficulty there is a twofold response. First, for those who can by grace, by reflection, by virtue practice the counsel of the Sacred Scriptures while studying the *magnalia Dei* [the great works of God] and to whom is addressed the promise, *qui elucidant me vitam aeternam habebunt* [those who shed light on me will have eternal life], the very consciousness of this destiny, the sight of the exigencies and of the ways of charity bring a light and a warmth of which, according to the expression of Diogenes, must contribute to illuminating and warming the obscure and cold body of this world. Here, as elsewhere and more than elsewhere, knowledge is a condition of security, of perfecting, of gains in action itself, and the act of charity will come out all the better to the extent that the divine epic in the universal supernaturalization will be better known and more intelligible.

But also, for the simpler, for the more stunted, the more rudimentary, the more childlike forms are sufficient for the divine seed to be taken in and take root in a life or perhaps only in a death or a submissive resignation; in short, there has to be a gift of self, a proof of devotion and of generosity to serve as vehicle and allow the advent of this new world to which we are invited and that, at times, a simple step enables us to attain; for, if we do not enter in without a toll, this price can be infinitely weak,—just as, no matter how great it seems, it is never anything but minute in comparison to the gift that God adds on to the merits of man.

It is even here that we find once again, but now to satisfy it, the appeal whose echo we had taken in: couldn't the goodness of God grant heaven instantly and quite gratuitously? We have seen why this gift could not be primitive and by itself; but it is exact to add that what God asks of most people is so little that, over this almost-nothing, which nevertheless opens the dikes of his magnificence, the ample flow submerges and carries away souls. In this sense the words of Saint James and of Saint Peter open before us the horizon of ineffable surprises, of which Saint Paul also gives us a glimpse according to the beginning of a personal experience. We are still only, and no matter how we could rise, babbling infants, at a still obscure dawn; "*initium aliquod creaturae*" [some beginning of a creature; James 1:18] "*quod Deus ipse perficiet*" [that God Himself will perfect; 1 Peter 5:10]: these texts suggest the thought of ulterior enrichments, of metamorphoses that, without destroying the continuity of memory and of personal merit, will realize this progress for which we have an irresistible hope, while the thought alone of an immobile and fixed contemplation makes many souls fear that the future life promised them would be a monotony rather than the reign of the spirit of love and of newness.

If it were permissible to speculate on this beyond what fortunately remains mysterious to us, would we not raise a corner of the veil by supposing that eternity itself, in its possessive and totalizing unity, does not prevent the movement of duration any more than the ecstasy of vision suppresses the discursive consciousness of oneself and of all beings? And what justifies this succession of progressive states is the very teaching given to us on the interval that separates the state of souls before and after the supreme Judgment, and what our *Credo* calls the "resurrection of the flesh"; there is then, beyond the present existence, a complementary history, a life ever increased and, as the Apocalypse says, a new land about which everything escapes us, but whose promise, as indeterminate as it may be, prevents us from restricting our explanations too much to the measure of our poor actual conceptions. In organic life where so many mysteries still subsist, it has been discovered that the colloidal equilibrium, ever unstable, can be modified by infinitesimal doses, since in the presence of these minimal data the synthetic unity or, as we say to mask a more profound ignorance, the synthetic dynamism from which proceed biological phenomena arouses, by catalysis, energies that seemed asleep and that are out of proportion with the minimal dose or the vitamin introduced into the organism: perhaps it is the same in this great spiritual body of the universe, and that which we can already glimpse allows us to suspect that, from the lowest degree of materiality up to the highest summit of mystical states, there is a continuity such that, although everything proceeds from above and tends to bring everything back toward this highest term, still this total work of God is worked out only by passing through the humblest forms: *ab imis ad summa* [from the depths to the summit].

3

RECONSIDERATION AND GLOBAL VIEW

Circumincession of the Problems and Unity of Perspectives

1

Twofold Inspiration of Our Inquiries

From the preceding considerations we can gather the twofold inspiration that has awakened and drawn forth our entire philosophical investigation. On one side, a preoccupation with method, a need for continuity, for rigor and for clarity, a desire not to lose sight of any of the points that make up the real and intelligible order of things, from the architecture of the physical world all the way to the development of the spiritual life; for these aspects apparently so distant, so disparate, even so strange, it seems, one to the other, nevertheless form a connection of states, a series of conditions such that the phenomena of the cosmic order (as well on the side of astronomic enormities as on the side of the inexhaustible particles of the atomic) serve as bedrock, as preparation, as alimentation for the labor and even the being of thought, and have as their final cause the advent of the spiritual life; for these sublime beings, which constitute an apparently acosmic and transcendent world, would still not subsist without this immense preparation from below, which is means, obstacle, stimulant, temptation, principle at once of opposition, of distinction and of union. Distinction and yet solidarity and reciprocal causality of Pascal's "orders": it is not enough to oppose them; they must be tied in together, *in eodem dramate* [in the same drama].

For another thing, if concern for a methodological exactitude corresponds to the orientation of thought that imperiously needs to establish among all its objects a connection and even a unity without which there would be no intelligibility, still what launches this continuous movement of investigation as well as the real interconnection of the beings that make up the total order of the world is a preoccupation that is no longer only scientific, but of a noetic, moral, and religious character: at issue is a question of explaining from top to bottom all this immense ordering of creation, of understanding the possibility and the reason for beings with only a borrowed being, of secondary causes that receive from a first Cause what Saint Thomas calls *dignitatem causalitatis* [the dignity of causality]; and then, it is no longer only a problem of intelligibility or logic, it is a problem of value, of goodness, of wisdom that arises: "how come and why are there beings capable of activity and of realizing a destiny that would be, thanks to gifts received, their own accomplishment?"

It is in going deeper into this fundamental problem that we are brought to discern the two gifts that, everywhere and always, Christian philosophy and Catholic theology have pointed to as constituting the enunciation of the vital problem we have to resolve:—on the one hand, the gift of a rational nature along with what it entails regarding knowledge of God and of the world, of freedom and of obligation, all of this granted, so to speak, as a deposit of funds we have to put to good use;—on the other hand, a gift still infinitely higher, a supernatural vocation, which does not allow man to remain legitimately at the stage where he believes himself to be at home; a gratuitous gift and nonetheless so obligatory for man that he cannot refuse it without being guilty and falling into debt; a gift that without return, without reconsideration, without repentance, which, even in the case of damnation and to make such damnation possible, just and terrifying, remains good, willed, loved in its indestructible core: it is what God has placed of his Being in our beings, which thus participate in something of the *Causa sui* [Cause of itself], of its Autogenesis, of its ontological and ontogenetic proof. Now the difficulty is to show precisely, and at once, the radical difference, the simultaneous existence, the rational explicitation and the justification of these two gifts, distinct and solidary, inconfusable and unseparable, in the concrete state that is ours.

To do so, is it enough to declare that the first of these gifts is simply a support for the second, which cannot remain suspended in air and which needs a preexisting prop? But then we do not justify the exigencies of the new gift, which does not merely rest on the rational nature, but penetrates it, raises it from underneath, and inserts in it unanticipated responsibilities. And besides, in speaking of nature simply as of a foundation, somehow in a physical way, for the supernatural, there is no explaining why the two gifts could not be granted together, in one and the same act. We have to go further then and discover a more radical, more complete, more precise explanation of this solidarity that entails, between two incommensurable data, at once distinction and a connection both equally indispensable. This is what we tried to give to understand in speaking of this genesis of the moral and the religious life in us, through the mortifying *offering* we have to make, in order to obtain what the Gospel calls "the second birth" or again "the spiritual birth": thereby it was possible to establish between the two gifts (which we have to make our own) a dynamic continuity and an intelligible relation. Indeed, the rational nature that constitutes our essential humanity is given to us as a property that is truly ours, but it is so that, for us to become wed to the divine will and to enter into the supernatural order, we have to become donors with regard to God Himself, by restoring to Him what He had given us as a means for obtaining Himself thanks to our generosity that shows confidence in Him and that, under the veil of the present shadows, gives itself over to the mysterious will of the "hidden God," yes, ever hidden in this world where, as Pascal says, our sacrifices always run the risk of seeming to be tricks.

How much there still remains to be done to redress the deviation that the influence of the pagan and naturist conception has brought on Christian thought and on the Revelation of love! According to that conception, God is an Essence, a Nature, a Force, that (Leibniz, still penetrated by this spirit, will say) fulgurates "possibles," arranges "compossibles," and ends up with "reals," having validated and made their rights to existence triumph; and this thesis evokes as well the idea of an original dualism, of a nothingness in the face of God, of a necessary proliferation of created things, of a sort of reservoir prior to creation or to divine freedom. Now, that is false and lethal: nothingness is not; God *is*, and that would have been absolutely sufficient, if charity had not, in totally gratuitous fashion, called to *being*, not antecedent possibles, but nonbeings, set in a case of conferring to this *given* (as to a loan) a value, a consistency, a plenitude of divine proportions. Let us dare to say that, according to the words of Saint Paul, God has somehow withdrawn and emptied Himself to create nothingness, to make way for virtual being, and to provide it with the means for remaking and resurrecting God. That was, according to metaphysical appearances, the impossible, as a kind of suicide of God seems impossible; and yet, that is truly the truth, *Deus seipsum exinanivit* [God emptied Himself], and it is for us to restore Him in his necessary being: hence the enormity of sin, the hatred of God for this refusal to recognize in Him the generosity of his love and the exigencies of his being. We must not say then that the work of this world was to go from the possible to being, but that God posited beings in spite of apparent possibilities, and that, if there is no congenital dualism, damnation underlines the indestructibility of the foundations of being in these creatures of love.

It is not enough to say that Christ is at once the God of nature and the God of supernature. It is already well to say (and how much this first thesis manifests that the run of men even of faith harbor a view that is shortsighted and even falsified) that Christ is not anti-nature, or that nature is not anti-Christ or aChristic, in spite of the dualism that persists in so many minds who have no suspicion that they are Manichean and that they belittle the power, the goodness of their God. We have to understand that, notwithstanding the difficulties and the dangers that nature entails, it is a provisional obstacle and risk to allow for the "deiformative" labor. And we must finally set intelligences and hearts at ease, in light and in warmth, thanks to a full, simple, and total exposition of the divine inventions, to begin, to continue, and to consummate the masterpiece, the creation, the supernaturalization, the assimilation of the *Unum totum* [One whole] where nothing is in vain and where the apparent or transitory renunciations and the destructive or purifying holocausts have a final sense of integration and of transfiguration, from the mount Tabor to the mount of the Ascension and of the Assumption, by way of the Calvary of this world.

In this everything truly hangs together: the world of nature has a consistency that is not fictional, and it is good to study this marvelous complex that ultimately brings us to the reign of the spirit; but, on the other hand, the whole of nature is only, so to speak, a currency of exchange, only a possibility for us to purchase with it infinitely more than it, through our detachment from it and by placing ourselves, through duty and through submission to the divine order, in the frame of mind of the merchant of whom the Gospel speaks, who sells all he has to acquire "the precious stone," in exchange for which all is nothing: so that in this sublime trafficking—which first seems an almost temerarious risk—we become finally "the good merchants," because we have gained at once God and, in Him, everything we had seemed to renounce for Him; for we can *have* nothing except by belonging to Him: *qui habet, etiam adjicietur ei quod respuerat* [to the one who has, will also be added what he had given up].

To sum up, we can posit these three assertions: (1) In us, thinking beings, there arises forcefully a total, indivisible, inevitable question, the very question of the unity of our destiny and of the term to which it necessarily leads us. (2) Outside of us, is given a response, it is also unique, total, indivisible, inevitable, and about which it can be shown, through a seamless and implacable analysis, that it alone resolves the anxiety of thought and explains the final end of life. (3) To this response, and to this question that human thought must raise for itself, that it cannot even fail to really raise for itself however vaguely that may be, and that it always resolves at least in an implicit fashion, there is, for all, direct access, possibility, and necessity to adopt a position, without the involvement of any preestablished philosophical system. And, if there is a philosophical truth, it is the one that consists in enunciating, in clarifying, in justifying this connection; otherwise, any system that claims to close in on itself or stop short sins by precipitation or by inconsequence; any doctrine that claims self-sufficiency is illegitimate and deficient. It is of the highest importance then not to leave thought halfway in its task, for, with the temptation it has to erect itself into a systematic solution, it runs the risk of shutting us in the artificially constructed prison where the horizon disappears and where we take the walls covered with ideological representations for the living truth and for the distant heaven.

On the whole, the capstone of our tetralogy in the study of thought, of being, of taking action, and of the Christian spirit, is this secret of the intentions and of the intervention of God, for realizing, verifying, "intelligibilizing," loving other himselves, for making what was not be, think, act truly, become an object eternally worthy of divine charity, and glorify the One and only, while being itself and rightly beatified and loved. To understand first the supra-metaphysical difficulty of this design, the supernatural difficulty of the solution, the tragic risks of this theogony of love and of truth, is what was imposed on us. This is about running through our thoughts, our actions, our subalternate forms of borrowed existence, in order to see both that there is to be explained how a thinking, an acting, a being, in the strongest sense of these words, are conceivable outside of God, even while remaining deiform and even deific, and how our natural and human ways are indeed the preconditions of a transfiguration and of an assimilation that make us live at once in God and as gods, which is to say that literally the reality of the *unum sint* [that they may be one], of the ultimate *unum sunt* [they are one] consists in this substantial union of charity that makes it so that those who love and those who are loved are such through a total donation and a reciprocal abnegation, all the more enriching for remaining fundamentally consented to. In short, the problem of action is the epic of this acting that is at once Theogenesis and Autogenesis; the problem of thinking is the sublime exchange of the Incarnation of the Word in created intelligences, who become, in one and the same light, other Christs: *verbum caro factum, ut caro fiat verbum* [the word made flesh, so that the flesh is made word]; the problem of being is the realization in the *divine fullness*, of a provisional *exinanitio* [emptying], allowing the *restitutio*, better still the *instauratio*, of a superabundant Divinity in those of whom it is said: *vos dii eritis* [you shall be gods]. Yes, but on what conditions? It is to the study of these conditions that we have had to apply ourselves.

2

Objections and Contradictions through Which the Enlightened and Enlightening Way Is Opened

(A) Misunderstandings encountered and dissipated

In order to shed better light on our positions, let us look back on the past and on the objections in the midst of which we have had to make our way laboriously in the face of contradictions.

(1) Concerning the nature of thought and of its objects, what we encountered first to block our way and to render our effort suspect and obscure for many philosophers and theologians, who were nevertheless open, is the materializing idea that things are like exterior realities (and even opposed) to the spirit; that these things are in isolation one from the other, and even isolated from all thought; and that the spirit subsists either, according to some, as a tacked-on epiphenomenon,—or else, according to others, as a transcendent substance entirely *sui generis* that comes down like a meteorite into the world, wherein this spirit, like a child found, makes its way as it can, always without succeeding in grasping anything else than intelligible natures or phenomenal relations.

Now we have contested all these presuppositions that, diversely and equally, succumb one by one before critical examinations and ultimately give an impression of being arbitrary or of unintelligibility. By following the line of the most concrete experiences and of the most verified experiences, we have quite naturally found our way out of this ever-abstract and extrinsicist way of breaking nature and spirit into pieces and into conflict. We took equal care to show the interdependence and the irreducibility of beings and of the thought that we acquire of them. We have seen that the objects of knowledge, as real and as distinct as they are one from the other, hang together, form a whole tied together, constitute thereby an intelligible given, and better still prepare and nourish our intelligence, which does not go without them any more than a mirror goes without its reflective tint or than organic life, even if it is not derived from physical and chemical causes, goes without its nourishment.

By the fragmentation that kept things and thoughts apart from one another, there was no understanding of the possibility of realizing the unity of the cosmos neither in the order of science nor in the spiritual order that nevertheless has to fulfil the divine will *ut unum sint omnes et omnia* [that all (spirits) and all (things) be one]. It is to remedy the dislocation of a triply deleterious extrinsicism (a) in the physical order itself, (b) in the order of knowledge, (c) and in the order of the relations between nature and spirit, that we insisted on the total connection that makes it such that, in the material and immaterial universe, nothing (according to the words of Aristotle himself) is in vain: so that the material, formal, final causes, without confusion of one with the other, complete one another, fit into one another and (as Leibniz was looking for) join the realm of finality with the realm of logic and force. Is this to say for this reason that the final causes themselves are determined and that they surge up mechanically or by way of immanence from internal data, so that supernature would be only the spontaneous, normal, terminal of nature itself? By no means; and it is on this second point that the readjustment with which we have constantly been concerned, as philosopher independently of any apologetic partisanship, has been most fought against, the most difficult to understand, but also the most important and the most fraught with consequences.

(2) When at the beginning of our effort we tried to show the unity of human destiny that (in fact and in the historical and concrete order where we really live) can have no solution except through supernatural life or death, we found ourselves beset by surprises, by protestations, by charges of heterodoxy. Yet we had done nothing more than enunciate dogmatic certitudes and take up these authentic data from Christian teaching in order to coordinate and to combine the normal attitude of reason and of philosophy with these truths officially prescribed and

required by faith. Whence then came the astonishment and the irritation provoked by this simple "exploitation" and explicitation of dogmas whose exactness and imperious character no one was contesting, but whose explicit consequences and connections in the philosophical order were misunderstood?

Unbeknownst to themselves, often many minds, tied to elementary formulas, had formed a sort of system, allegedly theological, whose principal articulations can be enunciated as follows:

Man is placed in a state of pure nature by the fact of the original fall, transmitted to all. In this state, reason is enough to organize a positive civilization, a spiritual philosophy, indeed even a natural religion, all within the human framework, all at one level; and any inquietude or higher aspiration one might claim to discover in man purely as man is taken as false mysticism, disturbances of sensibility, not to say of sensuality, romanticism condemned by a reason that is sound and firm. Far from seeing in the inquietude and the infinite élans of man a preparation or a stimulation toward the supernatural order, we must, it is said, see in the present order an external means for compressing, checkmating, putting an "end" to these romantic revolutionary agitations. The supernatural could not come except from without and impose itself by extrinsic dictate, like a historically demonstrable fact that we must take in purely by submission to the object, without any pretense of finding in the subject himself who accepts it and receives it any interior justification; so that what is at stake is only a question of a historical critique to establish the fact of the divine ukase and the miraculous proofs of its exclusively transcendent character; the two orders of nature and grace are like two spheres that can touch one another and do not in any way compenetrate one another; man remains at home in the positive artistic, political domain; on the other side, the believer belongs to the authority that shapes him and to which he submits with eyes closed; and it is even thought that the moral failings of natural man do not in any way suppress the favors that his docility can assure him in the supernatural order.

Is there not a feeling of being in a dream as we find ourselves before the enunciation of such theses? And yet, unknowingly, following from an imperceptible deviation of philosophical methods and of the spiritual sense, this is the attitude that has at times become violently and tenaciously manifest among certain people, in the face of a doctrine that was trying to balance, without sacrificing them one to the other, the exigencies of dogma, in what is inalienably supernatural about it, and the needs of an interior life without which there is no religion in spirit and in truth, not any more than there is living and efficacious philosophy.

(B) Permanent and opposed dangers of denaturation

What, however, contributes to justifying the fears and the challenges that still persist in spite of advances that would render impossible the initial incrimination and misunderstandings, is that in effect among those who were rising up against pure extrinsicism, many were running away from this peril and combating it only to lapse into the contrary excess, without any consciousness of doing so and even less any expressed will of doing so. Thus it was that some writers insisted on the mainly moral and interior character of faith; and even while recognizing that faith comes from on high as a divine gift and as a supernatural elevation, they were infusing this gift, which they were declaring to be transcendent, so profoundly into human nature that we had only to extract it from there, and to assure its development according to the habitual ways of our moral ascension to fulfil our destiny: so that the distinction between the personal and ethical character and the transcendent and religious character was erased, from which fact the latter characteristic was desupernaturalized in practice.

This danger was increased among some by a conception we can call intrinsically metaphysical of the content of Revelation, as if, in instructing us through his Christ, God was limiting Himself to making us know speculatively metaphysical truths, and as if we had only ourselves to go by to take this teaching into account. Moreover, it is not only a moral personalism, but even a metaphysical "charitism" that presents this peril of misconstruing the supernatural *quoad se* [according to itself], by reducing it as a whole to a hyper-intellectualism, to a metanoetic whose methods and characteristics remain without precision, or are limited to human modes of thinking, willing, enduring. If the *a, b, c* of the religious sense (*initium sapientiae* [the beginning of wisdom]), is the vivid sense of the inaccessible incommensurability and transcendence of God, we can say that, by misunderstanding that the Emmanuel cannot be such and can draw near and dwell in us only by a supernatural way, we are lacking in the religious sense at the same time as in the philosophical sense.

Finally, the danger was greater still for those in whose eyes the Redemption was supposed to have been only a sort of accident that came about to remedy the accident of the Fall and simply to get things back into the state of nature prior to sin; so that we have had to insist as forcefully as possible on the incommensurability of the supernatural and the life of reason, without forgetting that neither in the present, nor before the Fall, has man never been constituted in a state of pure nature. Hence there is nothing to authorize us, since we are bound to speak of what is really given, to speculate on a situation unknown to us and in fact alien to the divine plan and the total history of humanity.

(C) How even the misunderstandings and the errors can serve for the triumph of truth and show the goal to be attained.

The misunderstandings and the insufficiencies we have just recalled have not nevertheless been useless for making what is given in the problem more precise and for preventing hasty and inadequate solutions; as [Léon] Ollé-Laprune used to say, every fall can and must be a move forward; and it is in this sense that we can understand and approve the phrase of Saint Paul: *oportet haereses esse* [there are bound to be heresies]. The discussion of errors does not only push dangers back and reestablish acquired possessions, it ordinarily contributes to augmenting riches and to lending greater credence to unanticipated aspects of the truth, always susceptible of more light and of greater expansion. Also the conflicts, as painful as they may have been, between Modernism and integrism, have brought us into a broader comprehension of the supernatural, of its transcendence, and at the same time of its incorporation into human life, in the intimacy of personal consciences as well as in the development of social and international life.

We see better and better that the state in which humanity finds itself, even without the life of grace, is not a state of natural equilibrium: there is a disequilibrium, an unstable state that, to the extent that a ferment of civilization coming from Christian religion penetrates diverse peoples, results in what we can call a transnatural[1] crisis, as in an

---

1. Translator's footnote: The term "transnatural" is coined here by Blondel to focus on a crisis within the historical order of diverse civilizations as formed

ultimatum calling for a choice between a fall into moral and political disorder or an ascension toward ideas and virtues for which Christian religion alone furnishes the ideal and the means. Entering more deeply into this observation, we are brought to recognize that, even under obscure and anonymous forms, this supernatural vocation that is imposed on all and that consequently infuses into every conscience a motion from which we cannot legitimately abstract ourselves, is not simply a given that has come from outside under the form of a revealed teaching, but that penetrates human nature to its ultimate depths: this supernatural therefore, which, from one side, is proposed as an exterior and transcendent revelation, must also be sunken inside and, even without being discerned, remain active and inconfusable with the powers merely of human nature.

It is this last point that may be the most important and most difficult to establish rigorously and to safeguard without compromise; such is the task we have above dedicated ourselves to by showing the radical distinction between the two gifts of nature and of the divine vocation that properly speaking constitutes this supernatural order wherein it is given to us to be capable either of deification or of deicide: it is therefore all the way to this that we must come to discover the optical center from which, to speak as Bossuet does, all the apparent confusion of this world is unraveled and from which appear the continuity, the intelligible unity, the good and the excellent reality of all that in which we saw at first pluralism, opposition, unintelligibility, even scandal for reason or for the heart.

---

by their own use of natural resources, in relating to Christian religion with "ideas and virtues for which Christian religion alone furnishes the ideal and the means," which are in themselves supernatural as matters of faith and grace. The crisis is natural in that it occurs in the natural course of events. But it is transnatural in that it calls for a choice concerning an ideal and means for attaining the ideal that are beyond anyone's natural capacity to conceive and to achieve by means of one's own, thus requiring a revelation and grace from the Transcendent to learn about the ideal and the means to achieve the end proposed by the revelation, all of which is supernatural. Transnatural refers to the moment of choice in the natural order regarding all that is supernatural.

3

How Philosophical Thought Can Resolve the Enigma of Our Indeclinable Destiny

On the whole, we can sum up in two propositions all the effort of thought to resolve the enigma wherein thought is caught up as in a debate without ever resigning itself to not discovering its sense:

(1) To give some meaning to the wish of the spirit we need to become aware of the maximum conceivable goodness in this mute and mysterious universe that puts us to the test; and, when we read in Saint John that God loved the world *in finem* [unto the end], that is to the extremity of the possible, when we hear this word applied to this apparent chaos in which humanity lives, *plus et melius non potuit facere Deus* [more and better God could not have done], we cannot find any explanation for this paradox except by seeing in the extreme misery of perishable and even of evil things the condition for an integration of the lowest and the suffering beings into this assumption into God that only trial makes possible through which the creature becomes assimilable to and participant in the infinite beatitude: from this viewpoint we can truly say, *plus non potuit* [more he could not do]; and such an elevation of beings that were not and that become *consortes aeternae vitae* [sharers of eternal life] sweeps away all the objections generally addressed to the interpretation of the existence of evil through an alleged metaphysical limitation of the creative power.

(2) Once we have become aware of the sublime goal to be attained, what remains if not to discern the indispensable means and alone capable

of effecting such an inconceivable assumption: the goal freely and lovingly willed, the means necessary and lovingly inflicted,—necessary, not as a logical or a metaphysical constraint, but as a necessity of means in the order of spiritual realities that are required to be at once intellectual, moral, and religious; now through this threefold claim is justified in the fundamentally passive creature the inevitable necessity, for it to be able to participate in the divine acting [*agir*], to accept its subjugation, to espouse the divine will (*fiat voluntas tua* [thy will be done]), and to realize in it an act divinely pure by accepting and willing these passive purifications that, in diverse degrees, come to be imposed like a toll on every being capable of consciousness and free choice. Thus is consummated that sublime destiny of what the ancients called the *pleroma*, that is, that plentitude of a world arriving at being filled with all truth, all excellence, and completing itself as a perfect sphere without allowing for any vacuum, any lack, any fault in the unity that embraces all of multiplicity.

To sum up, it is therefore possible to bring out, from this viewpoint, the following advantages:

1. Rendered more intelligible are the immense generosity, the difficulty, and the coherence of the design of creation;
2. Found to be more manifest is the profound reason for the trial imposed;
3. Indicated is that there is no possible dispensation from this deific exigency;
4. Explained is the horror God has of sin that annihilates Him, kills Him, deprives Him of his glory of goodness;
5. Found integrated into this ensemble are the Incarnation and the Redemption, conditionally, but inevitably: *oportuit pati; factus obediens* [he had to suffer; made obedient];
6. Surmounted are all the objections falsely drawn from an apparent harshness of God, from his exigencies even toward his friends, from the apparent failure of some of his summons;
7. Perhaps illuminated to its depth the sublime, terrifying, and adorable drama of this extension of God into his external glory that consists in gods living from God, for God, in God, but who have passively and actively cooperated in this Theogenesis;

8. It can be understood thus that, if the supernature is entirely gratuitous and incommensurable with nature, on the other hand nature is condition for this supernature, posited in view of this supernature, even though nature may be a generative principle and an immanent cause of the life for which it is a support, a resistant and transubstantiable wild seedling.

All this brings us to a precise, illuminated, elevated conception of the supernatural, which does not consist in a form of taboo imposed and lifted, in a metaphysical elevation, in an imitation that would leave the copy and the model like two similar things, but not united, with a perpetual danger of confusion or of dissociation. What is at issue is a vital participation without analogue, in comparison to which all similitudes and analogies remain deficient and extrinsic symbols,—a participation where the transformation of love and the incommensurability of the lives united by charity surpass every expression and constitute a maximum of compenetration and of enriching distinction, a vitalizing and transforming assimilation.

4

APPENDIX

Clarifications and Admonitions

1

Remarks on Our Method of Implication against the Abuses of Abstractive and Constructive Methods

I

One of the most necessary questions, but also one of the most difficult to elucidate in depth, is that of the method we are using in contrast with that which, on the whole, has prevailed in diverse forms since Socrates. Nietzsche claimed that rationalism and scientism were derived from this falsified point of view. Boutroux, from an entirely different point of view, liked to repeat that, though applicable to the human world, since with Socrates at issue was the science of man and the governance of his life, the method that proceeds by generalization, induction, and deduction could not legitimately be apt either for nature and for the metaphysical order, because the Socratic procedures have a bearing only on what Xenophon calls "human affairs," pertaining to moral observation and leading to the regulation of our thoughts and our acts in the personal, social, and political domain. Socrates, in fact, set aside cosmology, no less than the study of divine things, regarding which he deferred to the religious means of information (divination, sacrifices, etc.). But he was misunderstood by those on one side as well as by those on the other side, paying with his life for his seeming impiety and witnessing his spirit deviated by his great disciples: the legendary words attributed to him about Plato: "how many things this young man has me say of which I never had the thought" is the spontaneous translation of a historical truth. It is certain that Plato, then Aristotle, and all the ulterior thought of Greece, of Rome, of the Middle Ages, of modern times have lived from a transposition of the Socratic procedures, unduly extended to the physical and the metaphysical order.

Now it is for us to take into account: (1) the nature of such a deviation and of the reasons that brought it about, the shortcomings it presents us with, the possibility and the urgency of remedying it; (2) to rediscover the route where thought, in order to remain faithful to its primordial élan, should have kept itself and must reenter. For philosophy, whose results, on the whole, have been too ordinarily weak, is in a state of bankruptcy, and it is that from a double point of view, in all domains: on the one hand, indeed, it has often been less thought of in the eyes of minds that are the most critical and the most enamored of precision, of probity, of a real sense, for having been content with unverifiable formulas and with abstract constructions; on the other hand, to the extent that it has claimed to develop practical, political, moral, religious consequences from the speculations into which it has ventured, the destructive work it has frequently produced has seemed, on balance in general, to surpass the services credited to it. Formerly, I used to get irritated at certain preachers who were in the habit—or who had it in principle—of thundering against philosophy, as if the word had only the sense of hostility regarding religious matters with which the eighteenth century had dressed it in France. But, upon reflection, and in seeing the evolution of the officially sanctioned teaching of philosophy, I recognize that the disorder, the dissolution, the anarchy results at times and all too naturally from the conceptions whose specious virtuosity and whose technical apparatus do not compensate for their incoherence, their partiality, and, in truth, their irrealism.

What happened then to vitiate in this way, for so many centuries and in spite of the genius of such great minds, a discipline that should normally be beneficial and that not only seems indispensable for civilization, but also appears as a preparatory and eminently useful for religious faith itself, for which, according to a consecrated expression, it has to establish the "preambles," to justify the credibility and to show a reasonable as well as transcendent character? Nothing is more important than to restore the true idea, the true practice of an integral philosophical method.

The false deviation seems to consist in this. Our knowledge develops only thanks to a reflection that is constructive of signs, of representational notions, of abstract constructions: that is not only legitimate, but indispensable and inevitable: only we must, from the start, avoid a temptation, a facile but ruinous precipitation. What is that to say? And by what slope do we slip into this abuse, so little attended to, although, so to speak, so universally committed? Let us borrow from Plato, the first one responsible, the very formula for this fraudulent operation. "It is undoubtedly," says he, "through sight and through touch that we must begin, and we cannot do otherwise"; then, starting from these initial data, the dialectical advance raises us into a suprasensible world, and then, led into the world of Ideas, we push off with our foot the ladder we had used to ascend into it; we constitute another world where, he literally concludes "everything is determined and is terminated in ideas." Aristotle does not, in any way, give the word "Idea" the same sense, the same value Plato gives it: for him, the Idea or essence or intelligible nature is, not apart from and on high, χωρίζω [separate], but immanent to the concrete and individual realities; but he sets aside as inaccessible to science, which has a bearing only on the general, these concrete data, these individual qualities, these *accidents* that no doubt constitute the existence of singular beings, but which philosophy cannot take into account. So that his doctrine ends more surely still—because it is apparently more positive than that of Plato—constituting in the world itself a world of representations, of which it will be said back and forth that it conforms to what is most consistent in things, and yet is foreign to the reality of the individual existences that one would be wrong to want to include in a science of being. Also the procedure constantly used to take us out of this positive reality, while seeming to keep us in it, is a spontaneous and immediate induction, ἐπαγωγή, the point of departure for a generalization that itself serves as a premise for all ulterior deduction, without direct and constant recourse to positive controls.

Hence, we find, otherwise than in Plato, but in a way equally or more bothersome, because it is dissimulated, the temptation to have the world of appearances "take a walk," even though it be the true support and as it were the necessary ballast for philosophical doctrine. Under the pretext of attaining the general, we emphasize the immediate data, we eliminate the troublesome particularities; and Bossuet may well say that the concrete alone truly subsists, we live in the abstract, while believing that is elevating, liberating, dominating from on high the real things themselves; and we build palaces in the sky, for an intellectual aristocracy to make use of. Whence comes a fault, committed more and more frequently: a fraudulent recourse to checks without funding. Our philosophy is constantly in a state of banking on what it has been unable to verify and attain; and the difficulty of establishing the foundation for induction in the experimental sciences can be overcome in the sense and to the extent that we shall indicate; but it is impossible to legitimatize in the order of abstract speculations this method of construction and of extrapolation that has become habitual, thanks to the plasticity of conventional formulas, thanks to the abuse of technical terms substituted for the real complex, thanks to the virtuosity and to the mutual accommodations among specialists who manipulate these artificial expressions, in forming a language among themselves about which Condillac said that after all science is but a series of verbal conventions, "a well-fabricated language," and for which M. Le Roy systematized the theory by bringing out exclusively the arbitrary and fictitious character of this terminology.

But, it will be said, how could we do otherwise? Philosophy has to have confidence in constructive reason or else renounce all science of the real, all metaphysics, to limit itself to being nothing more than a critique of the human procedures in the elaboration of positive science. That, indeed, is the delicate point to be brought to light. Let us say first that a duty of probity dominates all. No need could justify a reckless effort, and, to use Kant's image, we cannot fly in a vacuum; but precisely nothing is a vacuum: we have only to invent the airplane that does not cease to rest in the light and invisible air, sufficient nevertheless to furnish it with the support it makes use of to go about the world.

There would be a lot more to add to describe and stigmatize the abstractive method of construction or of critical demolition (which have been symmetrically interdependent for the last two thousand years in the history of ideas). We could also indicate the many, but fragmentary and timid, attempts made over and over again to escape from this false philosophy "that is not worth one hour's grief," for which Pascal had such a vivid distaste. But we must limit ourselves now to indicating in quick traits the method we have to use and which, in opposition to the procedures of abstractive constructions and of deductive extrapolations, can be called method of implication and of explicitation: these expressions signify simply that instead of having to step out, so to speak, of real data and of concrete thoughts, we have to bring to light what they contain, what they *suppose*, in the etymological sense of the word, what makes them possible and solid. A procedure that is the reverse of the preceding one, since instead of withdrawing into a more or less fictitious world of representations and of substitutes we fabricate endlessly, we do an inventory of the effective content of the complex data, of the certitudes natural and common to all, of the truisms, that is, of those truths so evident, so elementary that we do not even think of contesting them, that we do not notice any more than we do the movement of our heart or the air we breathe, which are nevertheless always in service.

But, it will be said, these common truths are not enough to nourish philosophy and to orient our life: must we not go beyond them, at the risk of being mistaken? And, like action, is not speculation (as the ambiguous sense of the word entails) a risk, a leap into the unknown, a hypothetical move into unexplored domains and beyond the very limits that we could not yet attain?—Therein lies the error; and what we would want to make manifest is the continuous and progressive force of these truths apparently quite simple, but solid, but grounded in the real, reinforced by all the experiences of life, capable of verification and forming together a coherent whole sufficient to hold up the highest wisdom. Instead then of turning our gaze upward toward fictions and more or less arbitrary considerations, let us return to this learned ignorance of which Socrates spoke and about which Saint John of the Cross said that it is at once the most reasonable of the uses of reason itself and the one most in conformity with the dispositions that the highest spiritual or even supernatural life calls for.

However, this would not be a matter of burning libraries and of bringing us back to what Lucretius sang about as *novitas florida mundi* [fresh flowering of the world] (cf. also the text of Louis Massignon[1] on the evolution of Arabic thought). We have to insert into over elementary truths the very existence of science, which corresponds to a natural need of the spirit and which, as we shall see, must, by relating back to its origin and to its true end, also serve the cause of thought and the spiritual life. We must then examine how and why we go through what Massignon

---

1. Cf. *La Pensée*, tome I (new edition, 1948), pp. 227–228.

calls a winding path and risks, which can be murderous, when they should be salutary... This is where we come to the most difficult turn in our itinerary, the perilous point of thought in the process of developing itself and that cannot dispense with having recourse to the abstractive and discursive method. We have only to become aware of the exact nature and the essential role of legitimate and indispensable abstraction, while avoiding giving in to the temptation that precipitates us toward handy constructions, all the more specious for being more artificial and more brilliant.

For one like Aristotle, there was no precise differentiation in the science of nature, whether it is applied to the law of phenomena, or whether it has any bearing in the metaphysical conditions of the physical realities themselves. On either side, one rose to generalities that never were called back to pass under the control of experience; so that this physics itself is composed of superimposed abstractions, and that is why it remained sterile relative to positive research and concrete applications. The effort of medieval thought consisted in discovering a method that never gets lost in notional fictions substituted for real data: positive science is in certain respects a continuous abstraction, for it never studies anything but aspects and phenomena; but that is an abstraction we can call of the first degree, in the sense that at each moment it remains in contact with the positive proofs and the confirmations of experience. Newton was, therefore, right in saying (in opposition to the metaphysical abstractions of Descartes in his *Physics*, hypotheses in a vacuum, etc., which Pascal had already radically criticized): *hypotheses non fingo* [I do not fabricate hypotheses]. It is on this basis that the sciences are legitimate, positive, and efficacious. No one today any longer sticks to the speculations on the quintessence or on the four elements, if not from the viewpoint of a historical curiosity and to show the distance between the mentality of the ancients and ours concerning the nature of science, the legitimacy of verifiable abstractions, the fecundity of a discipline of which Bacon could say: "Science is no longer for knowing, but for empowering."

Now, if we are disengaged from the ancient conception of the sciences of nature, our philosophy has too often remained in an attitude that is just as artificial and sterile regarding the sciences of spirit. Lacking any prudent and tried method, people restrict themselves to constructing theories starting from simplistic observations or from facts taken crudely but without being able to control these theories and these empirical pseudo-sciences. What conveys the illusion of a philosophical know-how in such a complex order is the use of terminologies and of technical formulas that create, so to speak, an artificial world of notions; and people believe they have given proof of the real when they have strung together a coherence of formulas and of technical terms. Hence the character of a philosophy addressed only to the initiated, only to technicians who have succeeded in determining a set of problems, themselves constructed with the help of conventional notions. Hence, also these successive fashions, this diversity of small clubs, the rapid obsolescence of alleged discoveries, the severity of the new recruits regarding yesterday's fashions, the contempt for works that had their success ten or thirty years earlier: all that manifests the instability proper to a false science, whereas true knowledge is such that it persists and is worthy of being inscribed with the celebrated word of Thucydides: "acquisition forever."

Well then, what it has been possible to obtain for the science of nature, which undoubtedly renews itself to the extent that explanatory theories have fallen before better-known facts, we may hope to obtain also for the science of the interior life and for the truths of the metaphysical order, which, also as well, should not be considered as something theoretical, abstract, constructed (that is the error of immanentism), but as something concrete, something positive in its own way, something universal implied everywhere and always.

We understand better now the sense of our effort to turn away from ambitious speculations and to tie back into these implications that support all the effort of thought, all the movement of the spiritual life. Here also, we are led to proceed by analyses and provisional abstractions; but they are analyses bearing directly on realities that are experienced or able to be experienced and commonly lived: they are abstractions we say of the first degree, which is to say that they remain subject to a control that is always possible and immediate. We can see the nature of this method at work becoming more precise as it can prove its legitimacy and its efficacy only by walking, as Diogenes did to prove movement against the sophistical arguments of Zeno of Elea.

If one reflects on this process, one quickly sees that the endeavor is weighty, since it is a matter of rectifying or even of entirely reversing the philosophical orientation. To characterize in advance the general sense of this reform, I lay out in a somewhat rough fashion the antithesis between the current methods and the one we have tried to set in motion. Ordinarily, one tends to fill in holes, to let people believe that one has found the solution, to bundle a system, to consider thought as victorious over difficulties and as arriving at the simplicity in which it takes satisfaction, solidly and definitely set on the throne it has set up for itself and where it has installed itself. We have taken exactly the opposite attitude. We have shown that thought is not homogeneous, is not a unique and universal instrument of solution, that it is itself a problem, the problem of problems; that it is shot through with an interior conflict, that its accomplishments are only partial; that each provisional victory adds precision to the internal or the ulterior difficulty that propels its movement and that it never succeeds in appeasing. Far then from exaggerating results and from becoming complacent with false solutions, ever surpassed and contradicted by history, we concentrate on discovering the fact and the reason of this semi-failure: semi, we must say, to underscore that there are in fact encouraging results that forbid us from turning back, from stagnating, from despairing; but failure nonetheless, because in fact the definitive solutions, which would quiet the congenital inquietude of man (that *irrequietum cor* [restless heart] of which Augustine speaks) is not obtained. But what is acquired, is itself an essential truth; it is that semi-failure whose importunate presence must not be covered over, that we must on the contrary scrutinize as a salutary warning, a philosophical truth par excellence that the first method criticized ignored or caused to disappear through more or less conscious frauds, but that we, on the contrary, have to bring before the eyes of all, because we cannot misconstrue it without failing in our interior sincerity, without sinning against the light and probity, without losing the spirit of science, without compromising both the functions of philosophy and the sense of our human destiny.

II

It may seem clumsy, and especially inept, to tell our reigning philosophers that, on the whole, they have gone down a false path and have usurped an authority whose influence, besides, has rather diminished, in favor of specialized experts, of industrialists who, with the financiers, have all too often taken possession of this world. We tell the philosophers, in order to console them, that in spite of it all they have the privilege of preparing the future and that their ideas, like silent workers, get more done than just noise. This is another questionable appreciation, and, in any case, an influence often more perilous than beneficial, to judge from recent results. In any event it remains that if we wish to effect a "rectification" of the philosophical method and philosophical doctrine, our delicate role is not to broadcast some pretense that would be self-promoting and a hindrance; but, at the same time, it is important to make known clearly the divergence of the ways we are following, in opposition to the orientation of most contemporary philosophers. Hence, without saying it brutally, but doing so with as much precision, calm, and force as possible, we must suggest for those who would declaim to us the necessity of a new examination of our intellectual consciousness, the return into ourselves, the sense that with so many failures and presumptions (that have discredited philosophers in spite of the treasures of ingeniousness and even of virtuosity put forth by them) follow from a false point of departure, from an original failing that can be discerned, prevented, and corrected.

Where are we to situate the indication for this reform, so often attempted that it seems an everyday theme for philosophy? And how are we to avoid the reproach of promising, like all the others, mountains and marvels only to beget a mouse? Let us keep in mind that Socrates was already claiming to accomplish a revolution by turning away from physical or sophistical curiosities to bring thought back from heaven to earth, that is, from speculation on the system of the world and on the principles of things back toward the earthbound study of man and his laws. Did not Plato base all his teaching on the idea of a return as expressed in his allegory of the cave? Did not Bacon and Descartes want, like Spinoza, to "reform the understanding," as if the spontaneous movement of the mind were turning against the truth: the effort, Malebranche said, was vitiated by the passions and by sin; and, after so many others, does not Bergson require another twist of the mind on itself and against our habits, to rediscover the pristine freshness of the intuitive gaze? So many precedents, which seem to end up frequently in debacles and in collapses, seem unfavorable for encouraging a new attempt to find a way that seems always to have been lost, sought after and missed.

But two answers are possible to this objection. On the one hand, it is fair to remark that all these attempts have not been without useful results: they have made way for a more complete science of the spirit by freeing it from certain illusions, which, for seeming natural, are nonetheless acquired, destructible, and avoidable. On the other hand, it is not for us to run away from our responsibilities; rather, we have to face them to the very extent that we ourselves, following the light prudently and scrupulously, are looking to resolve a constantly recurring problem and that nothing allows us to believe is insolvable. For centuries, positive science searched for its route in vain, through ancient dreams or medieval alchemy. It has not been useless to beat around all these false ways, since, as [Pierre] Duhem has shown, these errors did not prevent the fermentation that little by little prepared the explosion of the scientific era. It may be legitimate to hope that all the philosophical efforts, even the most fruitless, have prepared, be it only by closing off false escapades, the discovery of the happy passageway, which Descartes, Auguste Comte, and others thought they had found, without taking into account that starting from their principles philosophy would still only have to develop, with no less security than the sciences, the entire series of its truths.

But, here again, a distinction is called for. It was a mistake to have believed that the sciences themselves, based definitively on a few acquired principles, would acquire more like crystals juxtaposed to one another. No, the sciences, even by profiting from their past, are renovated by a reshaping of the whole, by an intussusception of rejuvenating truths. It would be a symmetric error to hope that philosophy would ever constitute a body of doctrine as fixed as a crystal, and that a single system will be enough to mechanically or deductively gather in all ulterior initiatives of a thought that, like the social life and the general civilization of which it is an expression, is always enriched from within and always needs a spiritual vivification.

With these reservations, which maintain the suppleness of the philosophical organism, we can still hope for what was the dream and the ambition of the Middle Ages, a philosophy common to all the spirits. Kant claimed that there could not be "classics" in philosophy, and Fichte added that, for philosophy, the issue is to affirm and not to limit the infinite resourcefulness of creative thought. That is an abuse against which we must protest, by calling for an equilibrium, always in motion to be sure, but constantly sustained by the very fixity of the orientation, without those sudden swerves that lead to catastrophes. Far then from being opposed as revolutionaries to the tradition of the *philosophia perennis* [perennial philosophy] and from the possibility of a continuous doctrine, firm and truly classical, we shall try to take hold of the direction glimpsed and wished for by all, but by becoming attentive to the deviations that have almost always made people miss the mark by reason of some precipitation or by a systematic desire we must beware of as of a deadly risk for philosophy.

In a sense, then, we are taking hold of all the programs we have enunciated. Like Descartes, we are leery of that single cause he assigns for error, docility to the prejudices caused by precipitation in judgment; like Descartes, we are practicing a sort of methodical doubt, by being on guard against constructive abstractions. Except that, whereas Descartes claimed he was clearing his mind all at once of all preventions slowly acquired and passively undergone, we recognize the impossibility of such a maneuver that looks good on paper, but is practically unrealizable: all these prejudices we believe we are getting rid of have, according to Pascal's expression, tainted and impregnated all our habits, all our ways of seeing, of feeling, and of judging. That is why this Cartesian method, that some, like Hegel, have dubbed heroic, as if Descartes had been truly the "hero who takes hold of the whole by its foundation and recreates the world and the spirit," seems to us temerarious in many regards, deprived of any consciousness of its difficulties and its impossibilities, incapable of making us take hold effectively of things in their principle and in their depth: it starts from what is precisely in question, from thought that is a mystery and that raises a problem before being an instrument of solution. All our effort then will consist in being leery of presuppositions and in examining the data, apparent or real, before pronouncing ourselves on their sense and on their bearing. To start by affirming the *Cogito ergo sum* [I think, therefore I am], or the objective validity of rational evidence, it has been said, is the bold stroke of the genius: is it not rather the rush of a lucid mind like that of a mathematician, but lacking in any sense of concrete life, of the complexities and the finesse of the real, as has been noted with a vengeance by Pascal, Malebranche, even Bossuet?

If we have insisted on these historical aspects of the problem, it is not to take pleasure in exposing difficulties of method and the needs of reform; it is to make you more completely aware of the line we have to follow in the contestations we have to rank in spontaneous fashion and almost without seeming to touch them. Let us not fear giving the impression of enunciating commonplace truths; what we have to do is try to have them follow and imply one another in the way they are in reality, so that in going forward and especially in ending the reading of a work, the courageous reader will have to be astonished that all these affirmations, seemingly insignificant, make up a coherent whole charged with consequences in the speculative and in the practical order.

The perpetual difficulty consists in keeping our mind and that of our readers from going too fast, from giving in to the temptation of exaggerating truisms, from wanting to draw partial and premature conclusions. Consider, for example, the volume on *L'Être et les êtres* [*Being and beings*]: it should be noted that the most deleterious and the most difficult error to prevent or to uproot is to substantialize and somehow to solidify different beings in isolation, as if each one by itself formed an absolute, an independent and sufficient whole. In the study of *La Pensée* [*Thought*], there is an analogous risk, constantly threatening, constantly to be avoided: supposedly at each stage one would like to conclude in a definitive fashion, as if it were a matter of laying down stones that must come before the next layer in a wall. Bergson, whose spiritual sense has been so rightly praised and who denounces quite strongly the danger of materializing internal duration and freedom, does not seem himself to have escaped this tendency to translate into a language of matter the most immaterial realities; thus it was that to those who were questioning him on the subject of morality about which he had announced a publication, he answered that for each hour there suffices its effort and its conclusion, that we must sequence questions and not pronounce ourselves in advance on solutions to problems that have not yet been raised nor studied: as if, in the intellectual and moral order, the question were about simple materials that depend on one another only according to the crude art of the bricklayer who uses weight to hold layers together with one another.

Everywhere we must place in evidence the character at once certain and provisional, incontestable and precarious of assertions that call for one another and that link into one another mutually. That is why, in opposition to the method of abstractions and of speculative constructions that holds sway in so many philosophers, we have spoken of a method of *implication*; for this word signifies very well what we wish to say: to imply is not to invent, to deduce, it is to discover what is already present, but unnoticed, not yet explicitly known and formulated. This word then suggests at once the idea of a real compenetration and of a logical dependence: on the one hand, facts entail a solidarity that does not allow for isolating them without tearing apart their conditions and their natural articulations; on the other hand, truths imply one another when one requires the other, even though, as Leibniz says, we had not attended to their being necessary for one another as *requisites* (he also uses the words *exigi, requiri* to underscore this interdependence that pertains, at once, to the concrete order, to the logical order, to the metaphysical order, without prejudice even toward the moral order of finality and of perfection).

Therein lies the center of perspective where we must find our place to escape all that is arbitrary, all that is artificial, all that is indulgence for the imagination, all impatience to rush to conclusion. Thanks to this systematic prudence, if we go slowly and almost humbly, we go at least surely, without ever having to backpedal. Pasteur has been justly praised for never having had to disavow one single assertion he had advanced after mature experiences. I remember my schoolmate, Perdix, after he had become his lab assistant, and who said to him one day, after months of research on the vaccine against rabies: "Master, I believe we are wasting our time and that we should abandon this long labor." Pasteur smiled and, the next day, he announced before the Academy of Sciences that the vaccine had been discovered. One could dream of a philosophy that would never venture beyond certitudes such as this, verified at great length, secretly and victoriously. Let us then try to be inspired by such an example by keeping to the near side rather than venturing beyond the certitudes of fact or of ideas confirmed absolutely by our method of rigorous observations and implications.

2

Some Precisions on Terminology

On "intuitive thought," some serious reservations are called for. Too often we adorn insights with this name that, far from being more profound, are quite superficial, brilliant, and confused altogether, like reflections of sunlight that blind us more than they enlighten us. To remain faithful to the etymological sense as well as the technical senses of this word, we would have to restrict it to a science that penetrates the concrete down to its finest details and especially disclosing the unity amid this multiplicity; in such a way that the intuition would focus, in the complex truth, on what is simple, not by reason of indigence, but by reason of richness, as Leibniz said of the *Vinculum*. Now, there is nothing such as that in the usual use of this term: everything about it, as we say popularly, is at the end of one's nose, without analyses turning back into syntheses; for this latter term evokes the idea of elements that would have priority if not superiority over the resulting finale, which is on the contrary the real principle and the true explanation of the total and final unity. We must be extremely wary therefore of would-be intuitions, either in the sensible order, or in the affective realm, or especially in the intellectual order and more so in the moral and religious order. In fact, there is not for us any first and complete intuition: even our perceptions presuppose elementary acquisitions that habituation bunches together, and what appears to us as given is always only partially acquired and constructed.

Regarding this, to turn to the other end of the field of our knowledge, there arises the problem of our acquired contemplation. Against M. Saudreau I had thought it possible and good to admit (along with diverse authors, among whom Rev. Garrigou-Lagrange is not the least authority), well below the unitive way and infused contemplation that itself, supernaturally effects a true unification of our powers, a preparatory and humanly accessible form, for which we could, by analogy, conveniently use the name of acquired contemplation. I fear now that this expression goes too far beyond measure and brings in false ideas and a presumptuous ambition. To be sure, after the discursive and ascetic period, there comes a more concrete, more one, simpler form of thought and prayer; but unity is obtained always in a fragmentary and an imperfect manner; and it is even less a unity than a simplification the nature of which is irremediably different from essential simplicity.

Let us recall, indeed, what we were saying (and that is the thrust of our stimulating inquiry on Thought and its final destination), namely, that never could the real aspects of our most intimate knowledge meld together in a veritable and complete union. Only in God can what we call, defectively, subject and object have, or rather are, a perfect unity by the very bond of the Spirit. In us, duality persists incurably; and it is in this sense that we can interpret the fundamental and so rich thesis of Scholasticism on the real distinction, in every creature, of essence and of existence, of the rational object, of the noetic, and of the pneumatic life, without ever having the union of the universal and of the singular realized apart from absolute Perfection.

And this brings us back to our last question: why should it be impossible for a finite thought to have an intelligible right to pure thought, without admixture of duality, without participation in a light that it does not find in itself? Well, you sort of see now that this would be like asking why there cannot be many Gods. With thought consisting essentially in the living and concrete unity of the knower and the known in a perfect spiritual reciprocity, such an adequation is manifestly impossible in a being that has received being, that is not all being, that does not possess all its being and all its thought through an interior auto-generation.

Let us further deepen this view. We all have the greatest difficulty in conceiving that God does not have a nature imposed on Him, that He is His nature itself, being at once necessarily and freely what He is;

for His intrinsic goodness is not a quality that, analogous to that of fire which is to be hot, renders Him good though an antecedent cause and in a somehow arbitrary manner: no, everything in Him is really light and love; and that is what is His being and His essence, without any conceivable priority nor separation. Now, that is forcefully what is lacking in any other but Being in itself and through itself. Therefore, either it should have been that God did not create, or it was inevitable that the creature, even the most perfect, the most assimilable to God, would have in it this fault, this secret hiatus, which resembles two lips of the abyss that it is impossible to make touch one another, but that can be as the prayer of a deifying expectation; and that is, in effect, all the mystery of creation for this supernatural vocation that communicates through grace and through adoption what it was absolutely impossible to give through nature.

The pages devoted to the problem of our *assimilation* to God and of the ways through which we are brought to the passive purifications (the highest of which is death itself) can be very enlightening to us by manifesting what is for the creature the only means of becoming *consors divinae naturae* [sharer in the divine nature]. Hence the truth that everything hangs together and that, from the first *fiat lux* [let there be light] to the summit of the unitive way and of the beatific consummation, the same design animates everything. The same problem runs throughout, of final destination, which we have tried to approach through the study of Thought, of Being and of beings, of Action, of Christian Life.

To replace the word "intuition" that we find to be improper and deceptive, some have proposed an attenuated expression, but whose success does not seem probable, the word "attuition"; for the term *attueri* designates a form of attention already recompensed by a semi-possession of the object under consideration, without penetrating yet to the inside and to the bottom of this object as seems to be implied in the term *intueri*. Besides, the word "intelligence" evokes an analogous image: it is an issue of "reading inside"; but reading is spelling, it is to work at progressive reflection, dissection, inventory; the metaphor is therefore more prudent than that of intuition, since *tueri* indicates a direct and full look granted to us in any case, especially when it is a matter of penetrating into the inside of beings. Nevertheless, *intelligence* implies the reflected distinction in the possession more than the global word of intuition.

I come back to the end of your long letter and to the complementary questionnaire relating to terminology. For it is important to be on our guard against equations and analogies that would make us fall into brambles absolutely to be avoided. Therein lies the most difficult point, but also the most fruitful, it seems to me, for methodological and doctrinal realignment.

The *noetic* element no doubt expresses what there is that is rational, ordered, coherent, substantial in the universe and, in one sense, that in what abstract thought with its pretenses toward intelligibility, universality, and unity aims to attain and to formulate. But precisely these pretenses are for the most part premature, deforming, often marred by a sort of improbity because of the precipitation with which, for lack of real beings, it fashions entities with which it satisfies itself and has no difficulty in organizing, but that are no more than a diminished representation, a partially deceptive substitute or a usurping substitution. For, note well, the noetic element is quite the contrary of an abstraction, of an ideology. From the first chapter in [the book] *Thought*, I insist as strongly as possible on the fact of concrete unity in the universe, where everything hangs together, historically, scientifically, metaphysically. At issue therefore is not a simple notional view, an abstract idea of the universe, taken in its logical sense; at issue is what Hegel called the "concrete universal" (cf. the *Vocabulaire philosophique* at this word), that is, a universal that is really present everywhere and in each singular, as it was said of that infinite sphere whose center is in each point and the limits are nowhere. It is therefore against such a misunderstanding that we must be on our guard, too accustomed as we are to substitute for positive data conceptual interpretations that we are inclined to prefer quite unduly to the authentic data.

I wonder besides whether the terms *noetic* and *pneumatic* are adequate to designate the objective and virtually rational aspect and the interiorized and virtually subjective aspect of thought. The word *pneumatic* might be more appropriate for the final synthesis of the two aspects, which expresses in a way the note of the Spirit, *osculum Patris et Filii* [kiss of the Father and the Son]; there is, it seems, corresponding to each Person of the Trinity, a proper reality of Thought, constitutive, intrinsic, creative thought, in the Father; reflected, adequate, mediating, illuminative, realizing thought, by the Word and in the Word; unitive thought, *ignis, caritas, spiritualis unctio* [fire, charity, spirited unction], which gives the science of the Father, knowledge of the Son, and perfects the divine spiration in the substantial Unity. But also this divine thought, to which we aspire as to a real knowledge and a spiritual possession, would seem (since it consumes the Pure-God spirit, the God-in spirit and in truth, the God in its being entirely act, entirely light, entirely goodness) susceptible to be called not only *pneumatic*, but *substantial thought*. Provisionally at least, to designate the two aspects of thought to be held together, I have therefore stayed with the terms "noetic" and "pneumatic," which correspond in sum to the connotations too often confused of thought-Thought-object [*Pensée-pensée-objet*] and thinking-Thought-subject [*Pensée-pensée-sujet*], the first being the universal strain, everywhere intelligible, the second being the genesis of spiritual and eternal life, *per gradus debitos* [through the due degrees].

But what equivocations to be unraveled! What idealist or psychological interpretations to be set aside! First, it is not an issue of knowing if thought has reality only in spirit, in God, or in man; the issue is to know whether there is, in itself, a thought projected into things themselves, that would not be a creation of our human thought, that would also not be vision of God, but somehow would be a distant creature, a reality *sui generis* [of its own kind], a subsistence at once positive and immaterial, such that we could call this sort of being a noetic element, a way of existing in no way reducible to materiality, nor to ideality, that is, that would be neither a body, physically characterized by traits specifically attributed either to phenomena studied in the sciences of nature, or to seemingly material beings,—nor an idea residing in a consciousness.

It is of course difficult enough to make this "noetic" understood: and yet that is an original, actual, indispensable element. You understand thereby how and why I refuse to assimilate noetic with abstract: in one sense, they are the most antithetic terms there are, since the noetic element (the expression, so to speak, of the creative work of the Father, inasmuch as it is the foundation of the entire order of things) is what there is that is most substantial, underlying everything, indestructible, infused in all reality, no matter how rudimentary or how rich it may be. I hope that in reflecting on these remarks you will grasp my primordial and permanent intention and that we must not allow deviation at any moment, lest we fall back toward the slope we are too inclined to follow and from which one must pull oneself no matter what the cost.

Conversely, the "pneumatic" is not akin uniquely to concrete, realist, knowledge; and although it supposes, in effect a sort of incarnation of the whole in each one of its parts, this spirit of finesse that, according to Pascal, gathers the broadest of views and the most diverse digressions into a single center from which everything lights up, still I estimate that this phase of concentration is only transitory and does not intimate the true nature nor the final destination of the pneumatic element. It seems to me, indeed, that the ultimate goal of this pneumatic reality, even though it is the contrary of the abstract, is not to remain in its singular isolation; it tends, on the contrary, to possess in it the universal itself, not by a centripetal egoism, but by a centripetal generosity that makes each being equal spiritually to the total life by infusing each with the divine will and integral charity, since thereby we shall live, without losing ourselves, or rather by finding ourselves better in this way, in the life of all others seen, willed and loved, so to speak, *per oculos Dei, per cor Christi* [through the eyes of God, through the heart of Christ].

3

On the Relation between the Philosophical Trilogy and the Study of Philosophy and the Christian Spirit

Why set apart and as if in a new series, you ask me, the final study on *Philosophy and the Christian Spirit*, while declaring that we entertain Christian religion only under the philosophical aspect, such that, from the standpoint of reason, it is legitimate to submit it to a methodical and integral examination? That is the precise point, it seems to me, about which you desire some explanations.

The trilogy has as its object the exposition of the conditions that make intelligible and realizable the beings, the thoughts, the actions that make up the world offered to our observation and to our initiatives. We are inclined to believe that these data have a sufficient bearing and that, lest we fall into an incurable skepticism, we can find in them a solidity, a certitude for which we do not have to discover the justification to be in a position to build on this factual foundation a stable, coherent edifice capable even of upholding transcendent affirmations with which traditional philosophy has crowned nature and humanity. Almost always these foundations are accepted as support strong enough by itself to uphold ulterior affirmations, even that of God, that of an order transcending nature and humanity.

There is in that, however, an incomplete attitude and one that can become disingenuous. All of our effort has consisted in discovering at once what is unfinished, inconsistent, indigent, but also all that is already indestructible, in these attempts at being, in these searches for intelligibility, these efforts at initiative. Far then from restricting ourselves to taking off from an accepted foundation, for want of something better, as a sufficient spring board, we have perpetually tended to reveal the impossibility of staying with these precarious supports, with these intrinsically ruinous foundations; hence also, it was becoming impossible to be content with obvious data, as if it were superfluous to look for the sense, for the raison d'être the conditions for existing of such data. Thereby we were brought to posing the problem preceding and encompassing all others: how to conceive that there could be created beings in spite of their radical deficiency, thoughts conscious of themselves in spite of the limits of their bearing and the obscurities they are plunged in, wills capable of free initiative, of personal responsibility, when so many unknown causes tie them to a determinism that seems to exclude for secondary agents all conceivability of an autonomous action?

Thus the entire ensemble of this trilogy has as its object to rise beyond the facts—undergone without being understood and justified—and, on the other hand, to make evident the unfinished, even unfinishable, character, of all thoughts, existence, actions creatures are susceptible of. Whence this double conclusion that could be called the testament of philosophy and its highest truth: impossible to annihilate all the order of things that impress themselves invincibly on every consciousness and that constitute a universe coherent in all its parts; impossible nevertheless to bring to intelligible unity and to the satisfaction of human aspirations this set of sketches, of movements, of desires that constitute the dynamism of nature and of the spirit, the perpetual infinitude of worlds that precipitate themselves we know not whence and of souls that live only for what they do not yet know how to define, nor attain, nor possess.

If the conclusion of the trilogy is such, one sees that it calls for a complement, that it causes the problem of a possible fulfilment; for, as it has been noted a hundred times, we would not have the sense of inquietude, of indigence, of effort, if there were not in us a presentiment, better still, an obscure presence, a means already for determining some fixed points, some simple sample to bring to consciousness this moving relativity and this imperfection in need of a complement. Now the problem thus raised encounters a solution offered, as with the mathematician who can legitimately suppose a problem resolved in order to then analyze and rigorously justify the data and the deductions that give the reason for what was at first only a hypothesis. We find in positive religion a conclusion to be verified, and that even independently of knowing if that hypothesis is grounded in itself. It is under this aspect that the philosopher can approach without taking sides the examination of a doctrine that seems foreign to his own horizons. But little by little the analysis that could first appear to be speculative takes on the character of something positive, verifiable, imperative; and if the philosopher (who is not dispensed by his scientific scruples from being a man, an actor more than a spectator in the mêlée of doctrines) undertakes this personal verification from which no one can be dispensed, he finds in his experiences, as Newman said, only reasons to adhere to the explanation of life, to the solution of the problem of destiny that Christian religion offers him.

Undoubtedly the task here no longer remains exclusively theoretical and rational; and that is why we had to set our essay on *Philosophy and the Christian Spirit* apart. This reservation imposes itself with all the more reason to the extent that we take better note of the absolutely supernatural character of Revelation and of the supernatural that confers on human nature or even on the entire created order a fulfillment entirely inaccessible to any created being. Far then from leaning toward the error of naturalism and of immanentism, our tetralogy, understood in the sense we have just indicated, serves to show first the natural impossibility of an evolution that would go from bottom to top and arrive by itself at the divine flourishing, then [it shows] the inevitably gratuitous and quite voluntary character of the grace by which God completes his work in order to assimilate it and make it participate in his own beatitude, finally [it shows] the conditions of this transformation that, to bring the maximum of union with God, or of personal felicity, and of dignity in creatures, could not go without some preparation by way of testing, which is one of the essential marks of Catholicism, the one that seems the most formidable objection, and yet that can and must be explained and transfigured into a proof of love.

Thus without stepping into the theological content, without ceasing to maintain contacts with the investigations and the conclusions proper to philosophy, we can, far from any apologetic servitude, give to the

Christian spirit a maximum of intelligibility, a significance of integral charity, without there subsisting any objection that could not be turned into a confirmation. In short, the coherence of the whole is such that there subsists no fissure, no hitch where it would be possible to slip in or hang a difficulty; and that is what we have a right to expect from a solution that claims to hold the total truth and the secret of eternal life.

4

Appeasing Clarities for Reason Projected by Revelation

To answer your first question finally, it will be good to insist in effect on supernaturalization in the creative plan and to show, with all prudence and all force possible, how this theogony is deployed in creation, along with the plenitude of sense it is appropriate to give to the "supernatural." Well chosen name: nothing natural can have a claim on it, nothing divine is compromised by it, and absolute transcendence remains inviolate. But, under these inviolate reservations, we dare say that God, without exposing anything of his unicity and of his incommensurability, withdraws somehow to make room for beings that will perfect their precarious being only by letting God take back in them and through them His sovereignty, His divinity; and so is explained the first duty of the creature, adoration. We have already seen how and why it is possible, indispensable, so that the vivifying and deifying plan would be consummated, and for there to be between the *being unworthy of being* and the plenary Being this marvelous realm of the supernatural, the heavenly Jerusalem, the overflowing of Charity, apparently a sort of metaphysical monster, the masterpiece of condescendence that some have been able to find "scandalous" and "foolish." And, from this center of perspectives, what intrinsic significance is given to so many commonly cited texts, so many metaphors we are tempted to reduce to symbols or to "pious exaggerations," but that we must take more than to the letter, so to speak, and according to all the intelligible force of their paradox! Do we not indeed understand, once we enter into this glowing ember, what divine interest God has for us, in us, from us? Do we sense that His own Being is brought into play, in some way, His glory, His honor, at the same time as His love not to let it be misunderstood and not to leave it unfruitful, for the common good of His Being and of our beings that have to become His beings, so that He may find His happiness in making theirs, even to the point of exposing Himself for that to deicide and rejection.

Do we realize, in Thought, this drama where power, logic, and love unify infinite efficaciousness, coherence, generosity, without any of these rigorous exigencies being suppressed, reproached, avoided? Let no one object that we exaggerate things; let no one fear to compromise the inalienable and absolutely sufficient Transcendence of God, nor the gratuity of His gifts, nor the indelible distinction of the natural order and of the supernatural theandric vocation. No, none of these confusions or of these excesses is to be feared, the moment precisely we have understood the authentic sense of this *excessus Dei* [excess of God] through which the work of the seven days conducts the work of love *usque ad finem* [unto the end]. God owed nothing: in creating nature He did not have to create humanity, in creating humanity and the world of spirits, He did not have to include the transformative union; but, in order to constitute the order of grace and of adoption, these preparations were settings for the edifice of His Wisdom and of His Charity; and consequently, if, from the higher term (which did not have to be, but which was willed and put in place in fact), we look back toward the degrees that mark the steps of the ascent, it is legitimate to show the conveniences that account, by their very finality, for the beauty, the unity, the sublimity of the divine plan.

It remains nonetheless that, considered in its ensemble and under the complementary perspectives, the notion itself of the supernatural appears with a salutary amplitude and clarity. *Omnia propter electos. Finis omnis motus naturae est producere plurimas homines ad vitam aeternam, et quasi plures deos, quam plurimos deos* [All things are for the elect. The end of every movement of nature is to produce a plurality of men for eternal life, and as it were more gods, rather than a plurality of gods]. And who will dare to say that this divine plan lacks unity, coherence, intelligibility *ab imis ad summa* [from the depths to the summit]? Is it not good to scrutinize, "to elucidate" this mystery of the Power, of the Wisdom, of the Charity, *ludens in orbe terrarum et delicias habens cum filiis hominum* [playing about in the sphere of lands and taking delight with the sons of men]? And here also, do we not have to understand this continuous and ascending disposition starting from the first *fiat lux* [let there be light]? What could one object to? That we risk compromising in this way the distinction of the two orders and the gratuity of the supernatural? But that is a false fear, which comes from a misunderstanding of this very distinction. There is more than distinction: there is incommensurability; and therefore, what we must fear, is, not to confuse, but rather not unify in a compenetrating life the infirmities of nature and the divine sublimities, all the more so because this union always implies the radical humility of the creature that is raised up by God and to God only by lowering itself before Him and for Him.

Let us not therefore hesitate in plumbing the foundations of the edifice and in describing the architectonic marvels that rise from the extreme baseness of the created to the summits of deific assimilation and adoption: we shall see better that God enjoys using what is not to "glorify His name," that what is proper to Him is to have pity, pardon, and mercy on those who confess their miseries and His goodness; that ὕβρις [pride] is in fact the unexplainable aberration, in the way the ancients already had the sense of it, but without explaining it through the very design of the divine love; that all that does not relate to or is opposed to the transformative union, through a false sufficiency of the creature, makes of it "a child of wrath" and takes on a character of indignity, of lèse-divinity, *confregit in die irae suae reges . . . divites dimisit inanes* etc. [in the day of His wrath He crushed kings . . . the rich he sent away empty]; that the world is only a parturition of eternal life or of imperishable death. And it is at once by a sort of metaphysical histology and by a spiritual genesis that we are prepared to face up to this theogony, this cosmo-anthropo-Christo-theandric ontogeny and phylogeny.

And how many ethical, social, mystical applications there are! Is it understood how, for example, we are forewarned against the two unilateralisms of Theocentrism and Anthropocentrism? How we escape from the equivocations of "pure love" and from the subtleties of quietism? How we grasp the sense of the precept: to love the neighbor and to love oneself in God, for God, through God, since it is God Himself whom we have to restore in ourselves as in all, to multiply, so to speak, to have reign, through an advent that could be turned into a deicide? *Adveniat regnum Dei* [May the kingdom of God come]; and this reign in souls is God loving enough to have given us the possibility of being his children and his generators. And do we not thereby elucidate a bit more the mystery of this "folly of love" of God and of the Saints, each soul counting as a God to be brought forth? The falseness of "pure love accepting damnation" follows from this that God cannot lack interest in his own coming forth through us and in us, and that we must therefore love His salvation in ours and ours in His will of unifying love. "Think of me and I will think of you," Jesus said to Saint Catherine. Why this absurdity of supposing that God would ask us to accept our pain and His pain? The idea of the multiplication of God through the mortification of the creature that makes God born again in it, is, in many regards, the key to everything and the center of the Christian and total perspective.

MAURICE BLONDEL (1861–1949) was a philosopher born in Dijon, France, and educated at the École Normale Supérieure. Blondel defended his thesis, *L'action*, in 1893 at the Sorbonne. Blondel at first was refused a university position on the grounds of having taken an improperly religious position in his philosophy but finally received a professorship in Aix in 1897.

OLIVA BLANCHETTE is professor emeritus of philosophy at Boston College. He is the author and translator of eleven books, including *Action (1893): Essay on a Critique of Life and a Science of Practice* by Maurice Blondel (University of Notre Dame Press, 1984).

www.ingramcontent.com/pod-product-compliance
Lightning Source LLC
Chambersburg PA
CBHW071405300426
44114CB00016B/2187